PATHFINDERS
THE DEFINITIVE STORY

SEAN FEAST

Published by Key Books
An imprint of Key Publishing Ltd
PO Box 100
Stamford
Lincs PE19 1XQ

www.keypublishing.com

ISBN 978 1 80282 211 3

Front cover image: Steve Fleming/Getty
Front cover design: Myriam Bell Designs

Typeset by SJmagic DESIGN SERVICES, India.

Contents

Acknowledgements

This book is the result of 20 years of research and personally conducted interviews with more than 100 Pathfinders Force veterans and their families, far too many to mention here. Sadly, there are very few still with us, but I hope they would have approved of this new history, and it is to them that this book is dedicated. One veteran, happily, who is still going strong is Mark Charness, and I would like to especially thank Mark's daughter, Marilyn Shank, for acting as a conduit for capturing some of her father's memories.

I would like to mention Dr Jennie Gray and Johnny Clifford, with whom I serve as a trustee of the Pathfinder Archive, and whose support for this project has been unstinting. There are few, if any, who do more than Jennie and Johnny in keeping the memory of the Pathfinders alive, and in making their achievements known to a wider audience through the archive and the further collections held at RAF Wyton. I would also like to thank Dave Wallace, Mike Benson, Philip Cleland and Kelvin Youngs, the latter of whom is in charge of the mightily impressive Aircrew Remembered website, for their help, and to Sally Barber who I met, now more than a decade ago, and promised to feature the heroism of her relative William Porteous.

My personal thanks go, as ever, to my magnificent team at work, and notably my friends and colleagues Iona Yadallee and Imogen K Hart, who help keep me largely sane, and to my two boys – Matt and James – and to the genius that is my wife, Elaine, who all seem to do their very best to achieve the opposite. The world would be a much duller place without you!

Chapter 1

The Land of Wishful Thinking

As 21-year-old John Mitchell headed out to his Armstrong Whitworth Whitley on the night of 29 July 1940, he had every right to be feel anxious. It was not the aircraft that worried him – the sleek-looking Mk V with its 1,145hp Rolls-Royce Merlin X engines gave a considerably better performance than an earlier variant he'd seen, although he very much doubted it could make the maximum ceiling the manufacturers claimed. No, it wasn't that. It was his lack of experience that troubled him.

His skipper, John Bartlett, was something of an enigma – a regular commissioned officer and flight commander – whereas John was a mere volunteer reserve (VR). In civilian life, John was a collector for HM Customs and Excise who liked rugger and the odd pint. Now he'd swapped his paperwork and scrum cap for charts and a compass and was expected to navigate his aircraft across the hostile skies of occupied France and into Germany to bomb a target he had little hope of finding, especially in the dark. He wondered if he should tell Bartlett that he'd only ever flown in a Whitley at night once before or, indeed, that his total night-time flying experience amounted to fewer than ten hours. Perhaps it was better keeping that one under his hat. He fancied his skipper didn't suffer fools.

The briefing, conducted by the commanding officer (CO), John Sutton, had been something of a gung-ho affair. The pilots and navigators of 58 Squadron gathered around a large table in the briefing room and were encouraged by their wing commander to 'go smite the Hun'. Sutton was a man who liked to lead from the front and used emotive language to inspire the men under his command. The detail of the raid came not in the briefing, but in a folder from the Air Ministry with precise aiming points and intelligence that if they could hit this particular generator at this particular point, they could put the whole of the Reisholz oil refinery out of action. It was nonsense, of course; John knew that even a near miss would unlikely damage a target to the point it was destroyed, and he also knew, from talking to other observers, that they'd been scattering their bombs all over the place. Finding the city of Düsseldorf itself would be a challenge, let alone a particular target.

After the briefing, John spent the next hour working out his route and trying to find Reisholz on the map. There was no station navigation officer to consult; they were all left to their own devices. The intelligence officer had suggested steering clear of the Friesland Islands but that was it. There was no such thing as the comfort of being in a 'stream', with all aircraft concentrated over the target to a set time to overwhelm the defences. That was a tactic that Bomber Command had yet to discover. Not at all. John had been given a time on target (ToT), but how he got there was down to him. The wireless operator was given the frequencies of known night fighter defences by the signals officer (at least they had one of those) but since he never passed them on to the observer, they were less than useless. It would just be a dozen or so squadron aircraft meandering their way across Europe in the dark, hoping they didn't bump into one another along the way or worse, bump into an enemy fighter. Fortunately, there weren't that many of them about.

As John settled into his new home behind the pilot and co-pilot's seat, he had a little panic as he couldn't work out how to connect his oxygen mask or find the radio transmitter (R/T) socket for the nav table. He had no clue about R/T procedure and use of the crew intercom, but figured he'd have to work that out as they went along.

As their take-off time approached, the engines fired into life and Bartlett began taxiing the inelegant Whitley, with its distinctive nose-down attitude, from its dispersal to the main runway. A blink of green from the Aldis lamp in the control caravan and they were off, slowly crabbing their way into the late evening sky.

Typical of Volunteer Reserve aircrew at the start of the war, John Mitchell had less than ten night time flying hours to his name. (Sean Feast Collection)

John had no sophisticated navigational aids on which to call upon. Finding the target would rely on dead reckoning which, in turn, relied on him being able to see the ground. That meant letting down through the cloud every so often in the vain hope of being able to pick up a prominent landmark or anything that might tell him where he was and where he had been. In the dark, only rivers, lakes or coastlines offered any positive identification and even those depended on the light of the moon or the half-dusk.

During every minute of the flight, John was learning. He learned, for example, that you can best see 'up moon' but next to nothing 'down moon', whereas the reverse is true with sunlight. He also learned the Germans did not take kindly to their presence, which was greeted by a bank of searchlights and intermittent flak. Being shot at was not recommended.

The German defences suggested they might at least be close to something important and so John left his nav table and crawled forward to the nose of the aircraft and the bomb aimer's position, peering through the angled Perspex at the inky blackness below. As observer, he was not only responsible for navigation but also for dropping the bombs. It would be another two years before the authorities recognised the absurdity of the observer leaving his navigation chart just at the point his expertise was needed the most, and split his role into two distinct new categories of navigator and air bomber.

John continued to look but could see nothing. He was not wholly convinced this was Düsseldorf. He hoped it was but his chances of being able to pick out the refinery were virtually nil. There was little option but to go round again, at which point Bartlett made John aware of his displeasure. John had never heard his captain swear before, but he did now, and in spades. As the minutes ticked by and their ToT came and went, sensible heads took charge. John reluctantly returned to his nav table, reconnected his oxygen and R/T leads, and set about trying to work out where they were. Somehow, he managed to take a fix and give his pilot a course to steer from home.

They landed at Linton-on-Ouse, with their bombs still onboard, in the small hours of the morning after a flight of six hours and 40 minutes. They had achieved absolutely nothing.

Three nights later, they tried again.[1]

* * * * *

John Mitchell's description and experiences of bomber operations in the summer of 1940 were a true reflection of the challenges facing Bomber Command and its crews in the early stages of World War Two. Not that the public was aware; they were being fed a very different story by propagandists writing about 'stout aircraft stoutly flown' by a force which, beginning with sturdy adolescence, was 'now on the threshold of manhood'.[2]

Winston Churchill, in a minute to Lord Beaverbrook[3] during the Battle of Britain, said that while the Royal Navy could lose the war, only the RAF could win it. Whereas the fighters were the country's salvation, the bombers alone provided the means of victory.

Churchill and Bomber Command's Chief of Air Staff (CAS) Sir Cyril Newall were very much invested in the bomber as the country's only way of fighting back in the dark days of 1940, when the German Blitzkrieg had swept through Europe and the Wehrmacht was now knocking on the door of Britain. Where and how Bomber Command's resources should be best deployed was being constantly changed through a series of Air Ministry directives. On the one hand, it had a stated plan – a strategy – to attack German industry (with oil as its first priority); on the other, it needed to meet an immediate tactical need and prevent an invasion. This meant attacks on enemy communications and airfields, aircraft production and what appeared to be an obsession with destroying anything that floated, from barges to battleships.

A glance at John Mitchell's logbook for the period between July and December 1940 is particularly revealing: it includes six attacks on docks and shipping (including an early raid on Genoa, just to let the Italians know they weren't untouchable), six raids on oil installations and three on aircraft production. Some of the big industrial names of the time feature on his target list: Škoda, Blohm und Voss and Fokker. He also went to Berlin (twice), including the night of 14 November, which became known as 'Black Thursday' for the losses incurred. That night a force of 50 bombers set out to attack the German capital but only 25 were believed to have reached the city, and dozens crashed on their return.

This was the reality of Bomber Command operations in the first year of war. No one was doubting the courage of the bomber boys: it takes a special kind of bravery to clamber into an aircraft with so little training or experience and with only the slightest hope of finding a target, while all the time an angry enemy is doing its level best to kill you. Mitchell was VR and had not even gone through basic training at an initial training wing (ITW), so perhaps some of his inexperience could be explained. But many of the regular commissioned men were also poorly equipped and ill-prepared for the task they were expected to perform. Their senior commanders lacked experience of modern warfare; none of their senior commanders had current flying experience, though some were more prepared than others to admit their shortcomings.[4]

Throughout the winter of 1940/41 and into the spring, Bomber Command did little more than muddle through. Newall was replaced, in what amounted to an unseemly coup, by Sir Charles Portal, the former Commander-in-Chief (C-in-C) Bomber Command, and his place was taken in turn by Sir Richard Peirse. Tactical expediency diverted the command from its desired objective of strategic bombing, as Peirse was obliged to switch targets and resources in support of the Royal Navy in the Battle of the Atlantic to which the Prime Minister had given absolute priority.[5]

Any pre-conceived plans for expanding the Command to become a war-winning force had to be put on hold. Worse than that, it promptly lost 17 squadrons to Coastal Command. Though some would later return, it constituted a threat to Bomber Command's whole existence. Not only was it losing aircraft to its Coastal friend, but its numbers were also constantly being depleted to meet the demands of other theatres, notably the Middle East in the defence of Egypt, and later to support ground forces in the Far East and India. Although, on paper, Peirse had inherited an impressive force of more than 500 aircraft, more than half of these constituted Bristol Blenheims and single-engined Fairey Battles that were not suitable for the task in hand. Taking into account other factors, such as serviceability, his realistic maximum strength for night operations was no more than 150 aircraft.[6]

This was not a happy time for Bomber Command. It was also a far cry from grand ambitions (which emerged in June 1941) to imagine a force of 4,000 bombers. This ambition, though laudable, seemed like an opium smoker's dream[7] in the context of a Command that appeared to be suffering death by a thousand cuts. At a point when it most needed to demonstrate its worth and justify the faith put into it by its supporters, it was failing, with a rapidly diminishing strength and a C-in-C who, as time progressed, appeared unable to face facts that were staring him in the face.

In a bleak and depressing period of trial and error,[8] the success of night bombing operations was being wildly exaggerated. The authors of the Bomber Command operations record books (ORBs) at a group, station and individual squadron level struck a consistently positive note of the damage being done and targets being reached. They appeared to suggest that not only were the bomber crews achieving an astonishing standard of navigational accuracy but also an ability to distinguish a wealth of detail about precision targets.[9] It was nonsense, of course, but this sense of confidence was reinforced by an unusual source: the Germans themselves, who reported extensive damage being inflicted by certain raids and praised the skill and bravery of RAF pilots. Peirse and his acolytes, who included the man who would ultimately replace him, Arthur Harris, the Deputy Chief of Air Staff, were only too keen to latch on to any publicity that could be generated in support of their success. Harris even complained at the time about the lack of interest from the Air Ministry's publicity department, who he dismissed as 'half witted'. Perhaps, however, they knew more than he did, or were more circumspect in what was reported.

An attack on Mannheim on the night of 16/17 December 1940 serves to illustrate the point. Until that time, bomber crews had been briefed to attack specific targets. Now, the War Cabinet authorised them to attack an entire 'area' in what John Mitchell describes in his logbook as a 'Blitz'.

Peirse marshalled a force of 134 aircraft to take part. The tactics were interesting: eight twin-engined Vickers Wellington bombers flown by hand-picked crews were to open the attack and attempt to start fires in the centre of the city with incendiaries. These fires were to act as a beacon for any aircraft that might be struggling to find the target, and as a de facto aiming point to destroy as much of the city as possible. The significance of the raid is immediately apparent: not only was this the forerunner to what would later be described as 'area bombing' (and the Germans would describe as 'terror bombing'), but it was the first in which an attack was orchestrated by a marking 'force' in its most generic sense. Through actions, rather than words, Peirse was acknowledging the need for greater accuracy, and for experience over enthusiasm.

Everything was in the attackers' favour: there was little cloud, a full moon and only light defences. Despite this, it was a shambles. At best, only three-quarters of the attacking force claimed to have bombed the target and the actual number may have been considerably less. The incendiaries dropped by the expert Wellington crews were not accurate and the largest fires were not in the centre of the city. The majority of the bombs fell in a residential area, hitting a school and two hospitals.

These results, however, were not immediately apparent. At the time, it was believed that the majority of the bombs had fallen in the target area, and the centre of the town had been left in flames. Peirse was so delighted that he sent a congratulatory signal to all those who had taken part. It was only several days later, following the return of a photographic reconnaissance unit (PRU) Spitfire, that a true picture of the raid emerged, to the dismay of Peirse's group commanders. Whereas Norman Bottomley at 5 Group welcomed the first real evidence of the accuracy or otherwise of Bomber Command's efforts, Arthur Coningham at 4 Group said it was clear the groups had no way of telling whether their people were doing good bombing or not![10]

The natives within the War Cabinet, the Air Ministry and at a Command level were becoming restless and wanted answers. Peirse blamed the failure of the raid on operational orders being too rigid – not allowing crews the freedom to identify and aim at the target themselves. Coningham spotted the elephant in the room and took a shot at it. He'd been impressed with how the Germans had picked their best crews to lead certain attacks during the Blitz and believed Bomber Command could achieve the same success if it, too, selected its best units to lead the charge.

But success was not confined to the accuracy of bomb aiming; more important was accuracy of navigation, and to this end, the results were depressing. Coningham knew of errors of up to 100 miles when the crew swore blind that they had bombed their target.[11] These same crews were also often the ones who failed to make it back to their home stations but landed elsewhere and returned the following day!

Mannheim, and the subsequent PRU photographs, was but one of many red flags being waved rigorously in the face of the C-in-C, and his confidence in the success of the raid seemed at odds with a conclusion he had come to a few weeks earlier: that, at best (i.e., on the shorter-range targets in ideal conditions), only one in three of his aircraft found its target.[12]

If Mannheim wasn't a wake-up call, then Peirse could surely not ignore a further report in December regarding two oil plants in Gelsenkirchen. Serious damage was said to have been inflicted by two raids involving a total of almost 200 aircraft dropping 260 tons of explosives and incendiaries. On 24 December, PRU Spitfires brought back excellent photographs of the two plants which, when closely examined, showed the bombs had missed by a country mile. Only a handful of craters could be seen anywhere in the vicinity.

Despite what appeared to be conclusive proof of the Command's failings, the significance of the report was not immediately appreciated, either by Peirse or those in the top levels of the Air Staff.[13] Neither was a paper by Duncan Dewdney, Portal's appointed oil adviser, which followed in early 1941.

Dewdney embarked on a tour of operational squadrons to learn first-hand how the pilots and observers felt about navigation and bombing accuracy, and their confidence in finding specific targets. Their views ranged from total confidence in their success and abilities to grave doubts that their bombs had fallen anywhere close to their intended target. Interestingly, the more experienced crews were the less optimistic. Perhaps more interesting still, nearly all agreed that a target marked by specially picked crews who could start a fire as a guide to following aircraft was much needed, and some threw out dark hints about the inaccurate claims of other squadrons.[14] It seems that while senior commanders demurred, those on the front line had already faced reality.

An attack on Bremen carried out in perfect conditions on the night of 12/13 March is another that suggests Peirse was still in the land of wishful thinking.[15] Fifty-four Wellingtons were detailed to attack the Focke-Wulf factory there, while a further 32 Blenheims went for the centre of the town. Thirty-three of the Wellingtons claimed to have hit their primary objective, and in the photographs that followed, 12 out of 132 bombs were plotted to have hit the factory and a further 28 had fallen within approximately

600 yards. The attack was heralded as a success, despite 21 of the Wellingtons failing to find the target at all. Worse, the results were seen as evidence that, in perfect conditions, the average aiming error would be 600 yards. The flaws in such thinking need little or no explanation and, in the words of the *Official History*, great concessions had been made to reality.[16] Bomber Command still had much progress to make before even the largest area targets could be found and hit with any certainty or regularity.

As the experiments continued, casualties began to mount. Evidence of the inaccuracy of Bomber Command's attacks also increased. Experienced crews were in doubt; post-raid bombing photographs confirmed their concerns. The misleading articles in the German press had now given way to more disturbing reports arriving at the Air Ministry, through neutral countries, that all was not well.[17] But the tipping point came not from Bomber Command or even the Air Ministry but from Churchill's favourite scientist, Professor Frederick Lindemann – Lord Cherwell. More precisely, it came from Cherwell's private secretary and one of the country's leading economists, David Bensusan-Butt.

Under the direction of Cherwell, Butt was tasked with providing a statistical analysis of the results of British bombing of Germany. He examined some 650 photographs taken during night bombing operations on 48 nights between 2 June and 25 July, relating to 100 separate raids on 28 different targets.

The results were little short of dynamite: of those aircraft recorded as attacking their target, only one in three got within five miles; for aircraft attacking the Ruhr, the proportion was one in ten. And this figure relates only to those that actually attacked the target in the first place!

The moon made a difference: in a full moon, two out of five found their target; in the new moon, it was only one in 15. Similarly, German defences also had an impact: an increase in the intensity of flak, perhaps not surprisingly, reduced the number of aircraft getting to within five miles of their target in the ratio of three to two.

The harsh fact of the matter was that the real damage being caused by Bomber Command fell far short of what was being claimed. In some instances, bombers were missing their targets by as much as 70 or 80 miles – the equivalent of a German aircraft dropping its bombs on Coventry believing it to be London.

Errors in navigation were enormous. Embarrassingly so. In one case, a crew from 49 Squadron who were adamant they had attacked Berlin had, in fact, bombed a town 60 miles further south. Another 5 Group aircraft reported as having bombed Mannheim was actually about ten miles north-east of Strasbourg – 65 miles south-west of their intended target![18]

When the contents were shared with Peirse, he did not deny the significance of the findings, but didn't wholeheartedly embrace them either. Cherwell conceded the figures might not be entirely accurate but were sufficiently robust to highlight the now critical importance of improved navigation.[19] Both Portal and Peirse found themselves on the horns of a dilemma. Limitations on bombing accuracy meant they would need every one of the planned 4,000 bombers to achieve the results they required; but that same inaccuracy might also mean they would never be given the force in the first place. Churchill, previously a strong advocate of bombing, began to waver, stating that the best a bomber force could wish for was some level of annoyance.[20] The belief that the bomber could be a war-winning weapon was fast disappearing, and with it the future of Bomber Command itself.

Churchill's response alarmed Portal to such an extent that he mounted a stout rearguard action in defence of Bomber Command, seeing no reason to regard the bomber as a weapon of declining importance. Churchill sought to reassure the CAS that his enthusiasm had not waned, but that no single method of waging war was certain to achieve victory. The only plan, he wrote, was to persevere.[21]

Thus, the Butt report proved both a blessing and curse. In the operations over the late summer/early autumn of 1941, Peirse no longer pursued attacks on priority targets that might fail; rather he directed his forces to other places of lesser importance but where the chances of success were improved.[22] Bomber Command appeared to be losing its confidence.

The beginning of the end to Peirse's somewhat miserable tenure as C-in-C came in November when he was summoned to see the Prime Minister at Chequers to explain the losses incurred on a recent attack on Berlin. On the night of 7/8 November, Peirse sent out a force of 392 aircraft to attack three targets, the largest force being concentrated on Berlin. Despite constantly being warned of poor weather en route and over the target, and objections from Jack Slessor, his new 5 Group commander, Peirse pressed ahead with his plan, with disastrous consequences. Of the 169 bombers despatched to the German capital, 21 were shot down. Less than half of the bombers reached the target, and very little damage was caused. Of 53 Wellingtons sent to Mannheim, seven were lost, and not a single bomb was recorded as falling in the city. Only the force attacking Cologne escaped without loss, but only eight heavy explosive (HE) and 60 incendiary bombs found the target, destroying two houses.

Total losses were more than double the previous highest for a night's operation and the fall-out was almost immediate.[23] Besides the poor weather, Peirse at first attempted to explain away the disaster by placing the blame on his men, citing their lack of experience and inadequate training. It did not take long, however, for his superiors to demand a more satisfactory answer, and although Peirse revised his initial thoughts, he still stuck largely to his guns. It was a position the Vice Chief of Air Staff, Sir Wilfred Freeman, described as 'objectionable' and a damning admission: if they were insufficiently trained, he argued, then it was the commander's duty to train them.[24]

Churchill was in no doubt that Bomber Command could not continue in the same vein, telling Portal '… there is no need to fight the weather and the enemy at the same time'. In the same minute, he added: 'It is now the duty of Bomber Command to regather their strength for the spring.'[25]

The year ground to its depressing conclusion. The bombers were still failing to find their targets with any certainty, and when they did, they were achieving little or nothing by way of any meaningful damage. A successful raid was a rare commodity, even in perfect conditions, and the Command was paying too high a price for failure. It was falling far short of its stated aim of destroying the foundations upon which the German war machine ran, much less bringing about German domestic collapse.[26]

Navigation and bombing accuracy had to be improved to justify a return on investment and vindicate the strategists who believed the bomber alone could bring about victory.

New voices were now being heard at all levels of command, discussing how such accuracy could be attained. Talk began accelerating of creating a new force, a 'target-finding force' (TFF), and 'raid leaders' to take advantage of new navigational aids coming on stream or promised for the future. Groups and individual squadrons began experimenting with flares and incendiaries. Perhaps the answer lay not in choosing the best crews on every squadron to lead independently, but in bringing those best crews together into a single unit, under a single command separate from the Main Force.

Peirse was sacked and, after a temporary hiatus, a new man was appointed in his place, Sir Arthur Harris. The stage was therefore set to write a new chapter in Bomber Command's history.

Chapter 2

Over My Dead Body

I f the champions of creating a dedicated TFF thought they would find support for their ideas from their new C-in-C, they were to be sorely disappointed. Indeed, rather than being an advocate, he would become their most stubborn opponent. From Harris' appointment on 22 February 1942, it would be a further six months before the new force was born.

Harris, famed for his occasional dogma, was not opposed to the concept of target finding per se; he had been experimenting since his days in Iraq in the early 1920s.[1] What he was strongly opposed to, however, was creating any form of elite group to carry it out.

The catalyst to the debate was the introduction of Gee, the first of a series of navigational aids that was intended to revolutionise standards of navigation and bomb aiming in thick weather.[2] Although first tried experimentally in the summer of 1941, it was not until the following March that the device was cleared for mainstream operational use. Bomber Command hoped it would get a clear six-month head start over the Germans before the enemy developed a successful countermeasure.[3]

As soon as Gee was introduced, it became evident in Harris' mind that the aircraft used to find the target and mark it in one way or another should be manned by specially trained and experienced crews, and particularly by highly skilled navigators and air bombers.[4] A new method of 'Pathfinding' attack was developed, known as the Shaker technique, as a portent of things to come.

Under the Shaker principle, the force in any future large-scale raid would be divided into three sections: illuminators, target markers and followers. The illuminators, comprising 20 Wellingtons equipped with Gee, would arrive first and drop bundles of triple flares at defined intervals with the objective of providing a 'lane' of flares approximately six-miles long, which would drift over the target (the Wellingtons would make their run up-wind) and keep it illuminated for 12 minutes. Next would come the target finders, also equipped with Gee, to drop incendiaries, with the hope and expectation that the following force (which did not have Gee) would be able to drop their high explosives on the target.

Shaker was an interesting target-marking idea in theory, but there was plenty that could go wrong in practice. Gee was, arguably, not accurate enough to provide 'blind' bombing with any degree of certainty; the effectiveness of incendiary saturation tactics had not been demonstrated. And it was also not known whether the flares would provide sufficient illumination for long enough to enable the raid to get off to the good start that was so essential to its success. It was this last point that was first tested in action.

The first full-scale trial of the flare technique was attempted, in the event without Gee, on an attack on the Renault armaments and motor factory at Billancourt in France on the night of 3 March. The factory was churning out 18,000 lorries for German forces every year and was a tempting target. The raid was a pleasing success: a total of 235 bombers took part and a considerable amount of damage was done. Happily, only two aircraft were lost, allowing Harris to glow in the raid's success. The flare technique appeared to have more than justified itself, but the success of the raid could be attributed to certain features that were not likely to be common in other attacks. The weather, for example, had been particularly benign, and the full moon on the side of the bombers. There was little or no cloud and defences were negligible. Even in World War One, they had managed precision bombing in such conditions. As the *Official History* cites: 'They were, however, conditions which, over the important targets in Germany, seldom prevailed, and, over the Ruhr, never.'[5]

Five nights later, on 8 March, they attempted their first full 'Shaker' for an attack on Essen. With more than 100 aircraft now equipped with Gee sets, expectations were high. Sadly, they were to be disappointed. Eight major attacks were launched on Essen during March and April using Shaker or a variation on the technique without any significant successes being recorded. Only 22 of more than 200 photographs taken showed bombs falling within five miles of the city. Searchlights and flak were a growing enemy, as was the famed industrial haze which was the attackers' constant adversary over the Ruhr.

Although Bomber Command enjoyed rather more success using the Shaker method over Cologne on 13 March, it was becoming clear that the introduction of Gee and the development of the Shaker technique were not in themselves enough to overcome the substantial difficulties associated with destroying a major city.[6] Gee was a proven success when it came to improving the accuracy of navigation and getting to the right area at the right time, but any hopes that it would be more than that had been quickly squashed. It was not an aid to actual target location and blind bombing. That would come later, with a different device,[7] but, for now, a more radical solution was needed, and it found its strongest advocate in Sidney Bufton, a group captain in the Air Ministry.

Bufton, a gifted electrical engineer, who had been commissioned into the RAF in 1928, was a man of considerable passion and energy. He also had an acute brain and a thoughtful way of expressing himself that was quietly compelling. Against Harris, however, he came up against a force of considerable magnitude, and one with considerably higher rank that was unlikely to take kindly to being dictated to by someone so junior (Bufton was 34), even if he was the deputy director of bomber operations at the Air Ministry.

Although flying a desk at the time, Bufton had considerable operational experience, having commanded 10 Squadron and 76 Squadron until the end of May 1941 and been station commander at RAF Pocklington in Yorkshire. From the outset, he had been concerned with the inaccuracy of their bombing, and it irked him that so many of his men were being lost to so little effect. He vividly recalled one night seeing a bomber 'coned' by searchlights and then shot down in flames on the way back from Cologne. He returned to find one of their crews was missing and knew he had witnessed their deaths. The death of one of his brothers, John, flying Hampdens with 83 Squadron, also served to heighten his opinion of the futility of incurring increasing losses for such infinitesimal results, and it led him to experiment with ways of trying to illuminate the target. He asked for barometrically fused flares to ignite above the aiming point and tried out such resourceful ideas as firing coded Very cartridges once a bomber skipper was sure he had identified the target.[8]

Bufton had proposed to Harris – by the C-in-C's invitation and while the Shaker technique was being trialled – that six squadrons should be located within proximity of one another and given sole responsibility for target finding as a dedicated TFF. To complement his ideas, he canvassed the views of 16 squadron commanders and station commanders about the concept of forming a corps d'elite and received universal support.[9]

These officers, many of whom consulted their own senior crews before responding, believed that creating a TFF was vital if Bomber Command was to succeed in concentrating its effort on any heavily defended German target.[10] They knew that any successes to date had only been achieved by good fortune and against the more easily identifiable targets in ideal weather conditions. They recognised that while many of the crews were willing, they were far from able. Leadership was also an issue, and one likely to only become more acute as the war progressed. Good men, in the vanguard, with the most press-on spirit, would be killed.

Charles Whitworth, station commander at RAF Scampton, wrote, 'I have shown it to the two squadron commanders here. We have some 100 sorties between us, so we have a little experience. I can't imagine anyone in their right senses and who has had bombing experience in this war not agreeing with what you say.' Whitworth went further, describing any objections to the idea of forming an elite force as 'wet'.[11]

Edward Corbally, Officer Commanding (OC) 78 Squadron, urged Bufton not to be put off by those who argued that forming an elite force would be to the command's detriment: 'The Army has never suffered because of the Guards

Regiments,' he wrote, 'and I would like to see a posting to the TFF being regarded as a reward for good service and proved ability in the "line" squadrons.'

Gus Walker, station commander of RAF North Luffenham, described the proposal as 'excellent' and one he had considered to be a requirement 'for some time'.[12] Willie Tait at Marston Moor said that while the best bomber pilot could drop his own small bomb load on the target, 'present tactics do not use his ability to drop the bombs of ten other aircraft flown by average standard crews'.[13]

Bufton sent Harris the results of his survey on 11 April, confident that the unanimous opinion of experienced frontline aircrews would convince Harris and his group commanders of the benefits of his ideas. He couldn't have been more wrong. Bufton's proposals were dismissed out of hand, which appeared to contradict Harris' former statement that he had 'a fairly open mind' on the subject of a TFF – his actions made it perfectly clear that he had no intention of creating one!

Harris organised his own cabal of five group commanders and five specially selected squadron commanders who, universally, agreed that a separate TFF was not only unnecessary but also undesirable, and that bombing results from recent raids were improving.

The hubris demonstrated by the C-in-C in the matter was breathtaking. He prefaced the meeting by declaring that he was totally against creating any elite force, and it is hardly surprising in this context that anyone at the meeting chose to disagree with him. Jack Slessor, one of those consulted, would much later admit that he should have spoken out against his boss but did not so at the time: 'I argued strongly against the proposal and am still not sure that I was wrong. I did not like the idea of special marker squadrons, and still less of a special group.'[14]

In truth, Bufton and Harris were not especially far apart in their assessments of the bombing situation. While, publicly, Harris was defending his men from criticism and adverse publicity, in private, he was deeply concerned about bombing accuracy and especially bombing discipline. The difference between the two men was this: Harris believed area bombing was the core strategy for his bomber offensive and would bring about the ends he sought; Bufton saw it as a temporary measure until the art of precision bombing could be perfected, and accurate and effective attacks upon specific targets could begin.

Bufton tried another tack: he analysed a series of raids mounted by Bomber Command against Essen between March and April and concluded that 90 per cent of the aircraft had dropped their bombs between five and 100 miles away from the target. On a particular attack on Rostock, which had been heralded as a success, more than three-quarters of the effort had been wasted.

Bufton's report clearly served to irritate the C-in-C and his staff. It was said that one staff officer would call for tweezers and 'pause for nausea' whenever a paper from Bufton crossed his desk.[15] Harris put his own 'expert' on the case, who described Bufton's conclusions as 'biased' and 'misleading'.[16] He had to concede, however, that Bufton's figures were close to his own. In the Essen attacks, for example, he placed 109 of the 131 plotted photographs as being between five and 100 miles from the target compared to Bufton's figure of 110 out of 122. Rather than being able to roundly dismiss Bufton's findings, Harris had unwittingly confirmed them.

The failures, Bufton argued, were due to a lack of 'unmistakable conflagration', which could never be achieved when second-class crews were mixed with first-class ones in the initial phases of the attack. More pointedly, he added: 'Even first-class crews will not be successful unless they are co-ordinated in one body and develop the specialised technique.'

It was in this conclusion that Bufton found obstinate stonewalling from the C-in-C. Harris had been opposed to the creation of any 'corps d'elite' from the very beginning. He was utterly convinced that forming such a force of hand-picked crews into a single organisation would have a demoralising effect on the rest of the squadrons under his command. It would also, he maintained, reduce their efficiency, taking away from each squadron the very men who were required to be flight commanders and squadron commanders in their own units.[17]

In his view, Harris repeated, he had the full support of his group commanders. He also had his own plan to train and form target-marking squadrons in each group, and in doing so breed healthy competition and generate new ideas that could be more easily tried. His proposal was that the bombing photographs of each squadron should be assessed on a monthly basis, and the honour of target marking given to the 'winning' squadron for the following month. Harris also stuck resolutely to his guns that things were not quite as bad as they seemed, stating in a letter to Bufton that he was 'not prepared to accept all the serious disadvantages of a corps d'élite in order to secure possible some improvements on methods which are already proving reasonably satisfactory'.[18]

(Harris' forthright opinions of elite bodies of men, which he believed went against the very ethos of the Royal Air Force, are remarkable given he subsequently went on to form, train and equip 617 Squadron, the Dambusters, and continued to support its status as an 'elite' squadron for the rest of the war.)

Bufton wholly disagreed that there were 'serious disadvantages' to forming a separate unit. Nor did he agree that results were 'reasonably satisfactory', especially as he knew that, in private, Harris was far from satisfied himself. Similarly, Bufton did not believe for a moment that morale in the 'ordinary' squadrons would be adversely affected – quite the opposite. He believed that an elite unit would be something that first-class crews would aspire to be part of and be proud to belong to.

This certainly proved to be the case. From the very beginning, rank and file aircrew, senior officers and even whole squadrons did indeed aspire to become part of the new unit: out of the 150 aircrew from 35 Squadron asked to volunteer upon the formation of Pathfinder Force (PFF), only seven declined to put their names forward.[19] It was a similar situation on 83 Squadron; they considered it a considerable honour to have been selected as one of the founding squadrons of this 'great new venture'.[20]

Later in the war, that same sense of pride and excitement prevailed. Laurence Deane, by then an experienced Pathfinder captain, was so excited upon being given command of one of the elite squadrons of PFF that he couldn't sleep.[21] Gwynne Price, a flight engineer with 195 Squadron, was so thrilled to be considered good enough to serve with the elite Pathfinders that he and his crew accepted immediately.[22] And when Peter Noble, an air bomber with 550 Squadron, was initially accepted for PFF only to see his posting subsequently cancelled, he lay in bed all day feeling sorry for himself.[23]

On 8 May, Bufton skilfully crafted a private and confidential letter to Harris, outlining his analysis of the Essen raids. This appears to have been the tipping point, notwithstanding Harris sought to discredit them. He countered all of Harris' wider objections, addressing issues of morale and promotion, as well as the technical aspects of successfully locating and bombing the target. He also tackled Harris' fixation with a corps d'elite in a brilliant sentence, which is a reflection of its time: 'No one,' he wrote, 'would dream of trying to defeat a rival school by not turning out the best house team, and that is what we are doing now. It is essential to put the best men in the first team and even that is not enough; they must train and co-ordinate their tactics as a team. Until we do this, we cannot start to beat the enemy defences.'[24]

In arguably the boldest and most controversial paragraph in the letter, Bufton stated that the arguments made for or against a target-marking force were a manifestation of a much wider issue, a conflict of ideas between 'the older officers of much general experience and the ever-growing body of younger ones who have been actively engaged in operations'. Only the younger officers, he argued, truly understood the real challenges they currently faced, but they were not being listened to by their older peers. 'If we could marry, at all levels of command, the mature judgement and wider experience of the older officers with the imagination, drive and operational knowledge of the younger, then I think we should obtain the highest possible standard of morale and achievement throughout Bomber Command.'

Bufton's letter went unanswered. A formal report on the bombing of Germany from Mr Justice Singleton served to drive the message home further. Having interviewed two operational officers 'of great experience', he said that both agreed in the effectiveness of Gee in bringing an aircraft to within four or so miles of the target, but it was in those last few miles that the real difficulties arose, and that not all crews were of the same calibre, determination or skill. 'The officers are firmly convinced of the desirability of a specially trained Target Finding Force.'

Remarkably, in the face of such an extraordinary weight of evidence, Harris still declined to give in gracefully. He continued to press his own ideas, including a proposal to create 'raid leaders' and distinguish them by allowing them to wear a winged eagle on their uniforms – a symbol that would later be adopted by the new force. He wrote: 'My Raid Leader Scheme provides all the requirement of the Target Finding Force fanatic' – a less than oblique swipe, one imagines, at Bufton himself. He argued that he could see no reason why a pilot in the corps d'elite would have any greater chance of seeing a target than anyone else, but in doing so, also defeated his own argument in regards to a raid leader who would surely experience the same difficulty.

It took the intervention of Sir Wilfred Freeman to break the impasse. With the complete support of Sir Henry Tizard, the Air Ministry's chief scientific adviser, Freeman briefed Portal, the CAS, and persuaded him of the need to overrule Harris' objections once and for all. A letter was drafted and sent on 14 June, in which Portal rejected Harris' proposals in clear and unambiguous language, calling out many contradictions.

Much of Harris' argument, for example, had been centred around the use of Gee, but if Gee were to be jammed and rendered useless within a handful of months of operation, they'd be back to where they started. Portal's letter said, 'We cannot expect immunity from interference for much longer. When it is denied to us as a target locating device it is clear that your proposals could not ensure to the bomber force the leadership which they must have if the average crews are to overcome their great and increasing difficulties.' He was also bemused by Harris' suggestion that his raid leaders be given a special badge, which seemed completely at odds with his dislike of recognising the elite.

Noting that Harris' position appeared to have changed from one of a complete refusal to countenance any form of target-marking force to his latest ideas to appoint raid leaders, Portal appealed to his subordinate's better judgement.[25] Whereas Harris had refused to consider bringing selected crews together into a single unit, Portal believed this to be the very essence of the solution. He argued that, without that close association, there could be no continuity of technique, no day-to-day improvement of method and no simple way of ensuring the plans and briefing for each individual operation were similarly and clearly interpreted and acted upon by the force as a whole.

The letter concluded: 'In the opinion of the Air Staff, the formation of a special force would open up a new field for improvement, raising the standard of accuracy of bombing, and thus morale, through Bomber Command.'[26]

Portal was reluctant to impose an order on one of his most senior commanders, and a meeting was arranged for the follow day, at which the matter was discussed further. Harris is believed to have started by declaring that a target-marking force would only be established 'over my dead body'.[27] Told to think it over, he at last relented, doubtless appreciating the implied ultimatum. Bufton was ecstatic. An inveterate letter writer, Bufton penned a note to his fiancée, Maureen Browne: 'We have won!' he wrote. 'Bert came to see the head man today and he hadn't a leg to stand on. It's a shattering result and is rather like the battle in the last war which was required to set up the convoy system.'[28]

In what would today be described as a U-turn, Harris now threw what appeared to be his full weight behind creating a new force in his own image. He wrote:

In other circumstances, I should not have accepted the position, but we were now faced with the fact that Gee had failed as a bombing aid and that the new radar aids which had been promised for the autumn of 1942 were not to be forthcoming until the end of the year. For the time being it was essential to improve our methods of finding the target visually and marking it, and this seemed to require the whole-time activities of a specialised force, not only for leading but for practical experiments.[29]

Harris was far from won over to the need for a separate unit, or that it should be in any way permanent, as his later actions would show. But for now, he took decisive action, refusing to call them 'target markers' or 'target finders' but insisting on his own, rather more dramatic name: Pathfinders.

Since anyone volunteering for 'his' new Pathfinder Force would most likely run greater risks and expose themselves to greater dangers at the vanguard of every raid, he similarly insisted they should all receive a step-up in rank and pay, which caused considerable consternation and arguments with the Treasury. On this point, however, Harris would not be moved. He was also insistent that Pathfinders should wear the flying eagle badge that he had originally proposed for raid leaders: 'As we were compelled by events to have a corps d'elite it seemed necessary to carry the principle through to its logical conclusion.'[30]

The scene was therefore set. His new force had a name. Now he had to find the men and, more importantly, the man to command them.

He had just the person in mind.

Chapter 3

The Main Imaginative Genius

While Bufton and Harris were having their spat, a 32-year-old Australian wing commander, who both men knew well and who the C-in-C subsequently earmarked for command of the new Pathfinder Force, was making a thorough nuisance of himself in an internment camp in Sweden.

Whereas some of his fellow uninvited guests would have been more than happy to sit the war out in the comparative safety of a neutral country, the wing commander was having none of it, constantly badgering British Legation and Swedish government officials such that they couldn't wait to see the back of him.[1] It worked: within weeks he was on his way home in a Lockheed Electra as a consignment of 'unimportant undiplomatic male',[2] and upon his return to RAF Leeming, via Leuchars, he resumed command of his squadron, exactly one month after his Halifax was shot down.

Donald Bennett had been interned having made it across the border from Norway into Sweden after being obliged to bale out of his burning Halifax following a particularly desperate attack on *Tirpitz* in the Norwegian Aas Fjord. At the time, he was in command of 10 Squadron, having earlier commanded 77 Squadron.

The attack on *Tirpitz* in April had been ill-conceived and, as Bennett would find out later, devoid of vital intelligence from the Admiralty about enemy defences which, had they been known in advance, could have avoided the losses incurred.[3] Two squadrons of Halifax bombers were briefed to come in low and lob cylindrical mines at the banks of the fjord, hoping they would roll down into the water to lodge below the ship's hull and explode. A further force was to bomb from height.

Detached north to Lossiemouth and Kinloss, the small force (including nine from 10 Squadron) took off on the evening of the 27th for the hop across the North Sea. All was quiet until they crossed the enemy coast at which point all hell let loose. Taking flak from both sides of the fjord, Bennett's aircraft was immediately hit and the rear gunner badly wounded. Even down at 200ft, the observer was unable to pick out the target, owing to a chemical smokescreen, and the pilot was forced to overshoot with the hope of coming around again. It was a forlorn hope, for by now a wing was on fire, the starboard undercarriage was hanging down and the starboard flap had begun to trail. There was nothing for it but to jettison his mines and make height so the crew – and especially the wounded rear gunner – had time to bale out.

As the crew left one by one and Bennett contemplated his own fate, in particular how he could reach his parachute, clip it on[4] and bale out without losing control of the aircraft, his flight engineer re-appeared, risking his own life to help his captain. Bennett needed no second bidding, clipping on his chute and following his flight engineer through the escape hatch. He pulled his ripcord immediately, heard and felt the canopy deploy and then hit the ground, landing in the soft snow, unhurt. Quickly taking stock of his situation, he covered his harness with the parachute silk and started walking, soon bumping into his wireless operator. After a series of heart-stopping moments when they were sure they would be caught, the two men eventually found help and were guided over the border into Sweden, with the chance to return to operations.

Bennett was no stranger to adventure. A tough, single-minded Queenslander from the city of Toowoomba, Bennett left Brisbane Grammar School – having failed to make any particular impression – to work on his father's cattle station. Recognising his work as a jackaroo was utterly devoid of prospects,[5] he reasoned on joining the Royal Australian Air Force (RAAF), much to his father's disappointment and his mother's concern, but was too young. He enrolled in evening classes to expand his knowledge of the sciences and joined the Australian Citizens Force as a non-commissioned officer (NCO). Both carried weight when he was finally old enough to apply to become a pilot, and it was on a cold, wet July morning that Bennett and 14 others reported to commence their training.

As a cadet at Point Cook, the Australian equivalent of Cranwell for the training of RAF officers, Bennett took to service life and flying with ease, learning the rudiments of RAAF lore very quickly – particularly that it was not so much 'thou shall not do' but rather 'thou shall not get caught'.[6] He enjoyed lessons on the ground and in the air, especially the longer-distance cross-countries, coming second in classroom examinations and first in flying. Having accepted a transfer to the RAF on a short-service commission, he was soon on his way to the UK, reporting first to the Air Ministry and then on to Uxbridge. After further flying training on Siskins, an aeroplane he described as undoubtedly one of the worst aircraft ever produced,[7] he was posted to 29 Squadron, delighted to become a 'fighter boy'.

With 29 Squadron, Bennett learned further lessons that he would take with him to senior command – how some squadron commanders would go out of their way not to fly, blaming the English weather, whereas others were positively dangerous in the other direction. He learned how some were driven by bureaucracy and red tape, while others were more cavalier in their attitude to paperwork. At a practical level, he learned how to fly a Siskin at night – his first experience of night-time flying – and deal with the challenges it brought, especially when it came to navigation. And he learned a very English lesson: if you dropped a clanger, everyone liked you; the only way to fail was to be right.[8] He also made a good many friends who would help him in his future career, among them was Ralph Cleland, one of three officers in the same flight. Ralph had been a Halton apprentice, one of Trenchard's famous 'brats' at No. 1 School of Technical Training, whose qualities had been recognised with an opportunity to fly and a commission.[9]

Bennett spent a comparatively happy year at North Weald before applying for a flying boat course, determined to gain more experience on different 'types' and especially 'heavies' such as the twin-engined Southampton, the most beautiful example of wooden construction he had ever seen.[10] Unknowingly, his acceptance onto the course was to be the turning point in his career.

Another happy six months at Calshot passed without incident, Bennett readily getting to grips with the flying boat despite being told by one instructor that he flew it like a fighter. His response was typically Bennett: the only way to fly any kind of aircraft was to be its master. On completion of his course, he was posted to 210 Squadron at Pembroke Docks and soon had the privilege and pleasure of meeting the CO, 'Bert' Harris. Harris, Bennett believed, was a man of fire and dash, with the intelligence to match,[11] and he was delighted when Harris later took over as the head of Bomber Command.

For the time being, however, large doses of night flying were punctuated with fishery protection patrols before a sudden and unwelcome return to Calshot as a navigation instructor at the RAF Navigation School. Whereas the thought of lecturing appalled him, he soon recognised that if you have to teach, you have to learn, and he used this to his advantage, significantly expanding his knowledge and becoming something of an expert.

In the early part of 1934, and with a determination to enter the England-to-Melbourne air race, Bennett studied for his First-Class Navigator's licence, sometimes staying up until two in the morning with his books. His hard work paid off and, in only two and a half months, he passed, thus becoming only the seventh holder of the licence in the world. He also managed to team up with a fellow Australian to take part in the race. With a clapped-out Lockheed Vega, which had neither the speed nor the range to make an indent on the record, they set off, eventually making it as far as Aleppo. On coming into land, however, the undercarriage collapsed, and Bennett damaged his knee and crushed three vertebrae in the resulting crash. It was a rather battered young airman who returned to Calshot a week later.

With the end to his short-service commission in sight and making plans for a career in civilian aviation, Bennett turned once again to study. It was time well spent; when the moment came to fledge from the RAF, he held a B pilot's licence, ground engineer's licences in A, C and X categories, his wireless operator's licence, and an instructor's certificate. He also racked up a few hours flying for Jersey Airways. By the time he left the service, he had more than 1,350 hours flying to his name across more than 20 types. And this was only the start.

Bennett's knowledge of almost every technical element of aircraft and flying was to stand him in good stead, inspiring awe and not a little fear in the men who would later come under his command. Every NCO who came before him for a commission, and all those standing in line to be awarded their Pathfinder badge as a testament to their ability and qualification, were tested on their own 'trade' and many admitted that Bennett knew as much if not more of their own individual skills than they did. Bill 'Andy' Anderson, a decorated wing commander who went on to serve on Bennett's staff in the PFF, noted that Bennett could take Morse as fast as any wireless operator whose trade it was, and he had a knowledge of matters aeronautical that were 'encyclopaedic'.[12] Hamish Mahaddie, who similarly served on Bennett's staff, described his boss as having an enviable array of qualifications and experience without equal.[13] Bennett wrote the definitive textbook on navigation – *The Complete Air Navigator* – while on his honeymoon! Indeed, one comedian said that Bennett's book was in three parts: one for beginners, one for advanced students and one for Bennett because he was the only one who could understand it.[14]

Bennett did not leave the RAF altogether willingly, but he understood its limitations and embraced his new career with typical vigour. Invited to join Imperial Airways (later British Overseas Airways Corporation, BOAC), he flew two trips as a supernumerary before being appointed first officer on the mighty Handley Page 42, revelling in its size and performance. Operating from Croydon, Imperial was a 'real' airline in full-scale operation,[15] and Bennett could only marvel at the skill of its pilots who, he believed, were the best in the world, with the greatest self-reliance and, ultimately, the highest competence. They were a mirror reflection of the types of men he would later seek for Pathfinder Force.

Posted to Egypt to fly the route between Alexandria and Brindisi, Bennett not only had to put up with the questionable performance of the fleet's three-engined open-cockpit Short Calcuttas, but also the equally questionable behaviour of the Italian fascists and their open antagonism towards the British. On one occasion, being marooned in Brindisis for five days, he used the time to write another definitive work, *The Air Mariner*, on the handling of flying boats.

Spirits rose with the arrival of the first of the much-heralded Short S23 Empire flying boats, and Bennett was given command of G-ADIX *Cassiopeia* with a first officer and permanent crew, the happiest flying arrangement Bennett had ever encountered.[16]

Don Bennett with Albert Coster after their historic flight in the Mayo Composite, July 1938. (Jennie Gray, personal collection)

In early 1938, Bennett applied formally and in writing to be put in charge of Imperial's *Mercury* flying boat, one-half of what was known as a 'Mayo composite' after its inventor, Major Robert Mayo. The Mayo composite was Imperial's temporary answer to providing a transatlantic/ long-range mail delivery service and comprised a small four-engined float plane (christened *Mercury*) sitting atop a much larger parent flying boat, *Maia*. In simple terms, the parent boat flew a certain distance, at which point *Mercury* was 'released' for the onward journey, and *Maia* returned home. It was a short-cut solution while experiments were conducted (in which Bennett also had a hand) on in-flight refuelling.

It took some time, and not a little bullying of the Air Ministry, to be allowed to conduct a proving flight to Canada, which finally took place in July 1938 and proved to be an overwhelming success. Bennett recalled the reception they received upon landing as being akin to how the early settlers in Australia must have felt when suddenly surrounded by the Indigenous people!

The euphoria of that first trip was somewhat dampened by Bennett's attempt to break the long-distance flying record, a route being worked out between Scotland (Dundee) and Capetown. Having been initially delayed by world events, and particularly the Munich Crisis, the day finally dawned for the attempt to be made. With the trip expected to take two days, Bennett's crew included a radio operator, who also held a B pilot's licence so he could share some of the load.

All went well to begin with, but after a successful separation, the loss of an engine cowling caused increased drag and higher fuel consumption, so although the seaplane record was broken, the absolute record was not. Bennett had to comfort himself with the knowledge that he had navigated his way down the length of Africa with little else than a sextant to guide him!

Perhaps not surprisingly, Bennett was in the air on the day war was declared, in charge of a C-Class flying boat conducting further flight refuelling exercises en route to the US. Part way into the voyage, his wireless operator intercepted an SOS – the first of the war – from the SS *Athenia* to say it had been torpedoed (a sinking later condemned as a war crime). Bennett's immediate thought was to go to help, but he quickly realised that, in the dark, there was nothing he could do and, afterwards, he felt helpless at their impotency.[17]

While Bennett contemplated how he might best serve the war effort, and whether he should re-join the RAF, he was deployed on a number of 'cloak and dagger' exercises in relation to enemy submarines, which he described as 'real story book stuff'.[18] He was also assigned the urgent task of helping General Sikorski, the leader of the Free Polish Army, to evacuate senior members of Poland's cabinet and general staff from under the noses of the advancing Germans. In fact, France had already surrendered, and the country was, in theory, occupied. However, British troops were still escaping via Bordeaux. Bennett flew Sikorski and his aide in an S30 flying boat to Biscarrosse to the south of the town, and although he had been ordered to give him every assistance (but not lose the boat in the process), he made it clear that if the general was not back by morning, he would be off. An anxious night followed without much sleep, and as dawn broke, he made ready to leave. Just as he was giving up hope, a party of four vehicles screamed into town, and in short order they were all on board and on their way. Aside from being fired upon by a British cruiser on their way out (fortunately their shooting was up to their usual standard, Bennett remarked acidly afterwards), Bennett landed at Poole without further issue, delivering his precious cargo as promised.

After the Sikorski episode, Bennett was called upon for one last special operation: flying the Duke of Kent to an international expo in Lisbon. Britain was keen to show that, despite world events, they were still able to conduct 'business as usual', by royal appointment if necessary. Accommodated overnight in a dubious hotel in the city, Bennett was somewhat alarmed to be sharing a dining room with his opposite number from Lufthansa!

This proved to be Bennett's last flight with BOAC (as Imperial was now known) before he was approached for another assignment. Reporting to the Ministry of Aircraft Production, headed by the bombastic Canadian media mogul Lord Beaverbrook, Bennett was ordered to America and tasked with setting up a new unit to ferry US-built aircraft to the UK. Beaverbrook saw in Bennett a man used to getting things done, and the feeling was mutual.

Before the war, the British government had entered into a controversial enterprise to buy US aircraft to bolster its 'order of battle'. The controversy was not so much regarding the deal itself, but rather the quality of aircraft being bought, many of which were far from fit for purpose. Among the unquestionably poor aircraft – like the woefully dismal Brewster Buffalo – were the undoubtedly good, like the Lockheed Hudson. The challenge was how to get them to the UK quickly and in one piece. Previously shipped in containers across the Atlantic, the U-boat menace had led to journey times being extended, and more practical solutions were sought. The obvious answer, at least for the larger aircraft, was to fly them across, but to do so safely required expert navigation. With his new title of Flying Superintendent, Bennett was in his element and there was much to organise. Not only did he have to find the crews, but he was also keen on test flying the aircraft himself, doubting the manufacturer's claims for how the Hudson performed. He was right to be cautious: on putting a Hudson through its paces at the Lockheed Works in California, he noted the aircraft was inferior to the estimated performance by approximately 8 per cent, and this, of course, would mean extra fuel for the crossing.[19]

It was some weeks before Bennett had assembled six crews and their aircraft, in addition to his own, to attempt the first crossing, finding time in the interim to add both the Consolidated B24 Liberator and PBY Catalina flying boat to his flying log. By mid-November, they were ready to go, with many sceptical they would make it; other attempts during the winter months had ended in catastrophe, but Bennett was confident of his own abilities and those of his men. Although the flight across was not without its difficulties, all seven Hudsons arrived in Ireland in one piece. The next day, they made the short hop across the Irish Sea to Blackpool where the aircraft would be serviced before being delivered to their squadrons.

Bennett had laid the foundations for a new service and proved it could work. Further flights followed and a routine was established, but Bennett had no intention of seeing out the war as a glorified delivery man. With the arrival of Sir Frederick Bowhill in charge of the newly formed RAF Ferry Command in July 1941, Bennett found himself back in London, seeking ways of becoming gainfully employed. Re-joining the RAF was not as easy as it seemed, and the best the service could offer him was the temporary rank of wing commander and second in command of an elementary air navigation school. It was a job that anyone could have done without any great knowledge of navigation![20]

On the suggestion of his new CO,[21] Bennett paid a social call on the personnel officer at Bomber Command, Henry 'Daddy' Dawes, and was welcomed with open arms. He was appointed squadron commander of a heavy bomber squadron pretty much on the spot and hardly had time to catch his breath before he was on his way to HQ 4 Group in Yorkshire. Here, he happened to bump into the Air Officer Commanding (AOC) Roderick 'Roddy' Carr, with whom Bennett was already acquainted and on friendly terms and was asked to take command of 77 Squadron at Leeming.

The squadron had been operating from the start of the war and moved several times before arriving at Leeming on 5 September 1941. At the time, it was operating the Whitley, the twin-engined strategic bomber, which had been billed as a war winner and did remarkable service in the early years, undertaking the first leaflet raid (3/4 September 1939), the first sortie over Berlin (1/2 October 1939) and the first bombing attack on mainland Germany (10/11 May 1940). Conceived as the first modern heavy bomber to be designed purely for night operations, it was an aircraft full of character, a hard worker and certainly an accomplished type for the period.[22] Sadly, it was already out of date by the time the first shots of the war had been fired, though Bennett – who was at first dismayed to learn that 77 Squadron flew Whitleys – later came to appreciate the type as a workhorse.[23] It is to its credit that it was still operating with Bomber Command at the end of 1942, long after its sell by date had expired.

Bennett formally took command at the beginning of December from David Young who, in turn, took command of 76 Squadron at Middleton St George.[24] Before he left, Young, an experienced civilian pilot, painted a vivid picture of bomber operations, and Bennett realised he had much to learn. But he also had much to teach, especially when it came to navigation, and was pleased to see that his time spent on improving navigation techniques soon had a notable effect on bombing results. He shifted squadron thinking from one where crews were delighted to bring home an aiming point photograph to one of being disappointed if they didn't.

A valuable lesson was the suggestion from the Leeming station commander, Bill 'Crack-em' Staton, that Bennett should fly a few operations first as second pilot, partly to learn the ropes but also as an opportunity to assess the flying abilities of his crews.[25] It proved something of an eye opener. Flying with a Sergeant Grace to Wilhelmshaven on the night of 16/17 December, Bennett was alarmed that the pilot failed to notice a sudden drop in oil pressure on one of the engines and even more concerned when he ignored his CO's suggestion that it was the gauge that was at fault and not the engine itself. With one propeller 'feathered'[26] and losing height, they went into attack, their aircraft being peppered by flak and the air bomber failing to spot the target. Just as they were about to start their third bombing run, and now dangerously low, Bennett assumed command, jettisoned the bombs, unfeathered the propeller on the 'faulty' engine and headed for safety. He later said he had no wish to undermine the sergeant in front of his crew, but he simply had more experience. He made a point from that moment on of nearly always flying with different crews to assess their efficiency. As he wrote later, he did not fault their bravery, just that they had little knowledge and even less experience of flying.

Among the dozen or so raids in which Bennett took part prior to his move to 10 Squadron and his adventures in Sweden was the attack on the Renault works on the night of 3/4 March 1942, taking 29-year-old James Spalding as second pilot.[27] It was, in Bennett's opinion, one of the most thorough and effective raids he had seen up to that point,[28] the squadron commander attacking the target from below 2,000ft. An equally memorable raid followed a few nights later on the MAT-Ford works near the Seine, Bennett being obliged to be over the area for almost two hours while his bomb aimer attempted to find the target. On his return, Bennett was given a fatherly talking to by the then Leeming station commander, Strang Graham, about taking unnecessary risks. Between them, they counted more than 50 holes in his aircraft and discovered that one of the control lines had been all but severed.

Throughout his time on 77 Squadron, and after transferring across to Halifaxes, Bennett kept in regular contact with the Directorate of Bombing Operations. By happy circumstance, the staff within the directorate included his old friend from 29 Squadron, Ralph Cleland, now a wing commander. It was Cleland, Bennett said, who ensured the directorate was made aware of his expertise as a navigator and as such would have much to contribute to the debate on how to find and mark future targets. Although something of an irritation to successive C-in-Cs, the Directorate of Bombing Operations came up with a number of worthwhile suggestions. Bennett was one of the 16 operational commanders who responded positively to Sid Bufton's proposal for the formation of a special target-finding force: 'The majority of captains would be only too pleased to have the target found for them and navigators and captains would aspire to qualify for a posting to the TFF as a reward for proficiency and professional ability.'[29]

On his return from Sweden, and after a debrief that obliged him to miss the first of Harris' showpiece thousand-bomber raids (much to his frustration), Bennett was summoned to see his C-in-C twice: the first was to be told of his award of the Distinguished Service Order (DSO), one of the highest awards for gallantry that could be bestowed upon an officer, for his part in leading the attack on the *Tirpitz*;[30] the second was to be given command of Pathfinder Force. Harris was only just in time: Bennett was but hours away from leading his squadron out to the Middle East when he was recalled, virtually from his cockpit.

Bennett vividly recalled the event in his biography. Harris, who he much admired, was blunt, honest and to the point. He told Bennett he had opposed the idea of a separate TFF from the start and had fought its creation tooth and nail but had been overruled. He also said that he categorically refused to call it a 'target-finding force' because that was the name put forward by Bufton – who he described as a 'junior' officer – and the Directorate of Bomber Operations and which he, therefore, automatically opposed. It may also have been the reason he was against the appointment of a doughty and unquestionably gifted group captain by the name of Basil Embry as its first commander.[31]

Harris was also clear that while he would waste no effort on supporting Pathfinder Force as a unit, that did not mean he would not support Bennett personally. Indeed, Harris much admired Bennett as a man and for his technical knowledge and personal operational ability, which he described as 'altogether exceptional'.[32] He believed his moral and physical courage to be outstanding and, as such, he was the obvious man for the job, despite his comparative 'youth'.

There was little doubt Bennett was the right man at the right time, and Harris no doubt also saw in his protégé something of himself: both could be forthright to the point of rudeness. Harris said of Bennett: 'He could not suffer fools… and by his own standards there were many fools.'[33] Both men also had phenomenal stamina and energy, characteristics that would be required in large quantities if Pathfinder Force was to succeed, for there were many battles to be won within the service before taking on the enemy.

To his men, however, Bennett was to become an inspirational leader. Jack Watts, who had been the navigation officer and bombing leader on 10 Squadron, described him as 'a leader by qualification, by example, and by performance'.[34] Andrew Maitland, a squadron leader and bombing leader with 7 Squadron, said he had never met a more brilliant man, describing Bennett's knowledge of aircraft and aircrew as 'frightening'.[35] Andy Anderson, an expert navigator and one of the first to join Bennett's

HQ team, also described Bennett as 'brilliant', a man who was essentially not a talker but a man of action.[36]

Stafford Coulson, a pre-war regular, was accustomed to the pre-war management of operational units, where squadron commanders and flight commanders were there to administrate rather than fly. 'It never dawned on me until people like Don Bennett, Basil Embry, Harry Broadhurst, Gus Walker and Sid Bufton turned up, that you led your flight commanders, your pilots, your crews by example, and by finding out what it was like. This was Bennett's forte which he brought to Pathfinder Force.'[37]

Harris, who rarely left his lair in High Wycombe unless it was to welcome home his Dambusters,[38] was a notably distant figure from his men, at least physically. Bennett, at the other extreme, made a point of being 'in the field', at briefings to see the men off or welcoming them on their return. Pilot Stafford Harris remembers Bennett as an ever-present figure who would often turn up unannounced: 'One night I put some petrol on the fire to get it going and ended up setting fire to the billet. Fortunately, I was in demand at the time and avoided being court martialled!'[39] Lawrence 'Nick' Nicholson says simply: 'Usually as an NCO you'd keep well away from an air-rank officer. But not Bennett.'

Bennett's key strength was that he could talk to his men on equal terms because, unlike the other senior commanders, he had current operational experience. He was the only one, in his words, who had seen a 'hot' war,[40] and it even embarrassed him that group commanders were sending their men to do things that they were not, it appeared, prepared to do themselves.

To these commanders, Bennett was arrogant to the point of impertinence, an arrogance born partly out of youth and partly, no doubt in their minds, from being an 'airline fellow' and an Australian to boot![41] He was, in short, 'not one of them'. Even Harris, who described Bennett to the Prime Minister as one of the finest and most efficient youngsters he had come across in his service career, also said of Bennett that he had, at times, 'the young intellectual's habit of underrating experience and overrating knowledge'. Regardless of this, however, Harris still considered himself 'lucky' to have secured the services of a man of such attainment to lead his new force.[42]

But perhaps the last word on Bennett should go to a man who would become one of his chief adversaries, Oberst Hans-Joachim 'Hajo' Herrmann, a senior Luftwaffe commander and expert night fighter. He identified Bennett as 'the main imaginative genius' of the bomber offensive and a man who would become a personal obsession, the enemy of all Germans.[43]

The scene was therefore set. Now Bennett had to prove his genius, and the faith put in him by his C-in-C.

Chapter 4

'A Very Definite Advance in Technique'

Flensburg is a pretty enough town in the northern German state of Schleswig-Holstein, close to the German–Danish border. Indeed, it was founded by Danish settlers at the beginning of the 13th century and steadily became an important trading port with direct access to the Baltic. It became famous for its smoked herring, which was sent inland and traded with almost every other European country, along with sugar and whale oil. Flensburg's merchants were active across the globe, from the icy seas of Greenland to the warm waters of the Caribbean, and every point between. By the turn of the 20th century, it had a small but nonetheless active shipbuilding presence, its construction yards not only turning out surface vessels but also the much-vaunted U-boats and, as such, was a worthwhile target.

Despite this, the planners at Bomber Command took little interest in Flensburg until the beginning of July 1942, when it despatched six Mosquitoes from 139 (Jamaica) Squadron to carry out a low-level raid on the port facilities. It resulted in the loss of the squadron CO, Alan Oakeshott,[1] and his navigator (both killed in action), and the loss of John MacDonald,[2] who became a POW.[3] Half a dozen Mosquitoes were sent in again a few nights later but, similarly, lost one of their number for little return. On the night of 18/19 August, Flensburg was chosen as the target for the first Pathfinder attack of the war. And it was little short of a disaster.

Since Bennett's formal appointment to command Pathfinder Force on 5 July, he had been frantically busy, getting the men and machinery required for creating a corps d'elite. This had meant a number of uncomfortable meetings with the various group commanders, all of whom were obliged by Harris to surrender one of their squadrons, and some of their stations, to their unwelcome peer for the foundation of the new unit.

Alec Coryton, the AOC 5 Group, was positively hostile. He neither approved of the idea of Pathfinder Force nor did he think much of Bennett taking his best crews.[4] Coryton had presided over the introduction of the first Avro Lancasters into Bomber Command and bitterly resented having to surrender his best unit, 83 Squadron, to PFF.[5] At the other end of the scale, Roddy Carr, the AOC 4 Group, was positively helpful and encouraging and promised to do everything he could to promote Pathfinder Force to his men and to 35 Squadron, which he had nominated to transfer to Bennett's command.

By the other commanders, Bennett was met with ambivalence rather than active support. However, with the exception of Coryton (and later Coryton's successor and Bennett's arch nemesis, Ralph Cochrane), none were especially obstructive. 'Winkel' Rice, AOC 1 Group, who Bennett had known when he'd been Wing Commander Training at RAF Calshot before the war, was friendly enough, surrendering 156 Squadron to Bennett's care, while John Baldwin, AOC 3 Group, bore more of a strain. His group not only had to hand over a squadron (7 Squadron) but also a number of airfields.[6] He also had the encumbrance of having to administer certain aspects of the stations, even though he did not command them operationally.[7]

Thus, by the middle of August, and the PFF's first order of battle, Bennett could call upon four full squadrons – 7, 35, 83 and 156 – as well as 109 Squadron from 2 Group, which was experimenting with 'special' equipment that was soon to play a major part in the Pathfinders' success.[8]

As his headquarters, Bennett chose RAF Wyton near St Ives in Cambridgeshire to which he also corralled RAF Oakington, thus giving him two 'permanent' stations that he added a further two 'satellites' to at Graveley and Warboys. His headquarters staff comprised an initial gang of four: Robert 'Angus' Buchan, an expert in navigation;[9] Andy Anderson, similarly qualified; 'Barney' Barnicot, an expert in armaments; and a personal WAAF corporal secretary, 'Sunshine' Ralph, the ultimate gatekeeper. Others were quickly snapped up, including one of PFF's most outstanding personalities, Arthur 'Artie' Ashworth, a magnificently moustachioed, buccaneering New Zealander who was the epitome of a wartime Brylcreem boy.

The challenges of creating a new force were evident from the beginning. Apart from 156 and 109 Squadrons, which both flew Wellingtons,[10] Bennett also had all three four-engined heavies: Short Stirlings (7 Squadron), Handley Page Halifaxes (35 Squadron) and the 'new' Avro Lancasters (83 Squadron). This not only gave him four types with vastly different performance characteristics, but it also presented a huge logistical problem in terms of servicing and repairs – a situation that was never properly resolved until much later in the war when Bennett was able to rationalise his aircraft strength down to just two types: the Lancaster and the de Havilland Mosquito.

Furthermore, PFF had neither history nor tradition,[11] both of which are extremely important in military life and in inspiring new crews to join. Tradition is created by individuals working towards a common aim and takes many years to become established. Bennett was starting from scratch.

In providing the four principal squadrons and their aircraft, each of the group commanders was also responsible for providing the men. Not every man on the squadrons selected was particularly 'special', and so the responsibility of 'weeding out' those aircrew not up to the mark was given, ultimately, to the individual squadron commanders. Some of those commanders were better than others and embraced their task with greater enthusiasm. For example, Jimmy Marks, OC 35 Squadron and a keen supporter of PFF from the beginning, immediately set to work with his flight commanders in selecting the best crews and posting those who he did not think suitable to other 4 Group squadrons.[12]

Jimmy Marks, a keen supporter of PFF from the beginning, was also one of its early casualties. (RAF Wyton Pathfinder Collection)

For the aircrew posted out, replacements had to be found to back-fill their roles, and the group commanders were, again, given responsibility for finding them. They were clearly instructed to select the best operational crew (other than squadron or flight commanders) from each of their squadrons.[13] This process seldom went smoothly, and it was perhaps not always the case that PFF ever received the pick of the crews from the respective groups.[14] The only group commander who gave any consistent support was the AOC 4 Group, the group, coincidentally, in which both Bennett and Sidney Bufton had served.

The criteria for aircrew joining PFF from an operational squadron were clearly laid out from the beginning:[15] they had to have completed at least 12 sorties and demonstrated a determination in pressing home their attacks. More specifically, pilots had to have above average navigational knowledge and be able to make rough mental DR calculations; navigators had to be competent in visual, direction finding, astro and Gee navigation and be quick and accurate in their log keeping and use of a computer; and bomb aimers had to be proficient at their main skill but also be good map readers. The importance attached to navigation in all three roles is immediately apparent. It was taken as read that a pilot could fly, and an air bomber could work a bombsight. It was also true of wireless operators who had to be proficient in obtaining loop bearings and able to use Gee for fixes, and air gunners who had to be able to take drift sights and map read from high altitudes. Flight engineers had to possess a thorough knowledge of their aircraft types and all their systems but also, perhaps more importantly, their aircrafts' cruising procedures and fuel consumptions.

A study of the 4 Group returns shows some of the first of the 'outstanding crews'[16] to volunteer never made it to a Pathfinder squadron. Cyril Spencer was coming to the end of his first tour of operations from Linton-on-Ouse when his name was put forward to join PFF on 7 July. On 31 July, he was shot down over Düsseldorf and became a prisoner of war. Also from Linton, Frederick White from 158 Squadron volunteered, having completed his tour. However, he decided on one last trip on the night of 26/27 July; he ditched in the North Sea and was never seen again.

At 32 years of age, Canadian Bill Lunan was comparatively old for aircrew, but that didn't stop him from putting his name forward or being recommended for PFF by the station commander at Middleton St George. He never made it either. Bill and the rest of his mostly Canadian crew from 78 Squadron went missing on the night of 12 August.

Another Canadian, Bill Swetman, volunteered and was 'strongly recommended' for Pathfinders by his station commander at Pocklington. At the time, he'd completed 27 operations with 405 Squadron. He never made it to Pathfinders either, for reasons that are not especially clear. As it was, he stayed with the squadron until October to complete his tour and went on to command a Main Force squadron in 1943.[17]

Not every volunteer, however, was to be drawn from an operational squadron. For every two crews selected who were already operating, a third was to be taken direct from training, either from an operational training unit (OTU) or a conversion unit. These would be crews who, in their commanders' opinion, showed the greatest promise as resolute leaders (and not necessarily the greatest, but adequate, efficiency in their trades). They would not, however, be deemed Pathfinders or be entitled to the badge until they had carried out a dozen or so operations.[18]

Despite Bennett's best efforts, and the best intentions of his small number of supporters, four comparatively 'ordinary' squadrons suddenly found themselves part of an elite group, three of them effectively squatting on airfields over which they were little welcome and had little control.[19] At Wyton, 15 Squadron had been obliged to move out to Bourn to provide the necessary accommodation, causing further disruption. In this state, and without any special equipment or special training, and aircraft of widely differing abilities, Pathfinder Force went to work, with nothing but unbounded enthusiasm and determination not to let down the rest of Bomber Command.[20]

As is so often the case, enthusiasm alone was not enough. With the squadrons formally transferred to PFF and dispersed to their new bases across Cambridgeshire and Huntingdonshire on 17 August, Harris insisted they should be ready for operations immediately. This was, in Bennett's mind, a completely unreasonable request – and just how unreasonable would become immediately evident – but the spirit behind it was so thoroughly 'press-on' that he made no attempt to argue.[21] In the event, it was actually the night of 18/19 August that a new era in Pathfinding began, when crews of 7, 35, 83 and 156 Squadrons set out to mark Flensburg. They may have wondered why they bothered.

The Pathfinder 'technique' was little more than the Main Force squadrons had already been experimenting with up to that point – flares and incendiaries. Contrary winds, a particularly dark night and haze on the ground made conditions far from ideal, and in the event only half of the 31 Pathfinder crews claimed to have marked or bombed the target, when subsequent intelligence suggested that most of those had done no such thing. German radio reported bombs being dropped many miles away in the Heligoland Bight and Kiel Bay areas.

Although there had been much excitement among the Pathfinder crews, and even a competition to see who could be the first into enemy territory,[22] they were frustrated. Peter Cribb of 35 Squadron spent the better part of 40 minutes over the target while he and the navigator, Bill Grierson-Jackson, peered into the darkness but could see nothing. He was obliged to dump his incendiaries after an engine failed and he returned on three engines. His experience was typical. Jack Partridge of 83 Squadron searched for the target for an hour before dropping his bombs on what he 'presumed' was the target area. But at least he got there. At Wyton, things were so chaotic that four of the 83 Squadron aircraft allotted to the attack never even left the ground. Bombing up was late because of a lack of the necessary bombs and equipment and one Lancaster went unserviceable (u/s) just after starting up.

Bennett was clearly frustrated too. He knew the eyes of the whole of Bomber Command were upon him, and the Pathfinders had fallen at the first fence. One of their number had also failed to return.[23] Bennett had not, however, been surprised. As he was to remark in his autobiography: 'Merely creating a Pathfinder Force was not magic; if you get no opportunity to train, no special equipment with which to work, and an inaccurate weather report, the result must be exactly what one would expect.'[24]

Pathfinder Force tried again a few nights later when 37 of its number led an attack on Frankfurt. They enjoyed modest success, but once again the weather was far from ideal, and the bombing was, at best, scattered. Perhaps more alarming was the loss rate: five of their number failed to return, including the CO of 7 Squadron, John Shewell.

This was a feature of those early attacks, and although the ORBs for Pathfinder Force suggest the raids on Flensberg, Frankfurt and other targets, including Kassel and Nuremberg, 'promised well for the future of target location',[25] it is difficult to see on what basis such optimism was founded. Kassel was successful up to a point, helped by a number of bombs falling on the Henschel aircraft manufacturing plant and doing considerable damage, and the raid on Nuremberg was not the success it was reported to be at the time, despite confidence among the PFF crews that they had found and marked the aiming point. What is noteworthy about this latter attack, however, is the first use of what constituted a 'target indicator' (TI), adapted from a 250lb bomb casing and referred to in contemporary reports as a 'Red Blob Fire'.

Such experimentation in tactics and tools continued throughout September and for the rest of the year as PFF began to find its feet. Over Bremen in the first week of September, PFF split its aircraft into three distinct roles: 'illuminators', which went in first to light up the area with white flares; 'visual markers', which dropped coloured flares if they had correctly found and identified the aiming point; and 'backers-up', which dropped incendiary loads on the coloured flares. While PFF evolved several variations on a theme as the war progressed, this basic pattern – illuminate, mark and back up – formed the basis of most future Pathfinder-led operations.[26]

A much larger marking device, known as a 'Pink Pansy' and converted from a 4,000lb bomb casing was used for the first timed over Düsseldorf on 10/11 September, with some success. Like the red blob marker, the TI was a crude form of 'super incendiary' using an explosive concoction of benzol, rubber and phosphorous, which gave it its distinctive colour. It was a sign of things to come.

In those first four months, PFF was learning. It learned that the first PFF aircraft over the target were at the greatest risk, and by introducing a new role of 'supporters', some of that risk could be shared; 'supporters' carried bombs but no incendiaries or TIs and were effectively Pathfinders under training. It learned of the unreliability of the weather and the difference that clear weather over the target could make to the success of a raid. It learned that a mix of TIs and different coloured markers were required, both because the Germans had already started to mimic the markers on the ground and create decoy fires to lure unsuspecting Main Force crews away from the actual target, and because some of the markers could be quickly lost in the fire and the dust caused by thousands of tons of heavy explosives and incendiaries falling on a target in short order.

They learned also to take their losses. Average losses hovered between the 4 per cent to 5 per cent mark, largely (and surprisingly) comparable to Main Force crews at that time, but it was the quality of the crews perhaps more than the numbers being lost that was of greater concern. In one of the first operations, Bennett suffered the personal loss of his navigation staff officer, Angus Buchan, who was killed while fulfilling Bennett's principle that all his staff officers must still operate regularly to be thoroughly in touch with the Pathfinders' job.[27] Buchan was only 22. A few weeks later, Jimmy Marks[28] was also lost, along with his gunnery leader and navigation officer. Marks had not only been a great supporter of PFF but, as early as 1940, had been experimenting with marking techniques while still a humble flying officer.

There were also some remarkable feats of airmanship in those early raids. While Bennett had always made clear his dislike for glory hunters and said there would be no living recipients of the Victoria Cross (VC) in Pathfinder Force, he was not ungenerous in recognising bravery when he saw it. In the period from 15 August to 31 December 1942, he approved no fewer than 40 awards for gallantry, almost half of which were 'immediate' (that is, granted immediately for a specific gallant action as opposed to non-immediate awards given to those for sustained achievement). One of those was to John Trench of 7 Squadron for an incident over Maastricht on the night of 10/11 September when his Short Stirling was hit by flak and he lost two engines, one quite literally tearing itself out of its mounting. The wireless operator, Ivor Edwards, wedged himself into the nose of the aircraft, putting pressure on both the control column and the rudder bars to help his skipper keep the bomber on an even keel. Struggling to maintain height, they crossed the Dutch coast at barely 200ft, jettisoning everything they could to save weight, including their parachutes. With huge amounts of skill and good fortune, they managed to make it to the English coast and crash land near Clacton, whereupon the Stirling immediately burst into flames.

With the unfortunate pilot and wireless operator knocked unconscious, the navigator (Crofton Selman) braved the flames to drag the two men clear. The flight engineer and air bomber, who had made it clear of the burning bomber, also went back into the aircraft to free the trapped rear gunner, at which point the petrol tanks exploded and they were killed. Not to be put off, the mid-upper gunner then had a go and managed to reach his fellow gunner and the two men escaped, despite being badly burned. Trench, Selman and Edwards received an immediate DSO, Distinguished Flying Cross (DFC) and Distinguished Flying Medal (DFM), respectively. The mid-upper, Raoul de Fontenay Jenner of the Royal Canadian Air Force (RCAF) received the George Medal (GM).

There were other incidents in those first few months of existence that would be considered remarkable by any standards and reflect well on the press-on spirit of the Pathfinder captains and their crews. Three involved skippers ordering their crews to bale out of what they took to be a mortally damaged aircraft, only then to regain control of their aircraft sufficiently to fly and navigate their way safely back to England.

The first of the trio was the PFF staff officer Artie Ashworth, who ordered his crew out when smoke started filling his nostrils and sparks began flying after a flare ignited in the bomb bay. This was not an uncommon problem in early Pathfinding.

Artie had 'borrowed' a Wellington and crew from 156 Squadron for his 65th operation but couldn't possibly have imagined how it would turn out. Stooging around over the target area, his wireless operator reported sparks coming from the bomb bay. Having told his crew to leave and sensing the bomber might explode at any minute (a Wellington on fire seldom lasted long, he later remarked[29]), he hurried them out and made to go himself but could not find his parachute. In the confusion, he decided, one of the others must have taken it. Desperately searching for a spare, his luck was out, and so he returned to his seat, momentarily stunned. Then his survival instinct took over. If he could side slip the aircraft down, he might just have enough time to crash land before the whole thing blew up. Then miracle of miracles, the fire seemed to go out, and Artie was once again in control of his aircraft. Leaving his seat once more to grab a map from the navigator's table, he plotted an approximate course home and after a few further adventures, landed at West Malling. When asked to account for the rest of the crew, he is reported to have said that they'd gone on extended leave!

Douglas Greenup, a fully-fledged member of 156 Squadron (unlike Artie), repeated the feat a few weeks later when his Wellington was struck by lightning on his way to Aachen. With his port engine out of action, 26-year-old Greenup jettisoned his flares but was immediately fired upon by enemy defences and steadily began to lose height. With his aircraft seemingly out of control, his crew baled out and Greenup went to follow, but such were the chaotic meanderings of his bomber that it was too risky to leave his seat. Managing some semblance of control, he crash-landed at Manston, none the worse for his ordeal but minus his five former crewmates.

The third, and perhaps best-known, example of a solo flight fell to Basil Robinson of 35 Squadron, returning from a raid on Turin. Mixed in with the 'usual' attacks on German targets, Bomber Command and PFF had also been asked to focus some attention on the Italians, to coincide with the Eighth Army offensive at El Alamein. Trips to Genoa, Milan and Turin were considered relatively 'easy' compared to some German cities, but they required traversing the Alps, which was not without its challenges, especially with a damaged aircraft or a misfiring engine.

Robinson also experienced an issue with flares igniting unexpectedly in the bomb bay, the extent and intensity of the fire suggesting there was no hope of continuing.[30] He ordered the crew to bale out, which they did with alacrity. Moments later, however, the flames seemed to go out, perhaps because of the escape hatches being opened, and the immediate likelihood of the aircraft being engulfed in flames was averted. Robinson took stock and flew his Halifax home alone 600 miles and across the Alps without further incident, even landing in bad weather. For a time, pilots – and especially commissioned pilots of senior rank – were not the most popular subjects of conversation in the sergeants' mess![31]

What is interesting is how the three incidents were treated after the event. Robinson was widely praised and awarded an immediate bar to the DFC he had first won as CO of 78 Squadron. Ashworth was also feted as a hero, at least publicly, being interviewed by the BBC and the press in his native New Zealand. Privately, he received a right royal rocket[32] from his AOC and was only slightly compensated by a mention in despatches. Greenup's heroics went largely unreported and unrecognised. He was later killed in a flying accident while being 'rested' at a gunnery flight.

Towards the end of 1942, an attempt was made to analyse the effectiveness of Pathfinder operations since the force's introduction in the summer. It was also made with half an eye on certain new technologies that were to be introduced that promised to transform Bomber Command's strategic offensive. The results were mixed but broadly encouraging, and not surprisingly the vagaries of the autumn weather in northern Europe played their part in determining the success or otherwise of every raid.[33] Of 18 attacks on Germany, seven were assessed as being entirely successful on the basis that almost a third (30 per cent) of the aiming point photographs taken were plotted to be within three miles of the target. All seven took place in good weather conditions. Of the remainder, six raids were deemed 'partially successful', all of which took place in weather judged to be 'moderate to better', and five raids were described as total failures. These five were all conducted on nights when the weather was appalling. On one raid, an attack on Hamburg on the night of 9 November, no identifiable aiming point photographs were taken; it was as though the Pathfinders hadn't even been there.

As well as exploring the raw facts, the report also canvassed the view of Main Force captains for their impressions of the value of PFF. The findings were rather more encouraging. In just over half of the 18 attacks analysed, the work of Bennett's force was considered an advantage. The summary states: 'Success by the PFF in executing their planned technique has almost always resulted in an improvement in the results achieved by the Main Force. Where PFF have failed, the Main Force has never been able, on its own efforts, to improve upon expectation.'

In the opinions of the Main Force captains, and the statisticians, PFF was indeed beginning to make a small but positive contribution to bomber operations. On one night over Bremen in September, the night PFF trialled its new marking 'system'. Well over half (58 per cent) of the aiming point photographs were within three miles the target – an error margin now regarded as 'success'. Over the whole three-month period under review, almost a quarter (24 per cent) of all photographs achieved similar standards of accuracy, and the average number of aircraft bombing within three miles of the target improved by 40 per cent. PFF, the report says, never succeeded in bad weather but never failed in good.

An undated Operational Research Section (ORS) report from the period surmised that the introduction of PFF had not brought about any marked or immediate improvement in Bomber Command's results,[34] although Harris in his despatch, written immediately after the war, believed that 'a very definite advance in technique had in fact been made'.

Such sober commentaries should not take away from Bennett the achievements he was already making in conjuring an effective fighting force with the multiple challenges and characters ranged against him. He had faced down formidable difficulties and was starting to see the results of his labours.

Such was the character of the man, and the force that he led, that he was even able to turn a major 'black' to his advantage. On the night of 1 September, while PFF was struggling to find its rhythm, a force of 231 bombers led by 19 PFF aircraft set out to bomb Saarbrücken. Only when the post-raid bombing photographs were analysed did they realise that they had not bombed Saarbrücken at all, but rather Saarlouis, 20km to the north-east, close to the French border. The fault lay fairly and squarely at the feet of one of the PFF captains who had dropped his markers incorrectly. Saarlouis was a legitimate target, and as such the bombs were not wasted, but it was an embarrassment, nonetheless. Harris, Bennett recounted later, was very good about it, saying that PFF did at least concentrate the bombs on a target, rather than scattering them vaguely.

While there were no doubt sniggers among his detractors, the example of Saarlouis was used actively in the months and years to come as a case study to balance PFF's successes with its failures. Rather than trying to hide it, the PFF staff and recruiting personnel positively embraced it and won respect from the men they were trying to attract. Even elite men could make mistakes; the important thing was to learn from them.

The mistake over Saarlouis also highlighted another problem, and one of the unintended consequences of improving bombing accuracy around a specific marker. Prior to PFF, each observer had been responsible for identifying the target themselves. This meant that bombing was invariably scattered all over a target, but the mean point of impact (MPI) was invariably close to the aiming point. In the seven months prior to the introduction of PFF, only about 14 per cent of the attacks showed any appreciable displacement of the MPI from the aiming point. In the seven months immediately following, this percentage rose to 67 per cent. As the *Official History* records, 'misplaced PFF markers were more potent in drawing attacks away from the aiming point than German decoys'.[35]

The major problem, the history recounts, concerned the reduction in the systematic error or, in other words, the distance between the centre of the bombing concentration and the aiming point. 'The chief factor in this problem was to find the means of enabling the PFF to lay its markers more accurately'.[36]

Help, as it happens, was just around the corner.

Chapter 5

Nothing but the Very Best?

For the men of PFF, Bennett insisted on nothing but the very best, but he didn't always get it.

While Harris had promised to help Bennett personally, he did little to help PFF in any material sense. Pathfinders may have been elite in name, but in practice it was viewed as simply another competitor for scant resources, and it never enjoyed absolute priority.[1] This was as true for aircraft as it was for the trained men needed to navigate and fly them.

From the outset, Bennett recognised that Personnel was a major headache, and he made several representations to his master, only to find his requests falling upon deaf ears. He argued that many men in the command were totally ignorant of how they could volunteer for PFF and what their conditions of service in the force were likely to be.[2]

Some group commanders, as recounted, resented having to surrender their best crews to PFF and did little to advertise or promote PFF within their squadrons. Some squadron commanders went further and steadfastly ignored any volunteers who did come forward to request a transfer. Further still, they saw PFF as a convenient route to offload some of their worst or most troublesome crews.

Hamish Mahaddie, one of the most famous names in PFF, was appointed PFF personnel officer by Bennett in the early spring of 1943 and given carte blanche to do everything in his power to persuade, by fair means or foul, the best quality captains and crews to come over to Pathfinders. The charismatic Scotsman who, according to one contemporary, 'could sell snow to the Eskimos',[3] detected problems from the start: in his opinion, the policy of manning in those first six months of PFF's life had failed. After the initial flush of good intentions, the standard of crews being earmarked for PFF was steadily deteriorating and needed to be urgently addressed.

With the notable exception of 4 Group, he identified that certain group commanders were using PFF as a dumping ground for crews who had made a nuisance of themselves: 'Their "selection" was not acceptable,' Mahaddie wrote, 'and we were sending more crews back than we were keeping.'[4] Referring to the RAF's psychiatric hospital, Mahaddie added: 'some crews were more suited to Matlock!'[5]

The paucity of quality was a concern, and one of the difficulties was clearly one of perception. After a particularly dismal attack on Hannover in the autumn of 1943, for which PFF received much criticism and Bennett put down to human error, one AOC told Bennett that he could easily provide

Hamish Mahaddie – Bennett's staunchest supporter and horse thief. (The Pathfinder Archive)

a dozen better crews as backers-up than the Pathfinders could muster themselves. If that was the case, Bennett enquired, then why weren't those crews within PFF where they belonged? As Bennett later suggested to his C-in-C, the AOC had clearly misunderstood the purpose of PFF, seeing it as a rival rather than a facilitator for successful operations.[6]

Mahaddie, therefore, knew from the beginning that if he wanted to find the best men, he'd have to go out and get them, and he promptly set about an exhaustive daily tour of the Main Force squadrons. On each visit he would use the previous night's raid as his theme to explain the difficulties of finding and marking a target, and why they needed the best – because the best was only just good enough.[7] He gladly spoke of PFF's failures, such as Saarlouis, as well as its successes, as if to say, 'come and have a go if you think you can do any better'. It won him the instant respect of the Main Force crews, including those who were not already impressed by a man who wore the DSO, DFC and Air Force Cross (AFC) beneath his wings, having been there and done it himself.

He also applied rational science to his thinking. After every raid, bombing photographs were sent to HQ Bomber Command, and Mahaddie began to use these as the starting point for crew selection. He found there were crews ('they were always the same crews,' he said) whose bombs fell near the centre of the target. There were crews ('they were always the same crews') who dropped their bombs around the perimeter. And there were crews ('they were always the same crews') whose bombs never got on the plot at all.[8]

In the early months of his appointment, Mahaddie quickly identified that crews who were consistently getting aiming point photos on the bomb plot were never being selected for PFF. In his lecture tours, he actively sought these men out, and almost without exception found that they had in fact volunteered for PFF – sometimes on multiple occasions – but their requests had been blocked. Mahaddie was both angry and frustrated but immediately on the case. 'It was a very simple matter to reverse this procedure,' he said, 'generally after some unpleasantness with the appropriate squadron commander.'

As well as visiting the squadrons, Mahaddie also sought out instructional staff at flying and navigational schools, many of whom were keen to get back on operations. Typically, after a tour of operations, bomber aircrew were 'rested', which in effect meant a stint instructing at OTUs, air navigation schools, bombing and gunnery schools, etc., depending on their 'trade'. Training units could be dangerous places, putting lives in the hands of dubious pilots flying often doubtful aircraft, and many 'screened' aircrew were happier with the thought of returning to the 'safety' of ops! In his endless lectures to the training groups, Mahaddie charged a 'fee': two tour-expired instructors! A large number of Mosquito pilots were sourced directly from blind approach training (BAT) schools – the hurdle being 1,000 hours on BAT flights. This experience would prove essential for the introduction of new blind-bombing technology.

Thanks to Mahaddie's methods, and the growing reputation of Pathfinder Force, the quality of aircrew began to steadily improve. Mahaddie also wasn't averse to using a touch of theatre to make his point. One apparently 'elite' captain who shouldn't have been anywhere near PFF was flown back to his group by Mahaddie himself, immediately 'arresting the trash from that area'.[9]

Regardless of whether the men were regular RAF, VR or had come from the Dominions (Canada, Australia, New Zealand, South Africa, etc.) or any number of Britain's Allies (Holland, France, Norway, etc.), aircrew were attracted to PFF for many different reasons. Some proactively volunteered, excited by the challenge and the step-up in pay and rank. Prestige, status and bragging rights were as important to young men then as they are today. One of these young men was Harold Kirby, who had trained at Halton as a flight mechanic; he was one of the first conscript entries as opposed to being an apprentice. He was the only Englishman in an otherwise all-Australian crew who flew 16 trips with Main Force (with 467 Squadron) before being accepted for PFF: 'Bill Ryan, our pilot, volunteered us, partly because he had heard it meant better pay and faster promotion, and partly because we had the impression that joining Pathfinders would be a step-up.'[10]

As well as those who actively sought a PFF posting, there were others who were 'volunteered', having been identified as being of the right calibre by their squadron commanders, once the earlier 'referral' issues had been overcome. Fred Maltas, a flight engineer with a 51 Squadron[11] crew, is a case in point. Like Harold Kirby, he was already deep into his tour when he found himself volunteering for PFF: 'The skipper [Bill Hickson, RNZAF] told us one morning that the CO had called him into his office and said that he had been watching us. The squadron had been asked to provide two of its best crews to go to Pathfinder Force, and Bill asked if we wanted to go. The prestige of the Pathfinders, even in those very early days, was already very great, and we had no hesitation on saying yes.'[12]

Canadian pilot Elmer 'Al' Trotter remembers being asked to see his CO, George Carey-Foster, not long after being awarded an immediate DFM in December 1943. On his fourth operation with 101 Squadron, 'Al' had returned with four feet missing from his port wing and a huge hole in the other:

Carey-Foster asked if our crew would like to be transferred to a Pathfinder squadron. The Pathfinders were generally recognised as the élite of the élite and so I said I'd be really honoured to go to Pathfinders. He told me he had talked to Bennett and told him what the crew had accomplished with 1 Group and Bennett said he would be pleased to have us. We went on a one-week leave and on our return were posted to PFF.[13]

George Hall, who arrived at 101 Squadron sometime after 'Al' had left, had settled in well to the unit but was keen to be further tested. The obvious challenge, he believed, was the Pathfinders, and a visit by Mahaddie was followed by a call for volunteers by Carey-Foster's successor, Bob Alexander.[14] George said he was 'desperate' to get into Pathfinders, as was his crew: 'We liked to believe we were good, but the only way we would know is if we took on another challenge. Most people on 101 thought we were absolutely out of our silly minds. To us, a move to Pathfinders was one further step up the ladder.'[15]

To men like Harold, Fred, Al and George, the prestige of Pathfinder Force was a major attraction. So, too, was it for Mark Charness, a 21-year-old Canadian navigator: 'We were aware Pathfinders were an élite unit and knew we had to be "invited" to be considered. We were honoured to be asked and immediately volunteered.'[16]

Fellow Canadian Bob Pearce also knew of the Pathfinders' elite reputation. He'd flown eight operations with 101 Squadron at Ludford Magna, before his skipper – an American flying with the RCAF – volunteered them for Pathfinders: 'We knew that the Pathfinders were the élite and our CO asked us if we wanted to volunteer. Pete Uzelman [the air bomber] didn't want to go, but he also didn't want to break up the crew. He was always very level-headed. We were shot down in December 1944 and only the two air gunners survived. Perhaps we should have listened to him?'[17]

Above left: George Hall, who went from VR 'sprog' to master bomber. (582 Squadron Archive)

Above right: Mark Charness was honoured to be asked and immediately volunteered to join PFF. (Marilyn Shank)

Like Pete Uzelman, Reg Cann was put on the spot by his skipper Bob Cairns, a quiet Scot. Like Pete, Reg didn't want to be the one who broke up a winning team. They'd done eight trips at 625 Squadron, but his skipper was keen to become a Pathfinder. Reg was rather less enthralled with the prospect: 'I couldn't see the attraction in even more training, but neither did I want to be the one to split the crew up.' Reg went along with his skipper and the rest of the crew and survived 47 operations.

Bill Hough, an Englishman, came to Pathfinders via 576 Squadron after 11 trips. His Canadian skipper, Art Green, had joined the RCAF pre-war and held the AFC. Both he and the navigator, Willie Mood, had clearly caught the eye of the selectors, the former for his skill as an aviator and the latter for the consistency of his performance and the accuracy of his navigation.

Sometimes, ignorance was bliss. 'Nick' Nicholson, who found himself as one of a headless crew after his first pilot 'flunked it', would have followed his new skipper 'Kiwi' Lawson, a New Zealander, to hell and back. 'When he volunteered for the Pathfinder Force, he asked the rest of the crew if we wanted to come. I discussed it with our wireless op, Ted Herod, and he fancied it. It seemed like a good idea at the time and so I went along with it.'[18]

Captains of aircraft were nearly always the ones driving the conversation. Air gunner John Smith remembers the decision to move to Pathfinders was taken very quickly and unilaterally by his skipper, Jimmy Brown: 'Mahaddie persuaded Jimmy that he was up to the challenge, and the next thing I knew we'd all volunteered.'

Wireless operator Doug Reed had a similar experience. He'd flown more than half a dozen trips on 166 Squadron with Bill Peedell after his first skipper, Peter Legard, had been killed over Nuremberg. Peedell was formerly of the King's Royal Rifles and had fought at Dunkirk. Now he fancied a go with the Pathfinders: 'Bill had done about ten or so trips when we found ourselves in the CO's office talking about Pathfinders. Next thing I know we had been as good as volunteered!'[19]

These examples serve to disprove a common belief that all men chosen for PFF had at least one tour behind them before joining. Whereas Bennett sought the most experienced captains and crews when he could find them, he also had to settle for those with less experience and even, in some cases, no experience at all but simply the promise of greatness.

In an exchange between Bennett and his C-in-C in September 1943, when the Australian suggested he was still not getting the very best,[20] it was proposed that PFF should have first refusal on any crews returning to operations after a rest, and so, by definition, these would be experienced men. Bennett was worried that the average experience of his captains in February 1943 was 32 operations but by September this had fallen to 20 and was part of the reason PFF was still making mistakes.[21]

It was also agreed at that time that no direct-entry 'freshmen' crews should join Bennett's force in future, but in practice this wasn't the case. Whereas there is no doubt that PFF had many highly experienced flyers in its ranks, some with a chest full of medals, there were also those plucked directly from various training units. So-called 'Gen' crews, those rated 'above average' in training, especially those with the best navigators, were highly prized, particularly later in the war when the calls upon the Pathfinders' time became more onerous.

Individuals, as opposed to whole crews, without any operational experience might also find themselves in Pathfinders almost by chance and through being in the right place at the right time (or the wrong place depending on whether your glass is half full or half empty). Les Hood had graduated top of his class at nav school and was told he was also going straight to Pathfinders, along with his great pal, Dennis King. At first, he refused until he learned his contemporaries were being posted to a glider towing unit and he quickly changed his mind![22]

Bill Heane, also a navigator, similarly had no operational experience at all when he was drafted into Pathfinders. He was at an OTU, waiting to fly out with his crew to the Far East. They'd received their various inoculations and were at the point of leaving when, at the eleventh hour, it was decided that only the pilot and the air bomber were needed. Therefore, Bill found himself as a spare bod and, as part of a 'headless crew', continued to a heavy conversion unit (HCU) with a view to joining 4 Group. 'It was here that we came across "Min" Mingard, a squadron leader who was looking for a crew and wanted to go to Pathfinders. And that was that.'[23]

Don Briggs came to Pathfinders in a similar way and with an experienced captain. He had just completed a flight engineer's course and was at an HCU in Lindholme, waiting to crew up. (In converting from two to four engines, existing crews that had crewed up at an OTU needed a flight engineer and an extra gunner.) As a Halton apprentice (40th Entry), Don had been an ex-corporal engine fitter before being accepted for aircrew training and, as such, he'd had a fair amount of experience in air tests on Wellingtons and Hampdens. So when a pilot approached him and asked whether he had any previous flying experience he said 'yes': 'I then learned that "my" pilot – Bill Neal – had already completed a tour of operations, as had the rest of the crew, and he had just finished a period instructing on Wellingtons. I thought if I had to fly with anyone, then this was a good choice! The only thing he did say, however, was that in joining the crew I had to understand that we were going straight to Pathfinders.'[24]

Gordon Goodwin was also delighted to have been approached to join PFF, and even more delighted to have a very experienced pilot, Philip Patrick, as his skipper. Both men were squadron leaders. 'Having spent three months establishing a navigation school, I knew I had to get back to battle to use my new-found expertise. Philip Patrick, like myself, was starting on his second tour and needed a good navigator. He'd already organised the rest of his crew, most of whom had served with him in his first tour on Stirlings. His reputation as an outstanding pilot was legendary and I had no hesitation in gladly accepting.'[25]

The hike in promotion and pay and the support of a good captain were not always sufficient to lure an airman or crew away to a new squadron. Even when PFF was given group status in the new year of 1943, not all were impressed. Some were asked to volunteer and refused. Some saw the risk as too great. Arguments and discord were not uncommon, and relations within crews not always as harmonious as they are portrayed in other books and films.

When Bob Lasham consulted his crew on joining PFF, for example, it was far from unanimous. At that point, they'd already completed 17 operations with 9 Squadron and probably felt they had a good chance of making it to 30 without taking on another 15 on top of that. Bob disagreed: 'I always felt I had a better chance of making 45 straight off rather than coming back after 30 and doing another 20. But in PFF you could still stop at 30 and that's exactly what our navigator did.'[26]

Canadian pilot Walter Thompson had a similar confrontation. When he told his crew that they'd been accepted for Pathfinders in early 1943,

Fred Phillips accepted the risks as a master bomber without question. (via Fred Phillips in Sean Feast Collection)

most quietly acquiesced except his air bomber, a fiery Scottish NCO called 'Pete' Henratty. Henratty told his skipper in no uncertain terms that he had no right to have volunteered them without speaking to them first. He believed they had little-to-no chance of surviving one tour, let alone two. Thompson said they would be going 'with or without' the incalcitrant Scot, who eventually agreed but only to the first 30 ops. He refused to fly a double tour.[27]

Others had no such qualms about the dangers. Fred Phillips, a young Australian pilot, came to Pathfinders via 622 Squadron in the autumn of 1943, thanks in no small part to the noteworthy skills of his Kiwi navigator, Dave Goodwin. The crew quickly excelled and, by the age of 20, Fred was leading a Main Force attack: 'We accepted the high risk without question.'[28]

Navigator David Spier was one of those who never got as far as a squadron prior to PFF. Indeed, he never even made it to an OTU. He had only just finished his course at an advanced flying unit (AFU) at Halfpenny Green near Wolverhampton when he was asked to see the flight commander. He said that David's navigational skill was of sufficiently high standard to recommend him to the PFF. David asked for time to consider:

> He suggested that I visit Intelligence and consider the statistics of losses. I learned that the loss rate in PFF was less than in the Main Force. I talked the proposal over with Tony Smith – who had been a friend since we had first met at Aircrew Reception Centre [ACRC] – and decided that I would not go without him; we were determined to stay together. The CO agreed, at the same time informing me that because of the installation of more up-to-date technical navigation equipment (i.e., H2S), PFF crews required two navigators.

'Syd' Johnson was another who completely bypassed Main Force and any OTU. He arrived in the UK after training in Australia and was at a reception centre in Brighton awaiting a posting to an AFU when he was called to see the CO, along with four other navs: 'With the CO was a visitor whose decorations included the Pathfinder Golden Eagle [*sic*]. This chap didn't keep us in suspense for long. He said the five of us had been selected to go into Bennett's Pathfinder Force if we so desired.' Syd didn't have a moment's doubt: 'I felt this wasn't so much a challenge, but rather an opportunity, and so did the others. Without hesitation, we were in like Flynn!'[29]

Syd and his contemporaries were not lacking in confidence, but not all men selected for PFF were so sure of themselves. Ron Smith, an air gunner, recounts that his skipper volunteered for PFF but didn't let on because he didn't think the crew would be accepted.[30] Pat Turner, a flight engineer from 44 Squadron, was especially surprised to find his crew posted to PFF as he considered they were not especially talented flyers. It was later discovered they had been posted on account of the pilot's fondness for the base commander's WAAF driver![31]

Dug Jarvis volunteered for PFF but realised the standards demanded were so high that further training was required. He devised his own, which included the gunners and the pilot sitting in the aircraft on the hardstand while the rest of the crew pretended to attack them on bicycles. Throughout the exercise, the pilot and gunners would keep up a running commentary for how best to counter the impending threat. The training may have seemed odd at the time, but was very successful in the long run, helping them escape danger on more than one occasion.[32]

Pathfinder crews had been encouraged to regard themselves as a corps d'elite, and many attempted to look the part. Jack Currie remembers the wealth of smoothly barbered hair; neat moustaches; cool, clear eyes; and well-pressed battledresses, which made a striking contrast to the more outré appearances of the Main Force men at Wickenby: 'Nobody wore Irvin coats or sweaters in the splendid mess. For once it was the other trades who seemed comparatively less sartorially aware.'[33]

Arriving on a Pathfinder squadron could be a daunting experience. Roy Pengilley noticed the differences between Main Force and PFF straight away when his comparatively novice crew (they had flown nine trips) found themselves immersed in a world of higher-ranking, highly decorated men. His motivation for volunteering was to be measured against the best; he also figured that the 'chop' rate in PFF could not be any worse than on his squadron (625 Squadron) in 1 Group: 'We had come from Main Force where a flight lieutenant and particularly a flight commander was a very exalted position. Most of us in Main Force were NCOs; when we came to 8 Group, wing commanders were two-a-penny. I'm not decrying that. It was just noticeable that when you arrived at PFF, there was a vast change – not a social change – but a hierarchical change.'[34]

Trevor Jones, an air bomber with 635 Squadron, felt much the same. When he arrived at Wyton, he could not get over the number of officers wearing a particular ribbon beneath their flying 'wings' that was unfamiliar to him. Only later did he discover it was the DSO.[35]

As the achievements of PFF became more widely known, several senior-ranking officers actively sought involvement. Stafford Coulson's experience had all been on fighters, but having missed the Battle of Britain, and read in the papers what the men of Bomber Command – and PFF in particular – were doing, he volunteered at the first opportunity. In advance of being accepted, he managed to sneak in what he called a few 'non-recordable' jobs: 'Tubby Baker [the OC of 635 Squadron] would let me go along with him on a trip or two. Bennett seemed to know of my shenanigans and if anything, I think it helped me. They took me readily. Nobody even asked me for an interview. I was just told I was going to Pathfinders.'[36]

Not all men of such experience and high regard were accepted, volunteered or asked. One notable exception from its ranks was Leonard Cheshire, a stalwart 5 Group man. Bennett said that while Cheshire was a Bomber Command pilot of the highest order, there were others in PFF with more knowledge and experience. Cheshire was an individualist who did not have the professional qualifications to make him 'special'.[37] Mahaddie never understood his master's antipathy towards Cheshire. Mahaddie's selection of 'Chesh', with whom he had flown in 4 Group, to take command of 35 Squadron in the early days of PFF was vetoed by his boss, with no reason ever given. Laurence Deane[38] believes Bennett thought Cheshire 'a gong hunter' and, as such, was unwelcome in his ranks.

Another famous Bomber baron, Hughie Edwards, was approached late in the war by Bennett to take command of one of the Pathfinder squadrons. Edwards said he would take a Mosquito unit since, in his mind, it seemed fairly cushy to be dropping a 4,000-pounder on Berlin from 30,000ft in a fast aircraft. Bennett called Edwards later and offered him 156 Squadron. Edwards declined on the grounds he was already operating Lancasters and was happy to stay where he was. Since no Mosquito squadron was available, Edwards saw out his war in Main Force, and Bennett asked him not to let the 5 Group AOC (Cochrane) know that he had been lobbied![39]

And what of arguably the most famous Bomber baron of all, Guy Gibson? In February 1943, as the call on PFF services was getting greater, a decision was taken to add two new heavy bomber squadrons to the Pathfinders' ranks. One was to come from the newly created 6 Group and intended as an all-Canadian Halifax unit (405 Squadron). The second was to come from 5 Group. A letter to this effect was circulated to the group commanders to which Coryton (the 5 Group AOC at that time) replied that rather than detail one of his squadrons to the task, he would prefer them to volunteer. He instructed his station commanders to consult with their squadron commanders accordingly: John Whitworth at Scampton replied that neither 49 Squadron nor 57 Squadron wished to volunteer; 467 Squadron at Bottesford was similarly unwilling and did not, on any account, wish to leave 5 Group, though 207 Squadron had no such qualms and actively wanted to be considered. At Waddington, only 50 Squadron was keen, and at Coningsby, 97 Squadron was even keener and even described as being 'anxious' to become part of Pathfinder Force. The station commander explained that although comprising relatively new crews, it had the makings of a first-class squadron and would be 'an even greater success' than 83 Squadron.[40]

Edward Bussell, the station commander at Syerston, discussed the possibility of joining PFF with 'The Boy' Gibson and other members of 106 Squadron and seemed confident they would volunteer. 'The squadron is in very good form at present,' he wrote, 'and has a well-balanced crew list which should put them off to a good start on Pathfinders.' Gibson's men were indeed in good form and at that time were leading the Bomber Command league table for the accuracy of their bombing. The letter was dated 23 February. On 12 March, Gibson flew his last trip with 106, and a few days later was invited by Ralph Cochrane, Coryton's successor, to form a new special squadron and do 'one last trip'.[41] It seems Gibson would have been more than happy to have been part of PFF, and be benchmarked against the best of Bomber Command, had it not been for Cochrane's offer. Fate, and history, demanded something different from him, although it is ironic that Gibson would ultimately lose his life controlling a raid in a role for which he had little or no experience or training.

There is an interesting adjunct to this story. It was a rare occasion that Mahaddie was beaten at his own game as a 'horse thief' and a potential 'target' stolen from under his nose. 'Recruitment' often took place in the Black Boy pub in Nottingham, a favourite watering hole of many in the rival 5 and 8 Groups.

Mahaddie recalled a terrible row with Gibson in a pub one evening. It followed an earlier confrontation during tea with Gibson and Cochrane at the station. Cochrane always made Mahaddie most welcome and had given him a list of 20 pilots who he kindly asked him not to recruit. Mahaddie did not know, of course, that these pilots had been earmarked for the 'special' squadron then in the making. As he went to leave, an irate Gibson told him, in no uncertain terms, to keep his hands off his crews. He specifically said to keep his sticky fingers off Searby,[42] one of Gibson's flight commanders (and designated successor on 106). John Searby was not on Cochrane's list and not, until that moment, on Mahaddie's radar, but he certainly was now. That same day, Searby was 'pinched' from 106 to command 83 Squadron while, in a tit-for-tat move, Gibson 'lifted' Dave Shannon from training at Warboys to join his Dambusters.[43] 'We had the same view in the end – he wanted his best crews, and I was certain that the best crews were only just good enough to be Pathfinders.'[44]

Max Hastings asserts that, as the war progressed, 'Main Force' became almost a derogatory term and the best crews were concentrated in 5 Group, 8 Group and Mosquitoes.[45] Bennett didn't necessarily see it that way. He never wavered in his belief that the best captains and crews were being denied to him. In a minute, dated 9 May 1944, the AOC 8 Group expressed ongoing concerns at the quality of crews being selected for PFF and even introduced a new pro forma for station commanders to complete to better assess a crew's suitability for PFF duties.[46]

Sid Bufton, commenting on Harris' 1946 despatch, wrote, 'I don't think 8 Group ever succeeded in obtaining the best crews from the other groups, and at times, struggled with a deadweight of ex-OTU crews.' Perhaps he was right. But then as Boris Bressloff, a navigator, said, 'Most of us were just normal chaps, highly trained, doing the very best we could.'[47]

Chapter 6

Tools, Tactics and Techniques

In the early days of the Pathfinder squadrons, the additional experience of some of the aircrew was the only real difference between PFF and the Main Force squadrons.[1] From late 1942–early 1943 onwards, all that began to change.

The difficulties PFF were having in finding and marking the targets in the first six months have been well documented. But during that period, the scientists had been busy, and so too had 109 Squadron, nominally on Bennett's payroll but were yet to play any operational role. All that, too, was about to change and in spectacular fashion.

The equipment with which 109 had been experimenting, and the first of a triumvirate of technical advances that would transform the fortunes and performance of PFF, was Oboe, the brainchild of Professor Alec Reeves and a clever team of scientists at the Telecommunications Research Establishment (TRE). Reeves had been the man behind Gee. But if Gee had been first division, Oboe transported TRE – and PFF – to the Premier League.

Oboe used the standard beam approach system of aural indication to guide a pilot along his course. The device was fitted into the aircraft but controlled from ground stations in England. Two stations were involved: the first, known as 'the mouse', directed a radio pulse over the centre of the target. The aircraft travelled along this pulse, the pilot keeping on track by listening to a continuous note (of an Oboe-like quality, hence the name) that sounded in his earphones. A system of dots and dashes would alert him to any deviation in course. At the same time, the pulse was radiated back by the set within the aircraft and received by the second ground station, known as 'the cat'. By measuring the time taken for the return pulse to be received, the exact location of the aircraft could be determined, and with incredible accuracy. When the aircraft approached the release point, 'the cat' transmitted the letters 'abcd', then a series of dashes, then a series of dots. As soon as the dots stopped, the bomb aimer pressed his button[2] and the bombs would drop, with an accuracy of between 60ft and 200ft.[3]

The advantages of Oboe were obvious: it was not weather dependent, therefore giving Bomber Command greater flexibility in its operational planning, and it was phenomenally accurate. Targets that were previously being missed by 60 or 70 miles could now be located by the same measure in feet. The fact that it could pinpoint a target even on the darkest night and through the thickest cloud promised not only heavier damage to German cities, but also fewer casualties to Bomber Command's own aircraft.[4]

But this new blind-bombing miracle also had three limitations. Being a line-of-sight device, the limit of its range was dictated by the curvature of the earth, and that, in turn, would be impacted by the altitude an Oboe-carrying aircraft could fly. The system would not work if the aircraft was lower than 14,000ft – beyond the reach of some Bomber Command aeroplanes at that time. Secondly, each station in England could only control one aircraft every ten minutes, thus, as the maximum number of stations that could be used was three, only 18 aircraft per hour could use the device.

The third limitation was perhaps the most dangerous, at least in the early days. To control an aircraft onto a target required the pilot to fly straight and level for several minutes, making him a potential target for night fighters or predicted flak. It was not difficult for the German flak crews to work out the point in the sky at which to aim if an aircraft was flying at a constant speed and not deviating from its course. As one famous Mosquito pilot remarked, 'Oboe was a nice exercise piece for the gunners'.[5]

Regardless of these shortcomings, Bennett had no doubt that its precise nature and independence of the weather were of tremendous value.[6]

Early Oboe devices were installed in a handful of heavy bombers for an attack on German warships in Brest, but it was quickly realised that, given only a small number of Oboe-equipped aircraft could be employed against a target at any one time, it's most natural home would be in PFF. While their numbers meant they could not provide the marking for a major raid, they could provide the preliminary marking if other aircraft were available for 'backing up'.

A delay in the introduction of Oboe proved, for once, to be a blessing, for in that time, a new and quite remarkable aircraft was entering RAF service: the de Havilland Mosquito, making the success of Oboe a virtual guarantee. Although considered 'useless' by some high-ups in the RAF,[7] its wooden construction and lack of armament fostering little excitement, the Mosquito proved to be a war winner and a particular favourite of Donald Bennett.

It was the Australian 109 Squadron OC and former test pilot Colin McMullen, however, who is credited with producing the final gleam of genius to put Oboe and the Mosquito together.[8] And only just in time. One week before the final decision to begin installing Oboe into the Wellington VI on a production basis, McMullen got hold of a Mosquito and installed four devices ahead of an important conference which, accordingly, rejected the Wellington in favour of the Mosquito.

Whereas the Wellingtons, with which 109 was trialling the device, had a maximum service ceiling of circa 18,000ft on a good day, the 'Wooden Wonder', as the Mosquito was dubbed, could reach almost twice that height. This brought two major advantages: firstly, it made the Mosquito virtually immune from German night fighters, and secondly – and more importantly – it significantly extended the range of Oboe. With 'cat' and 'mouse' ground stations set up on the east coast of England, it meant Germany's industrial heartland of the Ruhr was now within reach.

On the night of 20 December 1942, six Oboe Mosquitoes began their operational career with a small calibration raid on a coking plant at Lutterade in Holland, each aircraft loaded with three 500lb medium-capacity bombs. The first of those bombs were dropped, perhaps appropriately, by an aircraft captained by 'Hal' Bufton, the brother of the man who had done so much to bring about a target-marking force. Three out of the six Mosquitoes had trouble with their sets, perhaps not surprising given that most had been handmade.[9] Reliability was an issue that would plague Oboe in those early days, and indeed for several months, until an upgraded 'precision device' could be introduced.[10]

Results from the first attack were difficult to discern. It was supposed to be a virgin target[11] and post-raid analysis showed several bomb craters, but whether they had been caused by this or previous raids was impossible to establish. The Germans didn't know either and for the moment were none the wiser of the significance of these raids. Further attacks on Essen, Hamborn, Meiderich and Rheinhausen left the smart boys at the ORS similarly scratching their heads.

From December 1942 through to the end of February 1943, 109 Squadron flew more than 100 operations, testing its equipment and experimenting with new techniques. On the last night of December, the first experiment at marking a target in Germany was attempted, involving two Mosquitoes – one as a marker, and the second in reserve. The lead Mosquito successfully dropped 'sky markers' (a weapon ridiculed in some quarters[12]) for the following force of only eight PFF Lancasters (all from 83 Squadron) to aim at. No serious damage was recorded, and one Lancaster was lost, but a new technique had been established, however fanciful it appeared to some.

Raids involving small numbers of aircraft continued in January; on 9 January, two PFF Mosquitoes and 50 Lancasters of 5 Group attacked Essen. The Krupp steel plant was hit, badly, and the Germans began to suspect that a new device of some kind was being used to allow the RAF to 'see' a target through the clouds. The Führer himself, it is said, took a personal interest in the attack and refused point-blank to countenance that 'blind bombing' was possible.[13] He was wrong, as PFF and Bomber Command went on to prove in spectacular fashion.

On the night of 16/17 January, a new 'weapon' was introduced, a weapon that owes much of its development to the pre-war firework industry.[14] Towards dusk, a force of 201 heavy bombers set out to attack Berlin, the first raid on the city in 14 months. Three PFF Lancasters were to drop flares in the target area two minutes before zero hour, guided to the city not by any new navigational aid, but simple dead reckoning. By the light of the flares, ten more PFF aircraft were then to visually identify the target and drop new TI bombs as a guide for the Main Force that followed.

TIs had been a gap in the Pathfinders' armoury from the very beginning. Early tactics, as we have seen, involved using large numbers of incendiaries. Later, the RAF began producing hooded flares, with mixed results. Bennett believed Main Force had to be able to aim at pyrotechnics of some sort,[15] and so the TI was born, originally in three casings: 4,000lb, 2,000lb and 250lb. The first two were found to be uneconomical[16] and development was concentrated on the 250lb version. These were produced with red, green, yellow and white candles and first deployed on the attack on Berlin.

The intensity of the TIs was very great indeed, and while the Germans tried to imitate them – evidenced at first anecdotally and confirmed by an analysis of bomb plots – they never completely succeeded.[17] The multiple colour combinations made things even more challenging for the defenders to replicate, as did the barometric fuses which enabled the TIs to explode anything between 200ft and 500ft above the ground, cascading colours as they fell to earth but designed in such a way that the main burning period was while the marker was on the ground itself.

Early TIs were not without their teething issues: some of the casings were unstable and sometimes the fins would become detached, leaving the marker to tumble wide of its intended spot, leading some to question the Pathfinders' ability and challenging their commander's patience.

In the event, the attack on Berlin using the new TIs miscarried, though the intention was honest. They tried again the following night but with little success. However ingenious, without the guidance of one of the new navigational devices, the marker bomb was not the solution to the problem of inaccurate attacks on formidable targets.[18] Conversely, it did indeed begin to prove itself when a new navigational aid could be deployed, as was seen over Düsseldorf on the night of 27/28 January. This was the first occasion when Oboe Mosquitoes swapped 'sky marking' for 'ground marking' using the now standard Tis, backed up by Lancaster heavies. Pre-Oboe, this raid would undoubtedly have been doomed to failure, such were the weather conditions over the target. Thanks to Oboe, however, and the co-ordinated efforts of all PFF aircraft, a good concentration of bombs was delivered on the south of the city and a considerable amount of damage done. The portents were good, and things were just about to get even better with the arrival of an innovation that was to have a profound success on PFF and the bombing war in general: H2S.

One of the principal shortcomings of Oboe was its range; H2S was different. H2S was a self-contained piece of navigation equipment installed in the aircraft and, as such, range was no longer an issue. Like Oboe, it could also be used in all weathers, and all flying conditions.

Said to have stood for 'Home Sweet Home', a phrase coined by Lord Cherwell himself,[19] the principles of H2S were similar to those of the air-to-surface vessel radar used by Coastal Command to detect U-boats and other vessels at sea. It was not surprising, therefore, that the science behind the device – and the scientists – became something of an unseemly tug of love between Harris and his counterparts at Coastal.[20]

Described as being the most revolutionary device ever known,[21] H2S – like Oboe – was yet another lovechild of the scientists at the TRE and was, in essence, a ground-scanning radar that presented the navigator in the aircraft with an image of the terrain below, displayed on a rudimentary oscilloscope. Initially using the 10cm wavelength,[22] the scanning equipment itself was installed beneath the aircraft fuselage in a distinctive streamlined dome. It transmitted a fan-shaped beam that rotated about the vertical axis beneath the aircraft. Pulses from the beam were reflected back to the aeroplane from the ground and the time the pulses took to return was in proportion to the distance the object was from the aircraft.

Referred to cryptically as 'Y',[23] H2S was especially good at distinguishing between land and large bodies of water. But the earliest sets were not without their challenges. A flickering, often indeterminate, picture was all the H2S operator had, even when his set was working properly. Great skill was required to operate and maintain the equipment, and even though reliability was an issue, there is no doubt that the device was a boon to Bomber Command just when it needed it most. By now, the Germans had found a way of jamming Gee; H2S gave navigators another trick up their sleeves and could even be used as a target-finding device if no better means were available. As Norman Ashton of 156 Squadron said, operationally H2S enabled PFF to drop markers and bombs onto an otherwise invisible target: 'It was, in short, a target area navigational bombsight.'[24]

It was originally hoped that H2S would be manufactured in such numbers that every aircraft within Bomber Command would be equipped with it. While that was the case eventually, in the immediate term the few sets that were available were given to the people who could make most use of them: PFF. Thirteen Stirlings of 7 Squadron and ten Halifaxes of 35 Squadron were the first to receive their new equipment and began training immediately.[25] But there was a hitch. Just as Bomber Command and PFF readied themselves for operations, the War Cabinet got cold feet, perhaps egged on by members of the 'senior service'.

The argument centred around the use of the magnetron valve, without which H2S might never have come about.

The first magnetron valves generated no less than 500 watts of power on the high frequency of 3,000 megacycles, a breakthrough that meant radar sets could be developed capable of plotting targets with far greater precision than had previously been possible.[26] This power was soon after increased to an incredible 10,000 watts and, in March 1941, a magnetron-powered radar set was carried aloft in an aircraft for the first time, as a prototype for a new radar for night fighters. It was while these trials were being conducted that radar operators noticed the echoes from the ground were returned most strongly over built-up areas, and most weakly by countryside or the sea. The birth of H2S came about when it was decided to modify the device to look at the ground, rather than the sky.

Since the magnetron was top secret, however, the powers-that-be did not want it flown over enemy territory, in case it was captured. Some scientists, among them Sir Robert Watson-Watt, the inventor of radar, held the opinion that if the Germans laid their hands on a working model, it would take them only two or three months to develop a countermeasure.[27]

The alternative, they decided, was to use the less-satisfactory klystron valve, though initial trials were disappointing and not helped when nearly half the scientific development team working on the device were killed in a Halifax crash. Eventually, and partly through the intervention of Lord Cherwell and strong lobbying from both Harris and Bennett, the War Cabinet relented, but not until vital weeks had been lost. They would repeat the exercise later with the introduction of another innovation, 'Window', and again based on the fear that the enemy would learn something from it, a policy Bennett – never one to mince his words – described as 'cowardly and disastrous'.[28]

With H2S cleared, literally and finally, for take-off, Harris had to choose the target. He selected Hamburg on the basis that its proximity to the coast and prominent waterways would show up well on the navigators' displays. It proved to be a disappointing night in so many ways: a Mosquito burst a tyre on landing and blocked the runway at Wyton, preventing all the 83 Squadron aircraft from taking part; seven PFF aircraft returned because their special equipment didn't work; and one aircraft abandoned the operation because of icing.

The disappointment did not last, and H2S did not take long to start proving itself. Neither, though, did it take the Germans long to capture their first set intact. Two days after H2S became 'operational', a 7 Squadron Stirling was shot down over Holland and a set was retrieved. The Germans gave it the codename 'Rotterdam' as a result. Although somewhat battered, it was repaired by the German firm Telefunken, which then began exploring its secrets. They were staggered by what they found, as were the pilots tasked with bringing the bombers down.

To form an opinion of the accuracy of the equipment, Hajo Herrmann flew over Berlin in a Junkers Ju 86 equipped with a set taken from a crashed bomber. The East–West Axis, Unter den Linden, Tempelhof airfield and the lakes around Berlin could all be easily recognised: 'The equipment enabled them to display prominent geographical features on a screen in the aircraft.

The enemy had something like this, while our bomber crews had to rely on their eyesight. At night, our night fighter pilots operated in darkness, while the bomber crews could see almost as clearly as by daylight. I realised what we are up against.'[29]

His 'boss', Hermann Göring, agreed: 'I expected the British to be advanced, but frankly I never thought they would be so far ahead. I did hope that even if we were behind, we could at least be in the same race.'[30]

With Oboe, H2S and his target indicators and sky markers, Bennett now had the tools at his disposal to really show what PFF could do. He also had the aircraft, though he was acutely aware of the inefficiencies of operating so many different types. Delighted with the Lancaster and the Mosquito, and their incredible performance, he was less enamoured with the Wellington, Halifax and Stirling aircraft that still equipped the majority of his force.

The time of reckoning would come, but not just then. His ambition to have just two types and dedicated maintenance facilities capable of fulfilling planned maintenance before the concept had even been imagined, would eventually be realised. This was certainly helped by the elevation of PFF to full group status – 8 Group – notified on 25 January 1943 and effective from the 13th of the same month.[31] It was similarly assisted by Harris' apparent determination not to put a 'senile stooge'[32] in command of the group ahead of Bennett, but rather trust in his own man and promote him to air commodore.

From this point until the end of the war, Pathfinders had three methods of finding the target: firstly, by visual methods; secondly, by H2S; and thirdly by the highly accurate Oboe.[33] To the different techniques that evolved, Bennett allocated certain new codenames that were to become familiar to Main Force in the coming months, but to an outsider would appear to be a language all of its own.

For a target marked visually with ground markers (TIs) for Main Force to aim at, he gave the codename 'Newhaven'. When the weather was poor, and ground markers put down 'blind' using H2S, he used 'Paramatta'. And when ground marking wasn't possible, either visually or blind, and sky markers were the only option, it was 'Wanganui'. The pre-fix 'Musical' was later added to denote when Oboe was being used in blind-bombing scenarios.

How Bennett arrived at such names is the stuff of legend, though, as with every legend, not everything is quite as it seems. In his autobiography, Bennett says the names were derived from the birthplaces of some of his staff: his confidential WAAF clerk, Sunshine, came from Newhaven; Artie Ashworth came from Wanganui; and Bennett himself chose Paramatta. Ashworth tells a slightly different story:

> The residue of my stay with Pathfinders can be found in the codenames for two of the types of attack we used. After discussing with Bennett how we were going to use the new air and ground markers, I went about writing the two operations orders for their original use. I named the two types of attack first 'Wanganui' – I had a brother living there at the time – and 'Paramatta' in deference to Bennett. I know this is contrary to what Bennett wrote in his autobiography. He claimed Wanganui was my birthplace. The nearest I have ever been to Wanganui is the RNZAF base at Ohakea, some 40 miles distant.[34]

It is interesting to note, in the context of all that had gone before, that the first major success for Pathfinder Force with its new-found magic box came in an attack where the crews never saw the target.

The date was 5/6 March 1943, and the target was an old favourite – Essen. The scope of Harris' remit had been enlarged and a joint Anglo–American bombing offensive against Germany had been agreed at the Casablanca Conference. The disorganisation of German industry was the order of the day, giving the C-in-C virtual carte blanche to attack any industrial city with more than 100,000 inhabitants.[35] Essen had been first on Harris' list the year before, and it was Essen that now topped the list again as the largest and most important manufacturing centre in the Ruhr.

Bomber Command assembled a force of 442 aircraft, comprising an almost equal number of Lancasters and Wellingtons, with the rest of the force made up of Halifaxes and Stirlings. Completing the ensemble were eight Oboe-equipped Mosquitoes, the stars of the show.

The plan of attack was meticulously worked out in every detail with nothing left to chance. The Mosquitoes were to lead the attack, first by dropping yellow TI flares along the lines of approach to the target, in effect creating a corridor through which the Main Force would travel. These 'yellows' were backed up by PFF Lancasters. The same Mosquitoes would then drop salvoes of red TIs on the aiming point which, on this occasion, was to be the very centre of the vast Krupp works. These reds were to be dropped in defined intervals, the first at zero hour (Z); the next, three minutes later; the next, ten minutes later and so on until the last was to fall at Z+33. Backers-up were to attack two minutes after zero hour and continue until Z+36. They were to drop green TIs along with their heavy explosives, aiming at the red TIs with a delay of one second before releasing incendiaries.

Main Force was to attack in three sections: Halifaxes to the front, Wellingtons and Stirlings in the middle and Lancasters bringing up the rear. Secrecy was paramount, though the Main Force crews were briefed that the placing of the red TIs was likely to be very accurate, and they should use their utmost endeavours to aim at them.[36] No Main Force aircraft was to bomb anything other than the reds before the attack had been in progress for at least 15 minutes

For once, an attack in theory manifested itself well in practice. Timing was everything and Pathfinding was exceptional. Only a mere handful of aircraft bombed outside of their allotted timings – some too soon and some too late, but most within their defined periods. The attack had been going for no more than seven minutes when the first fires began to take hold, followed by a tremendous explosion. The new method had brought about the necessary concentration, and, at last, the bombs were falling on what they were intended to hit.[37] Only one cluster of red TIs was off target, the result of a technical defect in one of the Oboe-carrying Mossies.

The results of the night's operation were stunning. An area something in the order of 160 acres was almost totally laid to waste: 53 separate shops were damaged and 13 destroyed or put out of action. Three coalmines, a sawmill, an iron foundry and a screw works were also damaged and two plants – those of the Goldschmidt company and the Maschinenbau union – were partly gutted. There was damage too in the city itself, with the town hall, the exchange, the town baths, four post office buildings, nine churches, five schools and a theatre also hit. Of all this damage, one history records,[38] the most satisfying was that which occurred in the shops devoted to stamping of sheet metal, annealing, and the production of gun parts, pneumatic tools, excavators and gun turrets. The main gasometer in the city was never used again.[39]

The raid marked a new stage in the development of Bomber Command, and the effectiveness of Pathfinder Force. Although three of the Mosquitoes were obliged to return early, the five that remained along with the backers-up performed splendidly. Backers-up kept the pot boiling. Oboe by itself would rarely have worked – it needed the follow up of the rest of PFF.[40]

The planning, methodology and execution of the raid were to become the template for future attacks, especially in the period between March and July 1943, styled by Harris as the beginning of his main offensive and by historians as the Battle of the Ruhr.

But if the attack on Essen during the Battle of the Ruhr showed Oboe and PFF at their best, it was an attack on Hamburg – beyond the range of Oboe but ideally suited to H2S – that was to show Bomber Command and PFF at their most terrifyingly destructive. It was also an opportunity for Harris to play the last of his flurry of aces – a major tactical innovation that had been waiting in the shadows for more than a year.

Bennett described the Battle of Hamburg as the greatest victory of the war – on land, sea or in the air.[41] It had been in the making for several weeks, Harris having circulated an order to his group commanders to start preparing for an all-out attack at the end of May. He chose the night of 24/25 July to launch his assault, four major raids in the space of only ten nights.

In the first of the attacks in favourable weather, the marking (a mix of H2S and visual) was a little scattered but sufficient for some concentrated bombing to take effect. Only half of the force of almost 800 aircraft bombed within three miles of the centre, and the bombs crept back twice that distance. Because Hamburg is such an enormous city, however, a considerable amount of damage was caused, and a number of gigantic fires were started. Coal and coke supplies stored for the winter caught fire, essential services were cut and dockyards and industrial installations were severely hit.[42] It was the raid on 27/28 July, however, where the real damage was done – a night that gave rise to the common use of a new and terrible word: firestorm.

The firestorm started through an unusual and unexpected chain of events.[43] The weather was dry and hot, and the city a tinderbox. Concentrated bombing started a number of new fires, and the emergency services were quickly overwhelmed. Fresh fires began joining with the old, competing for oxygen with devastating consequences, as detailed in a contemporary German secret report:

> Through the union of a number of fires, the air gets so hot that on account of its decreasing specific weight, it receives a terrific momentum, which in its turn causes other surrounding air to be sucked towards the centre. By that suction, combined with enormous difference in temperature (600–1,000 degrees centigrade) tempests are caused which go beyond their meteorological counterparts. The overheated air stormed through the street with immense force, spreading the fire farther and farther, developing into a fire typhoon such as was never before witnessed, against which every human resistance was quite useless.[44]

Men, women and children were consumed by the flames, many to die a terrible death that even Dante could not have fully imagined. Perhaps upwards of 40,000 people died, many from carbon monoxide poisoning when the oxygen was sucked out of their basement shelters and chemistry did the rest.

It was not the end of their suffering: two further attacks were mounted on the night of 29/30 July and again on 2/3 August. On the first, PFF was a little wayward with its marking (as Bennett described it, a 'classic bloomer'[45]) and on the second, the crews were not able to mark at all. But by then it didn't matter. The damage had been done, and at very little cost to the RAF.

In all four attacks on Hamburg, Bomber Command used Window: strips of aluminium foil exactly 27cm long and 2cm wide released at various stages in the run over the coast and into the target. When dropped in sufficient quantity, bundles of Window played havoc with German radar, rendering the radar controllers virtually blind, and the night fighters and radar-laid flak guns almost useless. It is estimated that in the six Main Force raids carried out between 24 July and 2 August, Window saved anything up to 130 Bomber Command and PFF aircraft that would otherwise have been lost. It was a sobering lesson to those who had refused permission to use Window much earlier in the war, fearful that once its secret was out, it would be quickly countered: Bomber Command lost 2,200 aircraft during the Window embargo period, a large proportion to German radar-assisted defences. Many of these could have been saved, had the powers-that-be been braver in allowing Window to be deployed sooner.

Bennett was keen to press home their advantage. He believed that the morale of the German people could be crushed once and for all, but his opinion went largely ignored. The Battle of the Ruhr and the Battle of Hamburg had shown what Bomber Command, and Pathfinder Force, could really achieve, given the conditions, the technology and the men.

Soon Harris would turn his attention to the big prize: Berlin.

Chapter 7

A Promise of Permanency

T he elevation of PFF to group status and the promotion of its first AOC to air commodore at the beginning of 1943 gave Bennett equality of function, if not rank, with other group commanders. More than this, perhaps, it was a symbol of success, a promise of permanency.[1] More importantly, it began to free Bennett from the shackles of total dependency on other groups and allow him the scope to start organising the Pathfinders his way and in his new headquarters, Castle Hill House. He started with his staff.

Bennett was keen to surround himself with men who had 'current' operational experience as far as he could or appoint acknowledged experts in their particular fields. For his number two, the senior air staff officer (SASO), he was offered a man who was neither expert navigator nor operationally experienced. He was, however, thoroughly conscientious and dependable.

Clayton Descou Clement Boyce, known simply as 'CDC' after his initials or 'Bruin' because of his teddy bear build, had known Bennett before the war. Both had served under Harris in 210 Squadron at Pembroke Dock and Boyce had spent a large part of his early career on flying boats at a time when such aircraft were regarded as having a greater potential share in aviation's future than eventually turned out to be the case. Boyce and Bennett were not natural bedfellows – Boyce being a public schoolboy didn't help – and Bennett had been warned by his supporters not to count on Boyce's loyalty.[2]

Bennett's opinion of his second in command was cool and rather dismissive, which is surprising given that Boyce had commanded Blenheims in North Africa and piloted a Wellington in the thousand-bomber raid on Cologne. He'd also achieved the somewhat remarkable feat of converting an Airspeed Oxford navigation trainer into a makeshift bomber to quell the rebellious forces of Rashid Ali in the Iraq campaign of 1940! He was not averse to sneaking in the odd operation when time allowed – something that should have endeared him more to his master. On the night of the famous PFF-led attack on the rocket research establishment at Peenemünde in August 1943, for example, Boyce hitched a last-minute ride with the 97 Squadron crew of Ernest Rodley, sensing that the raid was going to be something special.[3]

Boyce's opinion of his boss was also somewhat complicated. While he was said to have greatly disliked Bennett personally, he admired him professionally, and the two made an effective and successful team throughout the war. Indeed, their relationship endured when many others did not.

Reporting to Boyce was a collective of Air Staff officers, typically men who had just completed their tours and were not all delighted at the thought of flying a mahogany desk. But if they thought they'd be bored, they were wrong, for the job of an Air Staff officer was an exhausting one.

Among the first in a clutch of highly experienced bomber crew given Air Staff responsibility was Ray Hilton, a VR officer and consummate captain of aircraft. With his hang-dog expression and craggy features, Hilton looked much older than his 26 years. He was a chartered accountant by profession[4] and had flown his first tour of operations in 1941 in Wellingtons with 214 Squadron, and his second with 83 Squadron the following year, picking up two DFCs in the process. He'd seen the best and the worst of Bomber Command, and of PFF in particular. To satisfy Harris' desire to experiment with the Lancaster in various precision raids in daylight, Hilton had been one of a small number of pilots sent to attack the Krupp works in Essen in July 1942 – and one of the few to make it through to the target. It had been a close-run thing. His aircraft had been attacked en route by German fighters but managed to avoid serious damage.[5] With the transfer of 83 Squadron to PFF, he'd flown in the first disappointing attack on Flensburg, failing to find the target.

John Slater had no Pathfinding experience but had been one of the merry band of bomber pilots flying against the barges and build-up of troops and materiel as the Germans planned to enact Operation *Sealion* in the autumn of 1940. While the plaudits have always gone to the Few, the Many were also risking their lives every day, often in outclassed and outdated aircraft like the single-engined Fairey Battle, to prevent a German invasion. Slater, a Londoner, had been a member of the Royal Air Force Reserve before the war, and relinquished his commission in the Reserve on appointment to a short-service commission in 1937. Posted to 150 Squadron after the Fall of France, he stayed with the unit after it swapped its desperately poor Battles for the vastly superior Wellingtons, taking part in the squadron's

first Wellington operation on 21 December 1940, an exciting trip to Ostend. By the end of his first tour in August 1941, he'd been promoted to acting squadron leader and was awarded the DFC. Slater brought not only practical experience of the difficulties faced by bomber crews in those early days, but he'd also been personal assistant to the AOC 1 Group 'Pip' Playfair before the war. He had some idea, therefore,

Ray Hilton, one of Bennett's first Air Staff officers, and one of the first to be killed. (RAF Wyton Pathfinder Collection)

of staff work, administration and the vagaries of dealing with officers of air rank on a regular basis.

Dennis Witt was another who might be described as the first of the Many. A former Halton apprentice[6] from Swanage, Dorset, Dennis qualified first as an electrician but had always yearned to fly and saw his dream realised by securing one of the very few pilot training courses open to 'brats'[7] before the war. He flew lumbering Handley Page Heyfords with 10 Squadron before converting to Whitleys and flying his first operation less than 48 hours after Britain declared war. By September 1940, while the Spitfires and Hurricanes were still leaving their smoke trails over the skies of the capital, Dennis had finished his first tour and been awarded the DFM. Soon after, he was commissioned and posted to 7 Squadron (where he had initially been sent after Halton), playing a key role in the introduction of the Short Stirling, the first of the four-engine heavies. His second tour was perhaps even more hazardous than the first, many of the operations being conducted in daylight, often using the Stirling as 'bait' to draw up enemy fighters in a war of attrition being fought by Fighter Command. On more than one occasion his aircraft was attacked by swarms of Bf 109s, and he only escaped thanks to the skill of the crew, the manoeuvrability of the Stirling and a huge slice of luck. On completing his second tour, by which time he had also picked up a DFC, he completed a specialist navigation (Spec N) course before leaving for Canada to assist with the establishment of the British Commonwealth Air Training Plan. With his experience of operations, navigation and administration, combined with his practical knowledge of a 'trade', it was not surprising that, on his return to the UK, he was quickly snapped up by Bennett and given responsibility for group training and the acting rank of wing commander.

Navigation was something of a religion within PFF, and Bennett its high priest.[8] With so many demands on the group commander's time, however, it was necessary to appoint a group navigation officer to support him in his role. It was a critical appointment – an entire operation could depend on his ability to instil the highest levels of skill within his fellow navigators. Bennett's original choice had been Angus Buchan, but Buchan had been killed and the appointment of group navigation officer was not a happy one at PFF as several others were lost on operations. One who survived, however, was the first to take on the role – the highly experienced Cliff Alabaster.

Originally from Willesden and something of a scholar, Cliff worked in the legal department of London Transport, during which time he enlisted in the RAFVR and began training as an observer. He started operating on Whitleys with 51 Squadron, just at the point Dennis Witt was coming to the end of his first tour and took part in various raids upon the German Navy's capital ships. On one occasion, his aircraft was badly hit by machine-gun fire and the crew were forced to take to their parachutes. Later it transpired they had been shot down by one of their own, in an early example of 'friendly fire'. At the end of his first tour, he was awarded the DFC and completed a Spec N course in Canada before applying to become a pilot. His application was turned down, however, on account of his navigator skills that Bomber Command didn't want to see go to waste. Alabaster's loss was Bennett's gain because, soon after, he arrived at PFF HQ to take up his new post.

Cliff's stay at PFF HQ coincided with the delivery of the first H2S equipment, and much of his time on Bennett's staff was spent overseeing its introduction. Like his 'boss', he also spent considerable hours visiting each of the PFF stations in turn, discussing navigational issues and challenges with individual station navigation officers and generally making it known that he was there to support them.[9]

Also given a senior navigation role within the group staff was Andy Anderson. Andy was a somewhat unlikely candidate for PFF and might never have made it into the RAF at all had he not cheated during his medical. A public schoolboy who himself turned to teaching at a boarding school, he was considered too old for aircrew and given an administrative role. A further attempt at volunteering, and the neat trick of memorising the eye test card, eventually led to him being trained in Canada and returning with the 'Flying Arsehole' – an air observer's brevet. An eventful and successful tour of operations, often flying with the squadron CO, led to the award of the DFC, gazetted while on Bennett's staff.

Another navigator was Gordon Georgeson, a married man from Muswell Hill. Like Anderson, he was a little older than the average airman at that time, and an officer in the VR. He'd flown a tour of operations with 12 Squadron prior to being awarded a DFC and was noted for his technical skill as a navigator.

One of the more unusual officers to be recruited to PFF HQ in the first wave was Reginald Otto Altmann – unusual in that his family tree could be traced back to Leipzig in the 12th century where, intriguingly, the cathedral contains a statue of a saint by the same name! With his round, cheerful face and early receding hairline, Otto (he was only ever called Reggie by his mother) looked a little older than his years. Commissioned in the Reserve of Air Force Officers he flew with 61 Squadron until late 1939 before joining 144 Squadron with which he went to war. The squadron was equipped with Handley Page Hampdens, the famous 'Flying Suitcase', which required only one pilot and, as such, his first operations were as an observer, often teamed with Peter Sooby, to conduct 'gardening' (the codeword given to the laying of mines from an aircraft) trips in the Baltic.[10] Posted to 106 Squadron in the summer of 1940 and awarded the DFC, he continued to serve with 106 as one of its senior aircrew until the autumn of the following year when he was posted to 83 Squadron as a flight commander and completed his second tour. After several months 'resting' in various training units, Otto was rescued from relative obscurity to join the growing team in Huntingdon as an operations officer.

'Wimpy' Wellington, who joined HQ PFF in the summer of 1943, remembered Otto well, and the gruelling routine of being an operations officer, managing shifts of 24 hours 'on' and 24 hours 'off'. The day would start early, at 0900hrs, although the real fun began when their masters at the 'Petrified Forest' – their name for Bomber Command HQ in High Wycombe – began to stir. A phone would ring and 'ops' were 'on', the target given, and the number of aircraft allocated. The first task of the operations officer was to work out how many PFF crews were therefore required and from which squadrons. Once this had been determined, and the relevant squadrons informed, a group conference was held, with the AOC, SASO, operations officers, navigation officers and various specialists, assembling to work out the method, route and timing for the attack. Often, planning involved not just a single raid, but rather multiple attacks – certainly later in the war – as well as diversionary raids and 'spoofs' by a small number of Pathfinder Mosquitoes to keep the Germans in their shelters. A PAMPA (photoreconnaissance and meteorological photography aircraft) flight by a 1409 Met Flight Mosquito would also be ordered to give the planners the most up-to-date picture of the weather over the target and – perhaps more importantly – to help predict what conditions would be like on their return home. Fog was a killer, literally, and returning aircraft often had to be diverted to airfields clear of fog or, later in the war, those equipped with a fog dispersal system (FIDO – fog investigation and dispersal operation). It was the operations officer's responsibility to find alternative landing grounds for 'his' crews, and woe betide if he was late in doing so and an airfield was already fully 'booked' by another group!

No two operations were ever the same: for every operation, the bombload, marking, armament, fuel, route, timing, etc., had to be calculated and a 'B' Form compiled, which outlined every detail of the proposed attack from start to finish. The B Form was on a continuous sheet of paper that could run to considerable length and was top secret in every sense. On one occasion, it was thought one of the forms had been blown out of the window on a breezy summer's day onto the streets of Huntingdon below. It proved to be a false alarm, but not before the story had become even more ridiculous in its telling.

With the B Form agreed and completed, it then had to be shared with the other groups, which invariably led to a long session of questions and answers via the scrambler phone that kept the ops officer on his toes. Pathfinder aircraft were always the first to get away, after which time the staff had little to do except wait and log any early returns (in PFF these tended to be few and far between) or other notable events. The real work started again once the aircraft returned, and squadrons began sending in their reports. A first assessment of the success or otherwise of the attack was then quickly compiled, along with a list of those aircraft missing or at least overdue. By 0900hrs the following morning, it was all over, with the chance to hand over the reins and retire for some well-earned rest.

Alongside the Air Staff were the 'specialists' to advise on intelligence, armaments, signals, equipment, photography, engineering and all things medical. There were also the administrators – those in charge of personnel and organisation.

One of the most important roles was that of the group intelligence officer, William Shepherd. 'Shep', as he was inevitably known, had been an intelligence officer at Leeming and volunteered to join his old 'boss' at PFF. As an intelligence officer, commissioned within the RAF's Administrative and Special Duties Branch, it was Shep's responsibility, with his team, to gather all the information he could about the target and German defences – searchlight belts, fighter stations, etc. – before the raid, and then collect the pilots' reports immediately after. It was a hugely responsible task that Shep executed with commendable rigour, being twice mentioned in despatches prior to the creation of 8 Group. He was, in Bennett's words, one of the leading characters of PFF HQ and one who invariably sought to see the funny side of life whenever he could.

Another great character was the group armament officer, William Rathbone, who, like Shepherd, had been transferred into the Admin Branch before a further transfer into the Technical Branch. Rathbone, nicknamed 'The Reluctant Dragon' by his boss, 'produced the fireworks and the bangers' and a great deal more besides. He worked closely alongside the group equipment officer, John Rose, a pre-war regular who had spent his entire career in the Equipment Branch, responsible for the procurement of all non-technical equipment, as well as setting up appropriate stores depots (the Equipment Branch had formerly been known as the Stores Branch) and packaging depots.[11] It was an unglamorous yet essential role to which Rose was well disposed.

A similarly unglamorous role of vital importance was that of the group photography officer, a task fulfilled by the 'master of improvisation', Howard Lees. Like Andy Anderson, Lees was considered too old for aircrew and was also in a reserved occupation, until such time as the categories were revised and he was accepted into the RAF's Photographic Branch. Originally from Leicester, he left school at 16 to join a firm of manufacturers' agents in the shoe trade. However, his passion was for photography. He'd always been something of a photographic innovator, being credited in the *British Journal of Photography Almanac* in 1934 as having taken the first photograph of a moving image on the cinema screen. It might have been a portent of what was to come, for later Lees perfected a way of capturing a photograph from an H2S screen at the moment the bombs were released as a further aid to assessing the accuracy of a raid. Perhaps his more famous achievement was the development of a two-shutter camera, which served to eliminate the frequent ruining by ground fires of the image obtained by a single prolonged exposure. With Bennett's near obsession with aerial photography and finding ways of improving the accuracy of wartime night

Howard Lees helped crews deliver clear, undistorted target photographs for post-raid analysis. (RAF Wyton Pathfinder Collection)

bombing, Lees was an extremely valuable member of the 8 Group staff, helping crews to deliver clear, undistorted target photos for analysis.

For his group signals officer, Bennett appointed George Adams who had joined the RAF before the war and been transferred to the Technical Staff. Adams was responsible early in his tenure at PFF HQ for the introduction of Oboe, the blind-bombing device, and would later be mentioned in despatches and awarded the OBE for his wartime work. What Adams started was continued by Edward 'Barty' Barton who was a qualified Marconi engineer with South African Airways before the war and a reservist in the Royal Army Service Corps. Called up at the outbreak of war as part of the British Expeditionary Force, he fought alongside a party of Welsh Guards during the retreat to Dunkirk. Swapping khaki for blue serge, he was posted to the Air Ministry as Director of Intelligence in the Signals Directorate, on one occasion being flown to neutral Spain to examine the radio equipment in a crashed Focke-Wulf Condor, a four-engined long-range reconnaissance aircraft. Bennett kept Barton, and indeed all of his officers, busy with late nights and early mornings, and Barton kept his knowledge of wartime operations 'current' by taking the navigator's seat in a Mosquito or as a spare bod among the crew of a Lancaster.

One of Bennett's major bugbears was administration, and the Australian held most of his senior administration officers (SAOs) in little regard. 'The Administration of the Air Force is something to me which should serve the operational side,' he wrote, 'and not the reverse.'[12] His first two appointees were Aubrey Martin and William Carr – two old-school administrators with whom Bennett had little or nothing in common. With 'Ferdie' Swain he should have been better suited, given Swain's pre-war flying experience conducting high-altitude experiments at the Royal Aircraft Establishment. Swain had astonished the world of aviation in 1936 by establishing an altitude record of 49,967ft in a purpose-built Bristol 138A monoplane, wearing a pressure suit and a windowed helmet. His administrative skills, however, failed to astonish Donald Bennett, even though he'd also been a SASO with 6 Group and a station commander earlier in the war. It was not until the appointment of Hamish White, much later in the war, that

Bennett finally found a man he could work with and 'who did a grand job and produced efficiency with the right spirit'.[13]

John 'Doc' McGowan was another who did a 'grand job' as the group medical officer, looking after the fitness and welfare of the men of PFF. He was not averse to flying on operations as a rear gunner – 'for usefulness of medical gen on the crews'.[14] He was precisely the kind of man Bennett wanted on his team, giving him current experience to add to his years as a fighter pilot on the Western Front in World War One where at least two 'Huns' fell to his guns.

McGowan became something of an expert in night vision on bomber operations, excusing himself from PFF HQ to interview aircrew on frontline squadrons and detail their experiences. He was especially keen to know the effects of dazzle and glare of the target indicators and flares over the target, and how certain landmarks stood out in the darkness below. He went along for the ride on several occasions – more than 50 times in fact – and was awarded the DFC.

Tall and greying, and more than twice the age of some of the boys with whom he flew, he became a familiar and much-liked figure among the PFF aircrew. His skills as a navigator were also put to good use, assisting young crews in what they could and couldn't see. On one occasion, when a Lancaster in which he was a passenger was 'coned' by searchlights, he gave calm and considered instruction to the pilot as he sensed the danger from the astrodome. They managed to make it through untroubled by flak or fighters. Back at base he asked the pilot whether his instruction had been of value. The pilot denied hearing anything, such was the strain he was under at the time, and yet had reacted subconsciously to everything that had been said![15]

As well as McGowan, an eye specialist who had given up his Harley Street practice to join the RAF, there were also the met men, their civilian attire in stark contrast to the mass of military uniforms, devoid of any medal ribbons or badges of rank. That's not to say they weren't deserving of recognition or didn't show some degree of bravery in facing down their 'boss' when it was needed. M J 'Tommy' Thomas BSc, the senior meteorological officer in the group was, in Bennett's view, one of the best forecasters. It was just as well, for on his word depended the success of the main bombing effort, and the technique and timing of every raid.[16] Get it right, and he'd be the hero of the day; get it wrong, and he could expect the wrath not just of the AOC but also the C-in-C himself. At the beginning, every group had its own met man; later it was agreed to centralise resources and co-ordinate their views in advance such that they could speak as one voice.

Arguably the most important job of all, beyond navigation and the weather, was that of the group engineering officer, and for his head 'plumber' Bennett chose 33-year-old Charles Sarsby. Sarsby was a brilliant engineer and former army officer who resigned his commission on appointment to the RAF in 1933. Business-like and efficient, one of Sarsby's first actions was to instigate a programme of planned maintenance for the group, long before it was adopted by other units, inside and outside of Bomber Command.

In Sarsby, Bennett was fortunate to have a man who was ahead of his time; Sarsby was similarly fortunate in having a young AOC who valued the importance of engineering and the need to have maximum aircraft serviceability at all times. Sarsby, like Lees, was an innovator: he enabled H2S to be successfully installed in Mosquitoes (albeit leading to a rather cramped cockpit!) and devised a bomb carrying mechanism that increased the weight of bombs a Mosquito could carry. Like 'Shep', he favoured personal visits to the men under his command over random memos.

Resourceful as well as highly skilled in his endeavours, he worked closely with Bennett in standardising 8 Group, transforming it from a varied collection of aircraft – a significant issue in the first year of the Pathfinders' existence – to a highly efficient force based on just the two. He also created dedicated maintenance hubs for both aircraft types at Wyton and Upwood. Each squadron had an obligation to produce 16 aircraft out of 18 available each day, and definitely to know they had the other two available for servicing without fear of interruption.[17]

It made good sense to rationalise the Pathfinder 'fleet', and Bennett had a number of potential candidates for PFF. One night, for example, at

Boscombe Down, home to the Aeroplane and Armament Experimental Establishment, he flew a B-25 Mitchell, a medium bomber, which allowed him a 'line shoot'. When asked whether he had seen the new American aircraft he was able to answer truthfully: 'No, but I have flown one!'[18] He did not consider it suitable for PFF, however; neither was it ever seen as a competitor to the Mosquito.

With both the Wellington and the Short Stirling effectively 'retired' from Bomber Command service over the course of 1943, it became a straight choice between the Lancaster and the Halifax to take on the heavy lifting. The decision was not a simple one. While on paper, the Lancaster was superior in just about every department, the men on 35 Squadron were proving the Halifax to be the better aeroplane, at least in terms of results. An examination by the Directorate of Bomber Operations looked at the performance of the Halifaxes and Lancasters on operations in PFF and Main Force in the spring of 1943 during attacks on Berlin, the Ruhr and certain major cities including Nuremberg, Stuttgart and Munich. In terms of aircraft losses in PFF, the ratio was 3.5 per cent (Halifax) to 5.5 per cent (Lancaster). In Main Force, the losses were almost reversed: 4 per cent (Halifax) versus 3 per cent (Lancasters). While the report admits that the numbers were too small to draw any reliable conclusions, it did suggest that experience (of the PFF crews) was more important than aircraft type when it came to overall performance,[19] a view shared by the AOC 8 Group.

But the Halifax had its problems. One Pathfinder flight engineer, Fred Edmondson, described the earlier marks (the Mk II and Mk V in particular) powered by the Rolls-Royce Merlins as 'awful': 'When you closed the throttles on a Halifax it would drop; do the same with a Lancaster and it would float.'[20] The Halifax had well-known problems with its tail and rudder assembly, leading to a number of fatal crashes before the problem was finally resolved. By then, however, many – including Harris himself – had lost patience with the type, even the new Halifax IIIs with Bristol Hercules engines, stating that to continue with the Halifax would result in losses that 'will ensue on an ever-increasing scale... if we persist in our present policy of sending men to fight in inferior machines'.

Bennett and Harris no doubt discussed the matter; Bennett had his own personal experience of the Halifax on operations and his own view of the Halifax III, which was said to be equal to, if not better than, its rival heavy. Its top speed had certainly been increased and it was less likely to fall out of the sky on its own accord. In the late autumn of 1943, Bennett drove to Graveley, home of 35 Squadron, to test one of the new aircraft. Ted Stocker, who'd flown more than 40 ops by this time on the Halifax, was asked to accompany his AOC.

Ted remembered the take-off well; the aircraft thundered along the runway as the throttles were pushed forward, and Bennett had to account for the swing. The aircraft fair leapt into the air: 'I was surprised, and I know that Bennett was too. It caught us both unawares.'[21] Bennett spent half an hour putting the aircraft through its paces. With only pilot and flight engineer on board, and without any bombs and only limited fuel, the aircraft handled well.[22] Bennett flew a few circuits and played with the undercarriage and flaps. He also tested the effectiveness and weight of the controls, paying particular attention to the rudders before declaring himself satisfied and coming into land. It wasn't much of a trial, but it was enough to convince Bennett to throw his full support behind the Lancaster as his preferred heavy bomber. It was a decision he had no cause to regret. He continued this support for the remainder of the war and was particularly invested in a more powerful version of the Lancaster equipped with the Merlin 85, which had better performance characteristics at height making it ideal for high-level PFF operations. Several of the airframes were trialled by 635 Squadron in late 1944 but despite showing considerable promise, they were never produced.

While reducing the aircraft types belonging to PFF, Bennett increased the number of stations and squadrons operating them. To Graveley, Oakington, Wyton and Warboys, he added Gransden Lodge, Marham (for a short time) and Bourn. Having started out with four squadrons, a year later he had ten, and by the end of the war, he had effectively twice that number.

The departure of 2 Group from Bomber Command's order of battle at the end of May 1943 enabled two Mosquito units to be hived off to

PFF: 105 Squadron became the second unit to be equipped with Oboe, its crews very rapidly being brought up to speed with the unfamiliar device and sharing a station (Marham) with 109; 139 (Jamaica) Squadron became the first unit of a unique force within 8 Group, that of the Light Night Striking Force (LNSF), which eventually grew to a strength of eight Mosquito squadrons flying diversionary and 'siren' raids to keep the air raid sirens screaming and rob the Germans of their sleep. It moved to Wyton to share with 83 Squadron, whereas another Mosquito unit, 627, joined 7 Squadron at Oakington.

Also unique was the arrival of 405 Squadron, a Canadian squadron from the newly formed all-Canadian 6 Group. While there was some pressure to create other stand-alone Commonwealth groups (e.g., an all-Australian group), only the Canadians were afforded the privilege. Some dedicated Australian and New Zealand squadrons were formed within Bomber Command, but never a group, and the men who served in RAAF or RNZAF squadrons were not uniquely Antipodeans. Alongside 405 Squadron was one other new Lancaster unit, 97 Squadron at Bourn, ceded to Bennett from 5 Group. Its keenness to become part of the elite had been rewarded.

To support the expanding force, Bennett also reviewed how his men were trained. A brutal written minute, dated 26 April 1943, assumes the 'wastage' rate of PFF at that time to require a total of 48 new crews every month to replace PFF losses or those who were tour expired. These 48 were to comprise 32 crews from existing squadrons and 16 from various training and conversion units. The Pathfinder Navigation Training Unit (PFNTU) was therefore formally created 'for the purpose of learning the technique and equipment which is peculiar to Pathfinder squadrons'. For those already with operational experience, the number of training hours was between eight and ten per crew; crews arriving direct from conversion units had to do more. They had to have 30 hours of heavy bomber flying time under their belts and have had gone solo on the type of aircraft they would fly in PFF; they could expect anything up to 25 hours of additional flying, both to complete their conversion and learn about the new equipment they would operate. Gransden Lodge was chosen to host the new training unit, though this would soon move and be shared between Upwood and Warboys before ultimately residing at the latter.[23]

Every new intake was greeted with an address by the AOC which, to many, was quite a thrill, since Bennett's reputation preceded him.[24] The eight to ten hours of flying training was complemented by an additional programme of ground instruction, including an explanation into the many and various roles that were steadily emerging. New crews understood they would first have to complete a number of operations as 'supporters' before they might graduate to a more specific role, an 'illuminator' for example, to light up the target for the 'visual markers' – equipped with a specialist air bomber – to drop their target indicators. They were taught the role of the 'visual centerers' and the differences between 'blind' and 'visual' crews, the former marking with the use of blind aids, primarily H2S. For the crews with a few operations to their names, the codewords given to the PFF marking methods were already familiar, for they were used in Main Force briefings. H2S was perhaps less familiar, especially in the early days, as was the concept of a Pathfinder aircraft having two navigators: Nav 1 – a 'traditional' navigator who managed the plot, and Nav 2 – typically an upskilled air bomber who operated the 'Y' set.

Tony Hiscock, a pilot with 156 Squadron, graduated to a crew of primary blind marker illuminators: 'We used H2S to identify the target area, and then would drop flares to illuminate the scene so that the specialist bomb aimers that followed could identify the precise aiming point. H2S could be temperamental and the picture a little difficult to interpret at times, but our bomb aimer (Nav 2) became quite expert.'[25]

As well as a training unit for the heavies, a similar facility was created in 1944 for Mosquito crews – 1655 Mosquito Training Unit (MTU) – at Warboys. It not only converted crews to the ways of PFF, but it also specifically provided training on both Oboe and H2S and bombing practice at the Whittlesey Range near Peterborough.

However, not everyone who passed through training made it to PFF; one figure suggests that only half of all crews who arrived at PFNTU actually made it on to a Pathfinder squadron. But for those who did came the prestige of being part of the corps d'elite that Harris had done so much to resist, and the chance of earning the coveted Pathfinder badge. The badge was awarded temporarily at first, after a dozen or so trips and a test conducted, whenever possible, by the AOC himself, and then permanently – either at the successful conclusion of a Pathfinder tour or on account of an individual being lost on operations.

Some of those who passed through PFNTU, and many others who were awarded their Pathfinder badge prior to the establishment of the training unit, came back to PFNTU as instructors. Among them was Frank Leatherdale, a screened navigator with 7 Squadron: 'NTU was divided into two flights: A Flight was for complete crews (that is to say those that had arrived at NTU as a crew) whereas B Flight was made up of individual pilots, navigators etc who were then put into crews. Even experienced men needed refresher training or to be schooled in the art of Pathfinder terminology and methods.'[26]

Among the experienced men that Frank instructed was Kenneth 'Bobby' Burns, a wing commander who had recently been repatriated from Germany. Rarely seen without a pipe in his mouth or his faithful hound at his side, Burns only had one hand and used to screw on a claw to his right stump to operate the aircraft throttles. Burns had been shot down over Berlin following a head-on attack by a German fighter and was seriously injured in the resultant crash. He was lucky not to have bled to death. Indeed, his injuries, which included a broken back, were believed to be so great that the Germans considered he was unlikely to play any further part in the war, and so he was returned home. It was a mistake, as soon after, Burns resumed his Pathfinding career, adding a DSO to his list of decorations.

Burns subsequently joined Bennett as an Air Staff officer later in the war, for the AOC maintained his policy of surrounding himself with young officers with current operational experience. Others among the pantheon of Pathfinder elite brought into the 8 Group fold included John 'Joe' Collier, the epitome of an RAF hero, who won an 'immediate' DFC in August 1940 as a pilot with 83 Squadron and within two years had added a further DFC and the DSO and joined the Air Staff soon after; Alex Chisholm, an air bomber, who'd joined the RAF on a short-service commission and similarly flew with 83 Squadron, being awarded the DFC just before arriving at PFF HQ; and Dudley Allen, whose medal ribbons invariably caused a raised eyebrow or two since he wore both the GM and the British Empire Medal (BEM). He'd won the GM for saving the lives of three of his crew from a burning Wellington, and the BEM for putting out a burning incendiary in extremely dangerous circumstances. He later added the DFC as a gunnery leader with 156 Squadron.

There was a Canadian, George Grant, whose lanky, cadaverous appearance betrayed a steely determination, and who, as a founding member of 109 Squadron in 1940, returned to command the unit four years later. Cyril 'Smithy' Smith was a serious-looking pilot who won the DSO and DFC within six months of one another and was a hit in the 83 Squadron mess for his piano-playing abilities. Herbert 'Tiny' Travers was a former pilot and 'ace' with the Royal Naval Air Service who'd been a pioneering long-distance pilot for Imperial in the 1930s. Past 50, he did not exactly fit Bennett's 'Air Staff' mould of a young officer with current operational experience, but the AOC clearly saw value in Tiny's experience as a test pilot and navigator.[27]

Some of those who served on the Air Staff were better known than others. Charles Dunnicliffe, for example, was a former Halton apprentice and flight commander with 97 Squadron who was only at PFF HQ for eight weeks before receiving command of 582 Squadron at Little Staughton. One of his flight commanders was Brian McMillan, a likeable New Zealander who, despite his seniority, insisted his crew called him 'Mac'.[28] Then there was Geoff Womersley, with his walrus-like moustache, who had been shot down early in the war and only narrowly escaped capture. He joined PFF as one of its first volunteers and was recognised as being one of the Pathfinders' most fearless pilots. He won the DSO while still only a flight lieutenant and later commanded 139 Squadron, by which time he had already completed 50 operations.

Then there was Bill Deacon, who'd won the DFC with 51 Squadron in 1940 and been awarded the DSO for a daring low-level raid on Montlucon. There was also Charles De Wesselow, who won the DFC and Bar with 97 Squadron and was described as a man of great skill and iron determination, and Roy Ralston, another Halton apprentice and former NCO pilot, who carved a reputation as one of the most brilliant low-level bomber pilots of World War Two.

Many did not survive the war; several were killed within months of leaving Castle Hill. Ray Hilton and Alex Chisholm, for example, died in the same aircraft on the night of 23 November 1943 over Berlin; Gordon Georgeson was shot down during an attack on rail communications on the night of 26/27 July the following year. Kenny Lawson, who succeeded Cliff Alabaster as group navigation officer, was killed in the first month of 1945, having won the DFC and two DSOs and had made the successful transition from navigator to pilot. His successor, Alan 'Pluto' Cousens, an accomplished leader and CO, was also killed, having had the unusual

Alec Cranswick on his wedding day. It was to Cranswick that Bennett dedicated his biography. (RAF Wyton Pathfinder Collection)

distinction of commanding a Main Force squadron as a navigator. Pluto left a lasting impression on the men under his command, and his mother left a silver cup to 635 Squadron in his memory. It is one of many such trophies and drinking vessels inscribed to the memories of those gallant airmen who failed to return.

Most tragic of all was the case of Alec Cranswick, the gentlest of gentlemen to whom Bennett dedicated his autobiography. Cranswick was something of a legend in PFF, a veteran at the time of his death of well over 100 and maybe as many as 140 bomber operations. His aircraft was hit during a raid on the marshalling yards at Villeneuve-Saint-Georges on 4/5 July 1944. Cranswick and all but one of his crew perished in the crash.

Chapter 8

'The Bitterest Part of the War'

Alfred Willetts was a man who liked to lead from the front. A regular air force officer and Old Cranwellian, he'd been commissioned as far back as 1925 and had always been destined for high rank. He'd excelled at Staff College, and in the early war years found himself a wing commander in Greece, attempting to bring order to an otherwise disorderly military situation. With the arrival of a more senior man, John D'Albiac, an air commodore, Alfred was appointed SASO and both men were given a step-up in rank. It had not been a happy time: Axis forces were in the ascendancy, the British could spare little, and what aircraft the Royal Hellenic Air Force had lacked spares and leadership.[1]

Acknowledged for his services by the Greek government,[2] his skills were also recognised by his seniors and, on his return to the UK, Alfred was appointed Air Adviser to Combined Operations HQ. This was an entirely new position, created at the behest of Mountbatten, the chief of the Combined Operations Command himself. Until that point, the RAF had taken a somewhat nonchalant attitude towards Combined Operations, believing there was not much additional training required. However, as the strength of Combined Operations grew, its position changed. Within weeks of Alfred's appointment, he took part in Operation *Archery*, a very successful raid on Vaagso Island. The RAF was tasked with dropping smoke canisters, to cover the advance of the Commandos on the ground, or bombs to take out enemy gun positions. Not content with helping to plan the raid, Alfred also hitched a lift with the lead Hampden so he could 'see for himself'. The citation for the DSO that followed in the *London Gazette* noted that much of the success that attended the operation could be attributed to his 'skill and devotion to duty'.

Alfred, now a group captain, was just the man of action Bennett looked for in his senior team, and when appointed station commander at RAF Oakington, he was still not averse to 'getting some in'. It was of little surprise, therefore, that on the night of 23 August 1943, and with Berlin the target, he should choose to fly.

There had been some mutterings at briefing. To many Main Force crews, Berlin was a novelty, a name to write proudly into a logbook. But many Pathfinders had been there before and knew what it meant to confront a flak belt that was 40 miles across and included some of Germany's highest calibre guns, where even a near miss could spell disaster. At least three men refused to fly, an almost unprecedented event, and perhaps because of this, Alfred decided his personal leadership was required. He was not alone. To the south at Bourn and to the west at Graveley, Noel Fresson and Basil Robinson, both group captains, had similar thoughts. 'Press-on' Fresson had been in charge of 51 Squadron at the start of the war and was CO of 97 Squadron when it moved to Bourn to become part of PFF. He was no shrinking violet, neither was Basil Robinson. Indeed, Robinson was something of a legend in Bomber Command as the man who had flown his aircraft back single-handedly over the Alps.

Harris had been itching to open a series of attacks on the German capital. His liberal interpretation of various directives he'd be given regarding how Bomber Command was to be deployed – and the famous Casablanca directive of early 1943 in particular – justified any attack that led to the progressive destruction and dislocation of the German military, industrial and economic systems and the undermining of morale among the German people to a point where their capacity for armed resistance was fatally weakened.[3] Whereas his primary objective was to attack any targets specific to submarine construction, the aircraft industry, transportation or oil, Berlin was also mentioned by name, which he should attack 'when conditions are suitable for the attainment of specially valuable results unfavourable to the morale of the enemy or favourable to that of Russia'. This was enough for Harris, and even though the original Casablanca directive was updated in June 1943, with a view to complementing the efforts of the Americans and their daylight raids, the C-in-C saw no reason not to go ahead with his plan.

Even though he was eager to raze Berlin to the ground, he was not foolhardy. On the morning of the 23rd, he'd decided to open his offensive but only if the weather over the city was acceptable. It didn't have to be completely clear – the Pathfinders now had different techniques to cope with a variety of challenging weather conditions, but it was important his plan got off to a good start. He would wait until the PAMPA returned before finally issuing the order. As it was, it was not until after four in the afternoon that the teleprinters at last started clattering out the plans that his operations staff had already prepared. It gave the Pathfinders little time to make their final preparations, as take-off was set for less than four hours later.

Alfred opted to hitch a ride with one of 7 Squadron's most experienced bomber captains, Charles Lofthouse. Only a few days before, Lofthouse had acted as backer-up to John Searby, the CO of 83 Squadron and master bomber for the attack on Peenemünde on the Baltic. While later in the war the master bomber role would become de rigueur, and the pinnacle of any Pathfinder's career, for the time being it was still something of a novelty, and this was the first time the tactic was used to control a Main Force attack. It was a novelty, however, that Harris was prepared to try again for this particular raid on Berlin, and to Bennett fell the task of selecting one of his best officers to lead the attack. Having only recently secured the services of 405 Squadron from 6 Group, he opted for its CO, Johnny Fauquier, to be master bomber. Fauquier, who had been Searby's deputy over Peenemünde, was never under any illusions about the dangers that would face him, but his professionalism, skill and confidence in his own abilities was clearly shared by his master.[4]

Lofthouse was slightly less thrilled to have his station commander riding shotgun. No skipper liked a 'second dickey' or 'spare bod' in their crew at

The OC 405 Squadron, Johnny Fauquier, Canada's greatest bomber pilot. (RAF Wyton Pathfinder Collection)

the best of times, but to have such a senior officer present was a pressure of a different kind. Not that Charles wasn't used to pressure. He'd flown 37 operations with 149 Squadron earlier in the war and received the DFC. He added an OBE (Military) for helping to rescue five men from a burning Stirling that had crashed while he was night duty pilot at Waterbeach, 'resting' after completing his first tour. He didn't resume operational flying until late June 1943 when he was hand-picked by Hamish Mahaddie to join PFF and 7 Squadron in particular as a flight commander, for the squadron had lost seven crews in two nights, including Bob Barrell who was on his 60th trip and would have completed his second tour had he returned.[5]

Charles welcomed his station commander onto his Lancaster with a cheery 'Don't forget to bring your sandwiches for the trip home, sir' and then instantly regretted it. And with good reason: tempting fate was never to be encouraged and, on this particular night, Alfred never got to eat his sandwiches.

The plan was a complicated one involving more than 700 bombers, almost half of which were Lancasters. Thirty of PFF's best crews were to fly past Berlin to the south, and then turn back sharply towards it in a north-westerly direction to a built-up area that jutted out from the northern edge of the city and that should show up clearly on their H2S radar screens. The aiming point had been chosen to allow for creepback, so the weight of Main Force bombs should have fallen in the right place. It was, in every sense, a pure area bombing plan, with the Pathfinders never needing to see the ground.

It didn't work – at least, not quite as planned. Marking was inaccurate, Main Force was late, and several bombers decided to cut the corner off the planned route, which meant many of their bombs fell harmlessly in neighbouring countryside. That's not to say that the attack didn't cause considerable damage; it did, but simply not where it was intended. By chance, some of the bombs fell in the government quarter, much to the anger of the Nazi officials.

Not all the Pathfinder aircraft made it to the target. Dennis Cayford, Charles Lofthouse's navigator, had been struggling with his Y set ever since they reached the Dutch coast. Had it not been for having the group captain on board, Charles admitted he probably would have turned back. Arriving a few minutes early and unsure of their position, Charles flew straight and level to allow Cayford enough time to achieve an astro fix and navigate by the stars. Trying to lose a little time in a turn, the sky was suddenly lit up by a tracer. He later recalled:

I looked across to the port engines and saw the outer brewing up. A deep blue flame was growing from the fuel tank which spread rapidly, producing a huge, bright yellow flame streaming behind the aircraft, which was becoming uncontrollable. I said it was about time we got out at which point Willetts was out through the nose escape hatch like a rat out of a trap and the rest of the crew quickly followed.

Both Charles Lofthouse and Alfred Willetts had their respective Pathfinder careers cut short, victims of a German night fighter. Also failing to return was Basil Robinson, flying as a guest of Harry Webster.[6] Robinson was among the most senior and highly decorated Pathfinder officers to be killed during the war. His was in one of four aircraft from 35 Squadron that failed to make it back.

Some 48 men of PFF lost their lives that night; the experience and seniority of those missing was alarming. Within the crew of Kenneth Fairlie of 97 Squadron, for example, was 36-year-old Joseph Forrest, a hugely experienced navigator who had won the DFC in 1941 with 10 Squadron and added a DSO with 83 Squadron almost two years later to the day. At the time of his death, he was a squadron leader and group navigation officer. The 83 Squadron crew of Brian Slade, shot down by a night fighter, could claim four gallantry awards and 330 operational flights between them. Slade's aircraft was shot out of the sky at the start of his bombing run. He was on his 59th trip.[7]

One of the unluckiest of all, although he survived to become a prisoner of war, was Alan Ball who was on his 58th operation and about to be married. He was 35 Squadron's signals officer and had taken the place of one of the three men who had refused to fly. Wilf Sutton, a flight engineer with an Australian pilot, was also unlucky:

We broke cloud east of Hannover and within minutes we were straddled with 20mm canon shells from a Junkers 88… as soon as the first shells hit us the skipper went into violent evasive action… when he righted the plane, I could see what a mess we were in. Canon shells had ripped through the fuselage within an inch of my flare 'chute position, torn the starboard wings apart, set the two starboard engines on fire and the 1,000 gallons of petrol. None of the seven crew members were touched.

This was their 30th operation; all survived to spend the rest of the war in captivity.

As for 'Press-on' Fresson, there was better news. He returned safely to Bourn, none the worse for his adventures.

* * * * *

Harris' long-anticipated attack on Berlin had not got off to the start he wanted. Much had gone wrong, though valuable lessons had been learned. He went twice more over the next few days, but the casualties inflicted on his own aircraft, and the Stirling and Halifax squadrons in particular, meant that the third raid was an all-Lancaster affair in much smaller numbers.

The Battle of Berlin, as it came to be known, was, effectively, in two phases. The first, preliminary, phase saw Harris finding his feet, pushing the capabilities of H2S to its limit and not afraid to experiment with routes that were designed to confound and confuse the enemy as to where they were actually headed. 'Spoof' raids also fast became the norm, with Mosquitoes from PFF dropping flares and markers as though beginning an attack but with no Main Force to back them up. The second phase, the main battle, got underway on the night of 18/19 November, by which time Harris felt that various factors were on his side. In terms of technology, a new version (the Mk III 3cm set) of H2S was now coming into play, with better resolution, as well as the ground position indicator, which made it possible to carry out accurately timed runs even in well-defended areas.[8] There was also talk of extending the range of Oboe by having 'repeater' aircraft to 'bounce' the signal. In terms of timing, the long winter nights would afford his night bombing force better protection. The converse of these benefits, however, was that even the new Y sets were still prone to regular failure, and the weather in that winter of 1943/44 was about the worst it had ever been.

The Pathfinder chief had serious misgivings. He recognised that his squadrons were entering their greatest conflict well short of the state of perfection that he both demanded and saw as fundamental to their success.[9] He set out his position clearly to his superiors, once again highlighting the inconsistent quality of crews reaching PFF and the lack of training time he was given to bring them up to the required standard. He also begged once again for permission to fly, stating boldly that he could never do the job as it should be done unless he was permitted to operate.[10] Harris was having none of it: he did not agree that training opportunities were any less in PFF than they were in Main Force and refused point-blank to allow Bennett to fly.[11]

Bennett had every right to be concerned. In the period from the end of August to the start of the main battle in November, Pathfinders lost more than 40 crews, the equivalent of wiping out almost two whole squadrons. Among the captains lost were one wing commander, nine squadron leaders and at least three other skippers of junior rank who had been NCOs and awarded the DFM. Numerous flight commanders and section leaders – men of considerable experience – were also missing. From Oakington, for example, 7 Squadron lost 12 crews in five raids. On the night of 23/24 September, two crews from Bourn failed to return and in doing so 97 Squadron lost both its navigation officer[12] and gunnery leader.[13]

One of the saddest losses was that of Syd Cook, shot down on the night of 4/5 October. It was the eve of his 22nd birthday; he was one of the youngest officers of squadron leader rank to be killed in Bomber Command and PFF during the war. Cook had volunteered for PFF with his crew having completed 20 operations with 103 Squadron at Elsham Wolds. He was another who fancied a shot at doing 45 operations in one go; as it was, he was on his 54th operation when his luck finally ran out.[14]

Just prior to the launch of the main battle, Bomber Command, along with PFF, notched up one of its most successful raids of the war. A mixed force of 569 Lancasters and Halifaxes set out to attack Kassel on the night of 22/23 October and recorded an outstanding result. While the initial 'blind' H2S marking overshot the target, eight out of the nine 'visual' Pathfinder markers correctly identified the centre of the city and the aiming point, and Main Force bombing was exceptionally accurate and concentrated, with some 90 per cent of the bombload falling on the target.[15] Huge numbers of industrial buildings were destroyed, and all three Henschel aircraft factories – which were making the famous 'Doodlebug' V1 flying bomb – were seriously hit. The fires that were started were almost on par with Hamburg, the fire service having to deal with no less than 3,600 separate outbreaks.

The success, however, came at a cost. Forty-three aircraft – 7.6 per cent of the attacking force – were lost; all, apart from one 35 Squadron aircraft, were from Main Force. A second PFF aircraft from 7 Squadron was lost on a diversionary raid to Frankfurt. A large number of the losses on the trip to Kassel were the result of bombers being intercepted on the way in and out of enemy territory, as well as by freelance single-engined aircraft over the city itself. For while the RAF had been busy, so too had the Luftwaffe in overhauling its night fighter, flak and searchlight defences. While Window had caused a significant tactical victory, it almost amounted to a strategic defeat.

In the early days of the war, aircraft and crews of Bomber Command were left to their own devices to find the targets. Arriving, as they did, in small numbers and at different times made them susceptible to fighters, and as early as 1940 the Germans created a defensive 'barrier' in front of the Ruhr through which the bombers were obliged to pass. Over time, the bombers learned to avoid the areas where the German defences were at their strongest, prompting the Germans to extend and deepen the line – known to the RAF (though not the Germans) as the Kammhuber Line after the general who invented it – further, and moving more radar-controlled fighters to patrol the areas they had created.

By 1942, the Kammhuber Line extended across the coastal areas of Holland and north-west Germany and had begun extending south-west towards Paris. It soon reached to the tip of Denmark, obliging the RAF to route their bombers hundreds of miles to the north and over the North Sea in order to drop round behind the defensive line to attack Berlin. Bomber Command's rate of loss on night operations rose from 2.5 per cent of sorties in 1941 to 4 per cent in 1942.

The effectiveness of German radar in finding the RAF bombers and in guiding individual night fighters onto their targets led to the development and use of Window, and for a brief period, Kammhuber's night fighter defence system, which had built up over the previous three years, collapsed completely. It also led to the concept of the bomber 'stream', swamping the German defences with sheer weight of numbers and passing through particular areas when the Germans were temporarily blinded to their presence.

The Germans soon recovered; individual control of night fighters was abandoned and a scheme of fighting over target areas was developed using both single-engined and twin-engined aircraft in large numbers. They were supported by a general 'running commentary' from the ground, which helped them find the stream. Thus, a bomber's strength suddenly became its weakness, since once in the stream, the night fighters could quickly move from one target to the next. The Germans also introduced radio and visual beacons to concentrate their forces in a particular area until the target was determined, at which point the fighters were despatched with all speed to intercept, working closely with the searchlight batteries on the ground.

Further measures and countermeasures were introduced as the Luftwaffe and the RAF fought a battle on the ground as well as in the air, for supremacy of the skies. The British developed 'Monica' to help them detect a possible night fighter attack; the Germans created 'Flensburg', to home in on its transmissions, and 'Naxos' as a countermeasure to H2S. The increased use of H2S, and other technical vulnerabilities, enabled the Germans to detect a raid early; steadily, the German night fighters began to build their scores.

The first six months of 1944 proved so successful that Luftwaffe officers believed, with real conviction, that the night-time air battle had been won and that Bomber Command would be forced to abandon its large-scale night attacks. The success was due, in part, to the steady expansion of the twin-engined night fighter force: in July 1943, it had 550 aircraft on its strength; by July 1944, this number had risen to 775. The quality of the aircraft was also improving as older Bf 110s and Dornier Do 217s were being replaced by the latest mark of Junkers Ju 88s with enhanced performance. Heavier armament had also been installed including 30mm canon and 20mm upward firing canon (the so-called 'Schräge Musik'), and the Luftwaffe's early warning system had dramatically improved, enabling German fighters to be 'fed' into the stream both on the way in and on the way out of the target, causing maximum disruption.

The Luftwaffe also focused on re-organising its ground defences. At the beginning of 1943, the whole of the flak defences in Germany were strengthened and reconstituted, in part due to the RAF's approach to saturation bombing that had rendered single batteries virtually useless when confronted by a concerted attack. Until then, the main tactic had been to concentrate searchlights and guns (typically 30 searchlights and perhaps twice as many guns) in dedicated sectors (usually around Germany's industrial towns). When a hostile aircraft flew into that sector, every searchlight would turn upon it, and once captured in their beams, every gun would then concentrate its fire on a single target. This was all very well for a time, but it actually meant the guns could engage fewer targets, and the number of victims of flak began to decline. The higher the concentration of RAF bombers, the fewer the aircraft lost.

The concept of 'sector' defence was abandoned in favour of creating 'Grossbattieren' – large batteries comprising up to three single batteries at all the large and important targets. In practical terms, it meant that areas such as the Ruhr, which had around 200 heavy batteries (mainly 8.8cm guns) in 1942, had almost twice that number in 1943. This was achieved by bringing in all of the mobile reserves, including railway flak guns, and increasing the number of guns in a single battery from six to eight. Not only did the number of guns increase but also their calibre. The trusty 8.8cm guns were complemented by the addition of 10.5cm guns. The former were capable of firing a 20lb shell up to 25,000ft, and a trained crew could fire a dozen such shells every minute; the latter could lob an even heavier shell of around 32lb at a rate of ten rounds per minute up to 30,000ft. Now, no aircraft flying at any height was immune to attack, and with the advent of the first of the mighty 12.8cm guns, the Germans were once again in danger of gaining the upper hand.

The build-up of flak defences ran steadily from August 1943 to the early summer of 1944, and by recruiting more women and students into the ranks of the Luftwaffe flak divisions, the number of guns per battery continued to increase. By the end of the first half of 1944, a typical battery now comprised up to a dozen guns, complemented by up to 16 searchlights. Heavy and light artillery were moved from the east and redeployed for Reich home defence while, at the same time, the production of new weapons was increased, such that the Germans were able to create a staggering 30 to 40 new heavy batteries – about ten light batteries and 12 searchlight batteries per month.

Perhaps not surprisingly, Bomber Command and PFF losses began to cause concern. The main battle against Berlin was not a week old before the Stirlings of 3 Group were withdrawn from operations; in the period from August to the third week of November, more than 100 Stirlings had been lost on raids over Germany, and since their bombload was not as good as a Lancaster's or Halifax's, their services were quickly withdrawn. A similar fate befell the Halifax. In an 11-week period from the beginning of December to mid-February, almost 10 per cent of Halifax IIs and Halifax Vs on sorties to Germany were lost and on one raid in the second half of February, the same aircraft type lost 16 per cent of its number. While the Halifax IIs continued to operate with 35 Squadron PFF, Harris effectively lost approximately one-third of his frontline strength of heavy bombers and at least one-fifth of his bomb carrying capacity.[16]

Of the 18 blind marking attempts led by PFF during the main phase of the Battle of Berlin, four might be considered a success. However, in eight cases, marking was so scattered that some of the Main Force bombs never even hit the city; in the other six raids, marking was confined to the limits of the city but failed to achieve the level of concentration desired.[17]

The most successful attack of all occurred near the beginning of the battle on the night of 22/23, a raid described as the most effective raid on Berlin of the war.[18] At least 3,000 homes and 23 industrial premises were destroyed, and 175,000 Berliners bombed out. More than 50,000 troops were brought in from the surrounding districts to help with the damage caused – the equivalent of nearly three army divisions taken from their principal duties. A few nights later, on 26/27 November, the raid inflicted damage on the

Berlin Zoo, which led to several dangerous animals escaping that had to be hunted through the streets and shot.[19]

The *Official History* and post-war historians have universally condemned the Battle of Berlin as an abject failure. The attacks on the German capital had not cost Germany the war, as the C-in-C had so famously promised, and in the operational sense, the battle was more than a failure; it was a defeat.[20] The conditions of unbroken cloud, which so often prevailed over Berlin and many other targets between November 1943 and March 1944, coupled with the exceptionally heavy gun and searchlight defences over the city, made it almost consistently impossible for Bomber Command to concentrate its attacks on the correct aiming point, nor were the Pathfinders wholly convinced that their marking was entirely accurate to begin with. Oboe was not available to them, which meant relying on H2S when approaching a target that had few, if any, prominent features for the navigators to discern with any confidence. And while there were a number of first-class set operators within the Pathfinder ranks, there were not enough of them, and even if they were available, the sets could not always be relied upon, to Bennett's constant frustration. He'd mounted what was effectively a 'smash and grab' raid from under the noses of the navy, to get the first of the new generation of H2S sets installed in his aircraft in time for the battle, and to see them fail in operation must have been galling.

Bennett had been concerned from the outset that his crews were being asked to do a difficult job when experience was in short supply. It was a point he made both at the time and in an official report that followed a year after the battle had begun. In it he dared suggest the reason for the 'failure', if that was the correct term, was that Main Force crews had 'baulked at the jump' and that fierce opposition, a high casualty rate and difficulties over hitting the target had led to 'a state of mind amongst crews which automatically reduced the chances of success to negligible proportions'. There was no doubt in Bennett's mind that a very large number of crews 'failed to carry out their attacks during the Battle of Berlin in their customary determined manner', and while great damage had undoubtedly been done in Berlin, 'the effect of each individual raid decreased as time went on'.[21]

Throughout that winter of 1943/44, PFF strength continued to be depleted. The negligible amount of bombing on the markers to which Bennett refers, however, cannot be solely attributed to low morale or indeed any single cause, but rather a perfect storm of unfortunate circumstances. As Harold Trilsbach, a squadron leader with 405 Squadron said: 'The Battle of Berlin was the worst part of my operational flying. The worst weather, the most flak, most searchlights, and by far the greatest fighter opposition.'[22] Laurence Deane, who went to Berlin on six occasions, agreed: 'The enemy's resentment of intruders did not make them enjoyable excursions.'[23]

Some crews undoubtedly lost heart – in Main Force and PFF alike – and some crews did indeed jettison their bombs early. It was drilled into crews from an early stage that height would be their salvation, but with the huge bomb and fuel loads the aircraft were carrying, height was a precious commodity that few could attain. Even the Lancasters, wallowing in their excess weight, became easy prey to the night fighters, prompting some, like John Searby, to advocate removing the gun turrets to give the aircraft a better fighting chance.[24]

But as much as there was despondency within certain ranks and stations at particular times, there were always volunteers ready to take the place of crews who were lost and, as such, morale held up remarkably well despite a loss rate that amounted, in the whole of the battle, to more than the daily average strength of the command during the period.[25] As one Pathfinder from 97 Squadron later commented, 'Of course the Big City scared us all but there was tremendous satisfaction in doing a trip there.'[26] Elmer Trotter agreed: 'My crew never discussed the heavy losses sustained by Bomber Command in general or Pathfinder Force in particular, nor did we ever discuss the odds of our completing a double tour of 45 operations, which was less than 4 per cent. It was not a case of trying to ignore a fact of life, but rather if we concentrated on doing the best job possible, we could be part of the 4 per cent.'[27]

Bennett described the battle as 'the bitterest part of the war' in which he lost a large proportion of very experienced and good Pathfinder crews.

Al Trotter (third from left) never discussed the odds of completing a tour of 45 ops. (Leslie Zwingli)

He even went as far as saying that at one point he believed the backbone of PFF had been broken. Of all the squadrons that suffered the highest casualties during the battle, two were from Pathfinders.

Different authors at different times have produced figures to show just how serious the losses had become. One quotes a horrifying six-week period in which 87 Pathfinder crews became casualties and states that PFF had to recruit and retrain to marking standards nearly 50 crews each month during the battle. There was never a shortage of crews, but the average level of experience within those crews continued to fall.[28] Indeed, this is the critical fact: whereas the quantity of aircrew lost provides the shock factor, it was the quality of crews lost that was particularly devastating. The heavy bomber squadrons of PFF lost something in the order of 1,200 aircrew during the battle, and more than a third of that number were lost in a single month. Among the missing were one group captain, eight wing commanders and more than 20 squadron leaders – the very backbone to which Bennett refers.

At Oakington, 7 Squadron suffered terribly. Scarcely a night went by when there wasn't at least one set of empty seats at the post-op meal. In a three-week period between the end of January and middle of February, they lost Ralph Young and James Tatnall, both wing commanders, and Squadron Leaders Richard Campling and John Hegman. At 40 years of age, Hegman, a New Zealander, need not have been flying at all. Tatnall was also pushing 40 and being groomed as the future CO, wishing to round off his career with an operational command. Such was the prestige of PFF that Tatnall was determined to 'get some in' before the war passed him by. He was one of the old school, who felt a duty to fight but could so easily have sat it out.[29] The group captain killed in action, Kenneth Rampling, was also from 7 Squadron. His aircraft failed to return from the penultimate attack during the battle on the night of 22/23 March. While his aircraft was seen to clear the target, it soon after caught fire and exploded. Two further squadron commanders from Oakington – Guy Lockhart and Fraser Barron – were lost in consecutive months.

Among the wing commanders killed was Bennett's good friend and former Air Staff officer Ray Hilton, who had only been a handful of days into his command of 83 Squadron when he went missing on the night of 23 November. Ray Hilton's successor at 83 Squadron, Jack Abercromby, also lasted only a few days before he went missing, and Laurence Deane arrived to steady the ship. Bennett also lost another good friend – and another Hilton – Frederick Hilton – three nights later, though happily Frederick survived.

One of the biggest losses occurred at the opening of the battle when John White, a wing commander with 156 Squadron failed to return. John was on his 43rd trip with the squadron and had been a flight commander since May 1943. He had previously played a key role in the success of the Peenemünde raid. Every member of his crew was decorated with either the DFC or DFM, and between them they could claim close to 300 operations.

Many lessons were learned during the battle, some of them painfully so. When Pathfinders were able to produce accurate and concentrated marking, Berlin suffered accordingly. It was no one's fault that the battle was not a success; the task of destroying Berlin was simply beyond Bomber Command's capabilities at that time. Indeed, the task of defeating Germany by bombing alone was similarly beyond Harris' reach, for to call it the Battle of Berlin is something of a misnomer. Throughout the battle, Pathfinders actually led Main Force attacks on a dozen other major German cities, including the disastrous raid on Leipzig when 44 Lancasters and 34 Halifaxes failed to return (and which led to the withdrawal of the Halifax II and V from Bomber Command's strength). The 9.5 per cent loss rate over Leipzig might have gone down in history as Bomber Command's worst night of the war had it not been for the events over Nuremberg on the last night in March, in which 11.9 per cent of the force despatched was lost. The disaster, for there is no other word for it, led to serious recriminations among the senior men and near mutiny on some stations, which Bennett blamed firmly on the other group commanders' unwillingness to amend a route that he believed would leave the bombers dangerously exposed.

The value PFF demonstrated throughout the battle should not be measured in its marking alone. If there was one silver lining among the gloom that inevitably befell PFF HQ, it was the performance of the Mosquito and the increased use of the LNSF. Deep penetration raids into Germany led to more sophisticated planning on timing and routes, and diversions and spoofs became mainstream. Bennett also fast recognised that as well as spoofs, when sufficient numbers of Mosquitoes were available, they could inflict serious damage as a bombing force in their own right.

As the *Official History* records, 'There can be no doubt that in addition to enjoying a negligible casualty rate themselves, the Mosquitoes made an important contribution towards reducing the much more severe losses inflicted on the heavy bombers.' The threat of the Mosquito, it continues, was not an empty one, since by now it was capable of carrying a 4,000lb bomb to Berlin. But while the value of the Mosquito as a bomber was out of all proportion to its numbers, it was strictly limited by the fact there were so few. And before the end of the battle, their numbers became fewer still, thanks to one of the more shameful episodes in Bomber Command and PFF relations.

The inability for PFF to consistently mark blind and from height led to their detractors, and the AOC 5 Group in particular, to suggest that alternative methods should be tried. Ralph Cochrane, flushed by the success and publicity of the Dams raids in May 1943, and something of a blue-eyed boy in Harris' eyes, was a strong advocate of low-level marking; Bennett was not. Whereas Bennett conceded that, on some occasions and in perfect conditions, low-level marking was an option, map reading over a densely built-up area such as Berlin – or indeed any major city – was impractical and unnecessarily dangerous. After all, he had tried it! An exchange of telephone calls between Harris and Bennett led to an outcome that soured the relationship between the two men and confirmed Bennett and his opposite number in 5 Group as unfriendly rivals for the rest of the war. Three of Bennett's precious squadrons – 83, 97 and 627 – were returned to 5 Group. Its significance was threefold: it meant Cochrane now had the 'independent' air force that he especially craved and was free to experiment with his own '5 Group' method of Pathfinding; Harris had returned 5 Group squadrons back to where he had always felt they belonged; and Bennett was robbed of crews that he had nurtured and trained, just at the point when their services were most in demand. While several new squadrons would be created in the spring of 1944, to bring his force back up to strength, and an entirely new group – 100 Group – would be formed to support future attacks with special countermeasures and spoofs to relieve 8 Group of some of its duties, it seemed for a moment that the whole future of PFF as a dedicated group was under threat.

And a second front was just around the corner.

The 'Wooden Wonder' would prove to be one of PFF's most effective weapons. (RAF Wyton Pathfinder Collection)

Although not a Pathfinder aircraft, this study of a Mosquito shows how many Mossies returned from operations with one engine feathered. (RAF Wyton Pathfinder Collection)

An incredible air-to-air study of a 405 Squadron Halifax in flight. (RAF Wyton Pathfinder Collection)

A Lancaster 'office'. (Sean Feast Collection)

The starboard outer of a 35 Squadron Halifax is given an inspection by the ever faithful groundcrew. (RAF Wyton Pathfinder Collection)

'Shep' Shepherd (right), the 8 Group intelligence officer who saw the funny side to everything. (RAF Wyton Pathfinder Collection)

Above: Len Judd (second from left) and crew, including his skipper Brian McMillan (third from left) who, despite his senior rank, insisted his men called him 'Mac'. (via Len Judd in Sean Feast Collection)

Left: Ted Swales (top), who stayed with his aircraft long enough to save his crew but lost his own life in the process. (582 Squadron Archive)

Above: Groundcrews took great pride in their aircraft and their aircrew. (The Pathfinder Archive)

Right: Ted Stocker, the only RAF flight engineer to win the DSO and a veteran of 108 operations, all in four-engined heavies. (via Ted Stocker in Sean Feast Collection)

Mosquitoes known as 'pregnant ducks' were modified to carry a 4,000lb cookie to Berlin and back. (The Pathfinder Archive)

A 7 Squadron Short Stirling, the first of the four-engined heavies, being bombed up. (The Pathfinder Archive)

Reg Cann (third from right), whose skipper, Bob Cairns (second from left), gave him little choice in joining PFF. (via Reg Cann in Sean Feast Collection)

Bob Palmer (right), seen here at Elementary Flying Training School, was shot down on his 110th operation on a raid that earned him a posthumous VC. (582 Squadron Archive)

Boris Bressloff (second from left) was a hairdresser before the war. As navigator to Alex Thorne, a former band leader, they went on to become a master bomber crew. (via Boris Bressloff in Sean Feast Collection)

The royal family were regular and welcome visitors to Pathfinder squadrons. (The Pathfinder Archive)

Cologne, seen from 18,000ft, was a popular target and the scene of a thousand-bomber raid. (via Mike King)

A 405 Squadron Lancaster showing signs of severe battle damage. (The Pathfinder Archive)

It was after a very accurate attack on Essen that the Germans believed the RAF must be using a new blind bombing device. (via Mike King)

Groundcrews give the port airscrew one last look before declaring the Mosquito ready for operations. (The Pathfinder Archive)

Left: A rare wartime photograph of Don Bennett with General (later Field Marshal) Wavell. (The Pathfinder Archive)

Below: Gerry O'Donovan (right) became virtually oblivious to the dangers around him. (via Sean O'Donovan)

Gwynne Price (left) took special pride in dropping food to the starving Dutch. (via Gwynne Price in Sean Feast Collection)

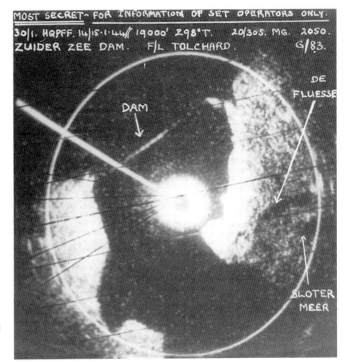

The Zuiderzee dam, as seen on an H2S screen. H2S was especially good at distinguishing between land and water. (The Pathfinder Archive)

Jack Watson almost shot down an Allied aircraft by mistake on D-Day. (Jack Watson)

Left: John Searby (centre), the first master bomber in a Main Force attack, in conversation with the 'Father of the RAF', 'Boom' Trenchard. (RAF Wyton Pathfinder Collection)

Below: At the going down of the sun... (RAF Wyton Pathfinder Collection)

Specialist air bomber Norman Westby had to demonstrate consistent bombing accuracy to within 100 yards of the target. (Ted Manners in Sean Feast Collection)

Above left: Joe Patient (second from right) considered his time in the Met Flight to be the most dangerous of the war. (RAF Wyton Pathfinder Collection)

Above right: Frank Leatherdale, an instructor at PFNTU, said that even experienced bomber crews had to undergo PFF training before being let loose on ops. (via Frank Leatherdale in Sean Feast Collection)

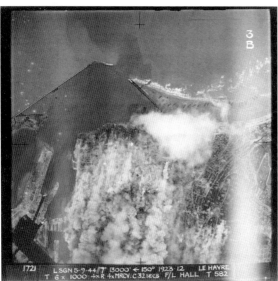

Above: John Smith (left) at a post-war event at the Dorchester. John survived a particularly hairy trip to Castrop-Rauxel. (via John Smith in Sean Feast Collection)

Left: Le Havre from 13,000ft. Circumvented by the advancing Allied armies, it was left to Bomber Command and PFF to soften the defences. (582 Squadron Archive)

An unnamed Main Force crew showing the relief of returning safely from a raid on Berlin in the summer of 1943. (Sean Feast Collection)

Above left: Stafford Coulson, a pre-war regular, led by example. (Jocelyn Finnegan)

Above right: Stafford Harris avoided a court martial as he was much in demand as a master bomber. (via Stafford Harris in Sean Feast Collection)

Stirlings operated with a pilot and second pilot until the arrival of a flight engineer. (The Pathfinder Archive)

Castrop-Rauxel – Pathfinders had no love for targets involving oil. (582 Squadron Archive)

Queen Elizabeth visits the Pathfinders of 156 Squadron, Warboys, to help keep up morale.

Chapter 9

D-Day, Daylights and Doodlebugs

I t was the afternoon of 5 June 1944, another typical day in the life of a Pathfinder station. Bob Lasham, an experienced pilot with 97 Squadron at Coningsby, remembered the briefing well. The squadron commander, Edward 'Jimmie' Carter, told them they would be taking out a battery of heavy guns on the French coast at a point called Saint-Pierre-du-Mont (Pointe-du-Hoc). Bob had never heard of it. In more peaceful days, the region had been famed for its Calvados brandy. Now, it was part of a defensive line overlooking Omaha Beach – one of the chosen Normandy beaches on which the Americans intended to land more than 30,000 of their troops on D-Day, and in doing so open the second front.

There was nothing particularly unusual about bombing a coastal battery. They'd been at it for several days, and everyone knew that the invasion must be close. Bomber Command was now under the direct control of the Supreme Headquarters Allied Expeditionary Force (SHAEF) and officially deployed in focusing its efforts on targets that would support the invasion. That meant attacking railways, marshalling yards, military barracks, ammunition dumps and explosives and ordinance factories throughout France and Belgium. It had also been carrying out a massive deception, continuing to bomb targets in the Pas-de-Calais to maintain the spoof that the invasion would be to the north, across the shortest part of the Channel, and not further west in Normandy. It meant for every bomb dropped on a 'real' target, a similar number – and often more – had to be dropped on the spoof.[1]

While the strategy was sound, PFF was being stretched. Instead of one major raid on a German city involving 800 or more RAF bombers, those 800 aircraft were now split up into 'penny packets' across anything up to half a dozen targets, with each packet nearly always requiring PFF support. The night of 19/20 May was typical: 143 aircraft were despatched to attack railway yards in Boulogne; 122 went to Orléans, 121 to Amiens, 117 to Tours and 116 to Le Mans. Sixty-four were to attack a coastal gun position at Le Clipon, with 63 sent to Merville and 44 to Mont de Couple. In each case, aircraft from PFF were involved, with the exception of Tours, which was an all-5 Group attack. Just a few days before, 156 Squadron had been bemoaning that it didn't have enough to do; now its skills were needed in spades.[2]

A particular feature of these attacks was the use of a master bomber – a technique that had been tried previously at Peenemünde and over Berlin but had been parked as an idea after it was recognised the use of a master bomber in an area bombing attack contributed little value. When it came to precision targets, however, the technique came into his own. The only problem was that to become the Pathfinder's most important asset required exceptional talent, and there was not enough of it to go around. It was not helped when master bombers went missing in action with alarming regularity; on the attack on Le Mans, not only was the master bomber, Fraser Barron,[3] a casualty, but so too was his deputy, John Dennis.[4] The two aircraft are believed to have collided. This was only a few weeks after PFF had lost Pluto Cousens of 635 Squadron, who was master bomber for an attack on Laon, on 22/23 April. Crews reported hearing his voice over the target, but then silence.

There was also the problem that 8 Group was now 'light' of three squadrons, and yet the 5 Group commander could still call upon marking support from PFF and Oboe Mosquitoes when he needed it – a case of having his cake, eating it and going back for another slice. While further heavy bomber squadrons had been added to PFF ranks in the spring of 1944, including 635 at Downham Market and 582 at Little Staughton, in the short term the additional squadrons only made up for the ones he'd lost, and even then, the men needed further training – and therefore time – to reach the standard required.

At 97 Squadron, they were growing accustomed to the short hops over to France as a refreshing change from the deep penetration and considerably more dangerous raids into Germany. As Carter briefed his crews about the target at Saint-Pierre-du-Mont, he seemed to be particularly animated, and his excitement was catching. Certain convoys were to be avoided and great emphasis placed on staying on the allotted track and at a certain height, which could mean only one thing: the invasion was 'on'. 'Thank God I'm still on ops and not at an OTU'[5] the CO said, dismissive at how easy the trip was going to be. They would be playing their small part in one of the greatest events in history.[6]

The wing commander should not have been so dismissive, and the attack proved anything but easy. Red target indicators were accurately dropped by three Oboe Mosquitoes from 8 Group and quickly backed up by greens, dropped – without quite the same accuracy – visually by 627 Squadron from 5 Group. While the Main Force bombing was concentrated, and defences over the target described as negligible, German fighters were soon on the scene and accounted for the loss of two 97 Squadron aircraft, including that of the deputy controller, 'Jimmie' Carter. He was last heard issuing instructions at 0504hrs, and then nothing. Within his crew was the gunnery leader, Martin Bryan-Smith, and the signals leader, Albert Chambers. They had both earned the DFC twice and all but one of the crew were decorated. The second aircraft lost was flown by Finn Jespersen, a Norwegian who had escaped to Britain after his country was invaded in 1940. He and four of his fellow countrymen were killed.[7]

Sixteen of the 18 aircraft from 97 Squadron that set out returned unharmed. As they flew back over the Channel, some had a chance to glimpse the greatest armada ever assembled. Arthur Tindall, on his 32nd operation, remembered the gunners getting particularly excited at what they could see below them, but it was only when they got back and were debriefed that the full scale of the operation became apparent.[8] Ron Smith, rear gunner in a 156 Squadron Lancaster, longed to catch sight of the vessels below but, in his part of the sky, the cloud frustratingly hid them from view.[9] Jack Watson, a flight engineer in another 156 Squadron aircraft, was manning the front turret of his Lancaster on his way back from attacking the battery at Longues-sur-Mer, and nearly opened fire on a twin-engined Airspeed Oxford that came a little too close. It was only on landing he realised that D-Day was underway, and he had nearly shot down what he assumed must have been a hospital plane.[10]

The Pathfinders' contribution to the D-Day landings involved the marking of no fewer than ten coast batteries. Bennett was asked at a conference prior to the invasion whether he could guarantee that no guns would be left firing as the troops hit the beaches. He would give no such guarantee and was annoyed to have been asked, the question suggesting that the senior commanders still had no real understanding of what was and wasn't possible.[11] Weather was still the Pathfinders' principal concern. As it was, however, the PFF and its Main Force charges performed admirably. As well as the guns at Saint-Pierre-du-Mont and Longues-sur-Mer, their targets included Crisbecq, Saint-Martin-de-Varreville, Merville-Franceville-Plage, La Pernelle, Maisy, Houlgate, Mont Fleury and Ouistreham. Thirty-one Mosquitoes from the LNSF also attacked Osnabrück. In addition to the 5 Group losses, 8 Group PFF lost just the one aircraft from the force sent to mark Longues-sur-Mer – a 582 Squadron Lancaster with Arthur Raybould at the controls. He had 78 operations to his credit and the DSO and DFM to show for his leadership and bravery.

The targets they attacked were, at least initially, scarcely defended at all, and being of short penetration, the raids were less vulnerable to night fighters.[12] The losses were particularly light in the context of the success they achieved. In a signal received from Harris via Bennett the following morning, PFF was credited with a famous victory: 'You did famously last night in the face of no mean difficulties. Fire from coastal batteries which were your targets has been reported as virtually negligible,' the signal read, 'and all four radar targets were put right out.' Harris warned that more would be expected of them: 'The next few days will necessarily be the critical period of this operation. Calls upon you may be heavy, and the weather may not be easy. I know that you will do your damnedest to meet all assignments with that efficiency and determination which has characterised the whole of your share of *Overlord* to date.'[13]

Calls upon their services were indeed heavy in the coming days and weeks, and the pressure told, not just on the aircrews but also the groundcrews. The level of aircraft serviceability throughout the period was exemplary. Harris attributed the success of the D-Day attacks in no small part to the work of the countless fitters, riggers, electricians, carpenters and armourers who kept the aircraft and their equipment on the top line. Bennett himself was more than aware of the contribution being made by his senior non-commissioned officers (SNCOs) and other ranks in toiling day and night through 'snag' lists, engine checks and major overhauls to keep his aircraft in the air, as well as the miracle repairs to battle damage inflicted by flak or fighters. A 105 Squadron Mosquito, for example, returned to base from an Oboe marking sortie with several large lumps of metal embedded in the main spar, a job far too big for the squadron carpenter. Since it had flown home and made it back in one piece, it was decided it could continue its journey to Hatfield, where the aircraft had been built, for repairs. The SNCO in charge, 'Butch' Foard remarked what a wonderful aircraft it was, to land, fly and take off with the main spar effectively cut half through.[14] Aircrew were also prepared to lend a hand if needed. When it was known that a highly polished airscrew could add another four or five knots to a Mosquito's airspeed, they were all too eager to be out there, polishing cloths in hand.

In the days immediately following the opening of the second front, Pathfinders continued to lead attacks on key rail and road junctions to disrupt the flow of enemy reinforcements to the battle area, as well as airfields in case the Germans opted to bring further troops in by air. In an experiment on 14 June, PFF led a force of more than 200 bombers on an attack on Le Havre, where motor torpedo boats (E-boats) and other light naval forces were a threat to Allied shipping in the Channel. It was a stunning success: at Le Havre, nearly every ship in the dock, more than 60 all told, were sunk or damaged – a convincing demonstration of the effectiveness of air power.[15] A convincing demonstration also, it should be said, of the effectiveness of Pathfinder Force.

The attack was unusual for several reasons: firstly, it was conducted in daylight, the first daylight raid in over a year; and secondly, it included a fighter escort, their presence no doubt contributing to the low loss rate. The novelty of entering enemy territory in broad daylight, escorted by hoards of friendly fighters, was indicative of the air supremacy achieved.[16] Only one Lancaster failed to return.

The attack on Le Havre – and a similar raid on Boulogne the next day – highlighted a number of practical and moral challenges for the men of Bomber Command. At a practical level, the switch to daylight operations necessitated the replacement of nose turrets in some aircraft where they had been eventually removed to save weight and improve performance, something John Searby had advocated during the Battle of Berlin. Now the guns were needed to fend off the day fighters. It also meant continuously swapping from night to daylight ammunition, imposing further heavy strain on the armament staff who, in many cases, were now working 18-hour days.[17] At an ethical level, attacks on French targets inevitably put French civilians in the firing line, testing the Entente Cordiale to the limit. While the bomber boys did all they could to signal their arrival in advance, and enable the French to take cover, casualties were unavoidable. More than 200 civilians were killed or injured during the attack on Le Havre, for example. However, on the plus side, the E-boat threat to the invasion beaches was all but eliminated, with hundreds – potentially thousands – of further casualties avoided. It was a judgement call, and one never taken lightly.

Another new menace and test for PFF were the V1 flying bombs, the famous pilotless cruise missiles that were quickly christened Doodlebugs by terrified Londoners. The first was launched in the early hours of 13 June, exploding in Swanscombe, to the west of Gravesend. The second fell six minutes later in Cuckfield, Sussex, and a third in Bethnal Green, killing or injuring at least 15 people.[18]

The Germans had built a series of well-hidden and superbly camouflaged launch sites in Pas-de-Calais, more than 40 in all, and the RAF and its

American counterpart argued as to the best way of taking them out. As well as the ramps (colloquially termed 'ski sites'), from which the V1s were propelled into the sky, were also the storage facilities and an important railhead from which the V1s were delivered. On the night of 16/17 June, four sites were attacked, with promising results – all being successfully marked by Pathfinder Oboe Mosquitoes. PFF Mosquitoes also provided the marking for 19 Lancasters and a further two Mosquitoes from 617 Squadron to attack the flying bomb store at Watten. The 5 Group men managed to get one of their special bombs – a 12,000lb 'Tallboy' – to explode within 50 yards of the concrete store.

The need to attack small targets of this nature stimulated a dramatic development in the technique of precision bombing.[19] One that divided opinion among Pathfinder crews was 'Heavy Oboe'. Until then, Oboe had only been used in Mosquitoes. Now it was decided to install the precision device in a Lancaster, and within the newly dubbed 'Musical' Lancaster crew would be a Mosquito pilot and navigator to help control proceedings alongside the 'regular' skipper and his team. Rather than each aircraft bombing independently on a given marker, they were to drop their bombs in salvo as soon as the leader dropped his. The technique would bring far greater accuracy, especially when the target was obscured by cloud, and allow a much greater tonnage of bombs to be dropped on a single point.

The new technique required additional training. Allan Edwards, a PFF flight engineer, remembered his crew practising flying in formation; it scared the life out of him. Many PFF crews felt the same. Formation flying in daylight was something for the Americans. Most preferred flying at night, where they couldn't see the gun crews rushing to their guns in a race to tear them down, or the looks on the faces of their compatriots in a stricken bomber as they fell to their deaths.[20] Men were exposed to terrifying scenes in daylight from which they were spared at night. Peter Johnson, a very experienced pilot and Pathfinder who later went on to command 97 Squadron, described his first encounter with heavy flak in clear daylight as being a 'muddling and distressing experience'.[21]

Heavy Oboes did not always go according to plan. Flying straight and level in daylight over enemy territory was not without significant risk. On 20 July, 20 aircraft led by a Musical Lancaster set out to attack a site at the Forêt de Croc, with John Weightman[22] and James Foulsham[23] in the lead aircraft controlling the attack. The aircraft were in line astern with slight variations in height to avoid being caught in the slipstream of the aircraft in front. Jeff Chapman, a wireless operator in one of the Lancasters playing follow-my-leader, poked his head out of the cockpit astrodome to see the Musical Lancaster open its bomb doors and start its bombing run. They were no more than 30 seconds from the release point when he heard and felt a huge 'whoomph' as a flak shell burst with deadly accuracy, hitting the leader whose port wing immediately caught fire. Jeff could clearly see the terrified expression of one of the crew. The leading aircraft kept on its track but within moments the wings collapsed, and the blazing aircraft turned onto its back and smashed into the ground. At the very moment that the flak shell exploded, the flight engineer in Jeff's Lancaster, who had his thumb on the bomb release 'tit', inadvertently pressed it, at which point all the aircraft behind them also let their bombs go, believing the signal had been given. Down went the whole load, missing the target by at least a mile.[24] Nobody in Jeff's aircraft spoke until the captain came on the intercom and asked for a course to steer for home.

With the striking power of Bomber Command now fast approaching its zenith, both in quantity and quality,[25] it was perhaps frustrating that such capability should have to be spread so thinly and at such risk, for PFF was still losing some of its best captains and crews. Two further master bombers and a deputy were lost on raids on 23 June (George Ingram of 35 Squadron[26]), 29 June (Sydney Clark of 7 Squadron) and 14 July (George Davies of 156 Squadron[27]). Also lost were such luminaries as Bill Blessing of 105 Squadron,[28] Stephen Watts of 692 Squadron[29] and, perhaps saddest of all, the death of Alec Cranswick.

The flying-bomb targets also presented the occasion for the first of three VCs to be awarded to PFF aircrew. Ian Bazalgette, 'Baz' to his friends in the RAF and 'Will' at home on account of his middle name (Willoughby), had been desperate to get into Pathfinders. He'd flown a tour of operations with 115 Squadron in a ten-month period between September 1942 and August 1943 and had remembered a visit by Hamish Mahaddie lecturing on PFF techniques. Mahaddie was impressed by Bazalgette's operational record and suggested that he might like to volunteer for PFF on completion of his first tour. Baz did just that, only to see his application quietly squashed by higher authority,[30] and faced a long 'rest' languishing in an OTU in Scotland. He wrote a despairing letter to Mahaddie, in which he said he was convinced that he would be of more value at PFF than as a flight commander at a training unit. 'Anyone missing ops this autumn has had it,' he implored, 'and I entreat you to rescue me. The incentive is very strong.'[31] Mahaddie did eventually come to the rescue, but even his influence could not prevent Baz from being posted to fulfil his training duties.

'Baz' Bazalgette had been desperate to get into PFF and not be left languishing at an OTU. (RAF Wyton Pathfinder Collection)

It was not until the spring of 1944 that Baz finally got his wish and joined 635 Squadron. With his good looks, beaming smile and friendly manner, he fast became one of the most popular pilots on the squadron. He inspired confidence in all who flew with him[32] and was also quick to make others feel welcome, especially new boys like Alex Thorne and Boris Bressloff – a future master bomber crew – who were at first in awe of such illustrious company.[33] His skills as a pilot and leader were also recognised, and Baz was soon given responsibility as a deputy and then master bomber. By the beginning of August that same year, he had completed 54 trips. Then came the brief to attack a V1 storage depot at Trossy St Maximin, Baz being detailed as a supporter, much to the delight of the master bomber, David Clark, a Kiwi and one of the squadron's flight commanders. It meant sharing the load over the target.

David remembered the long run into the target in line astern, having flown cross-country in the very loosest of loose gaggles. They made no attempt to fly in formation; it simply made them a bigger target. The Oboe Mosquitoes went in first and accurately put their markers on the aiming point. Then came the first of 64 heavies, all PFF crews.

A supporter aircraft a mile or so in front of Clark flew through the target virtually unscathed, taking the enemy flak defences by surprise, but the Germans soon made up for their slow start and accounted for the loss of deputy master bomber Bob Beveridge. David saw his friend die – flak hit the Lancaster in the tail, forcing the aircraft into a steep dive, which then became inverted. Bob and his crew never stood a chance. Then David was over the target himself, weaving frantically as his Lancaster took hits in the fuselage and starboard elevators before releasing his markers and not waiting for the photograph as he threw the bomber into the tightest turn to avoid the flak.

David was so frightened and relieved to be out of the firing line that he momentarily forgot that he was the master bomber controlling the raid. He was quickly brought back to his senses by his visual air bomber, 'Junior' Linacre, who identified the red markers as being the place to bomb, and David started issuing instructions accordingly. Very quickly the area became a mass of exploding bomb flashes and smoke, and David did not have to hang around the target for long. He was spooked by the amount of flak they encountered, so much so that he weaved all the way back to the coast, even when over friendly territory.

At some point during the attack, Bazalgette's Lancaster was also hit, both starboard engines being put out of action and the starboard wing and part of the fuselage bursting into flames. The air bomber was severely wounded, an arm and part of his shoulder torn away, and the mid-upper gunner was overcome with the smoke and flames that filled the body of the aircraft. The rest of the crew valiantly fought the fire as Baz struggled to regain control of the burning aircraft. He not only managed to get the Lancaster on an even keel but also complete his marking run, determined to fill the place left by the stricken deputy, turning away from the target, with his aircraft pouring fire and thick black smoke. A quick consultation with his flight engineer confirmed there was no hope of making it and they needed to bale out fast. With two injured crew, Baz ordered the others out of the aircraft, by which time the Lancaster was no more than 1,000ft off the ground. He then attempted to land.

Approaching the village of Senantes, he was seen to turn away from a cluster of houses and farms and put down in a nearby field. It was a textbook crash landing. Then the Lancaster exploded. The four men who baled out all survived; the three left in the aircraft, including the gallant skipper, died in the explosion. On the rest of the squadron's return to Downham Market, the mood was grim. Of the 14 Lancasters that set out, two were missing and all but one had been hit by flak, some seriously. Norman Perkins, an 'erk' (aircraftman) in charge of one of the Lancasters, remembered the crew walking around the aircraft after it landed and their shock upon seeing the damage. 'The Lancaster looked like a monster tin opener had attacked it; some Lancasters had holes big enough to put your head through.'[34]

Only when the full story of Baz Bazalgette's heroism became known was he recommended for the VC, gazetted on 17 August 1945, three months after the end of hostilities in the West.

The attacks on the V1 and V2 weapon sites were seen as a 'distraction' by the senior air commanders at the time. Sir Trafford Leigh-Mallory, the C-in-C of the Allied Expeditionary Air Force, for example, described the pilotless aircraft as 'tiresome'.[35] The more attractive targets – beyond the railway marshalling yards and oil production and storage facilities that had now been added to the priority list – were those that supported the army's advance on the ground, as the Germans tried to hurry in reinforcements of tanks and armour.

On 30 June, Bomber Command responded to intelligence that showed two panzer divisions – the 2nd and the 9th – beginning to assemble in the area of Villers-Bocage to strike at the Allies that night. More than 250 bombers were assigned the task of destroying what they could and were devastatingly efficient. Almost 1,200 tons of high explosives were dropped on an area not much bigger than Wembley Stadium, an eye-witness reporting that he had seen one tank blasted into the sky and resting atop a two-storey building.[36] Even though several of the Oboe marking Mosquitoes had to abort through technical failures, the raid was an overwhelming success. In gem-blue skies, the master bomber controlling the raid, Brian McMillan of 582 Squadron, ordered the Main Force down to a height of 4,000ft, so that there could be no mistakes. Not everyone in Main Force was excited at the prospect of flying so low: 'Mac was exhorting the Main Force to reduce height to bomb, but they were reluctant to come down,' remembered Len Judd, Mac's flight engineer.[37] It was understandable. Even PFF crews were not keen on flying so low. George Hall recalled how the Lancaster made a much bigger target for the gunners: 'At 20,000ft you are shot at by the 88mm guns, the same things they had in Tiger Tanks. But at 6,000ft or lower, all of the light flak that was there is aimed at you – 30mm stuff – and you could even see the people who were firing at you.'

Despite the dangers, the Main Force crews ultimately relented. Doug Tidy, a pilot with 105 Squadron who waited around the target area until the dust had cleared, reported that the ground looked like it had been excavated.[38] Another 105 Squadron aircraft, piloted by Ken Wolstenholme,[39] was obliged to abandon its run due to enemy action,[40] but aside from this, only two aircraft failed to return. Harris was to later remark, sardonically, that the village of Villers-Bocage had been thoroughly liberated.[41]

The attack on Villers-Bocage was tactical; what the Pathfinders and Main Force were asked to do next was more strategic, as part of the ground forces' main battle plan. An attack on 7 July as a pre-cursor to Operation *Charnwood* was a triumph for Pathfinder Force. With British and Canadian troops poised to attack Caen, which had become something of a barrier to progress for Allied forces, Bomber Command was asked to take out various strongholds that stood in the army's way. Oboe Mosquitoes, again, did their bidding with expert precision, and the hero of the hour was Pat Daniels, the master bomber from 35 Squadron, who ensured a fine concentration of bombs on the target. Their only frustration, and one expressed by Bennett after the event, was the apparent inability of Montgomery and his men to exploit the opportunity that the air force had given them. It was to become a familiar feeling in the weeks ahead, as Montgomery's reluctance to commit his troops became something of a bone of contention with his contemporaries in the 'third service'. It became worse when the army began complaining that the advance of its tanks was being hindered by the craters and smashed buildings that they now had to navigate their way through!

Another triumph for the Pathfinders was recorded 11 days later on the eve of an armoured offensive given the codename *Goodwood*. This was to be another move on Caen, since only the northern part of the city was currently in Allied hands. Again, various strongholds were identified and, once more, Oboe Mosquitoes marked the targets well. On one of the targets where the Mosquito's precision device failed, the master bomber, Keith Creswell, another 35 Squadron professional, opted for visual means and great havoc was caused. Significant elements of two German divisions were badly affected, prompting one of the senior German commanders to write to Hitler and describe the Allies' total dominance of the skies as having 'an annihilating effect'.[42] His men had been shaken to the core – in direct contrast to the heartening effect it was having on the Allies.

The dangers of bombing so close to the Allied ground forces, however, was not lost on any of the senior commanders. The fear of hitting their own troops was very great.[43] Andrew Maitland said it was always a relief to see his markers dropped in the right place, for even a small error might see bombs falling on advancing troops.[44] Bennett was so concerned that he opted to see for himself, perhaps now safe in the knowledge that should his aircraft be attacked, he was no longer likely to fall into enemy hands. He was pleased to see that his Pathfinders were performing so well. The challenge, much like the rolling barrage of World War One, was to bomb far enough ahead of the advancing army that they weren't in any danger, but not so far ahead that they weren't close enough to seize any advantage that may have been gained.

Between D-Day and the middle of August, Bomber Command dropped 17,560 tons of bombs on German troop concentrations in the battlefield. These were delivered in eight separate attacks. It was estimated that 1,000 bombers could deliver the equivalent in weight to the shells of 4,000 guns, and the bombers could strike with only a few hours' notice. Perhaps it was inevitable that something should go wrong, and when it did, it was to have tragic consequences.

It was, in the words of Cliff Alabaster, who had responsibility for marking the target, a simple daylight raid in support of Canadian troops who were being held up by a German stronghold. As the target was close to the UK in distance, it was decided to use Gee for blind marking, since the weather was foul. It effectively meant sliding down one co-ordinate from roughly north to south until crossing another co-ordinate, at which point the TIs would be released some 6,000 yards in front of the Allied lines.

The co-ordinates had to be set up manually in flight by the navigator, who would then give directions to the pilot to maintain track on one co-ordinate until crossing the 'release' co-ordinate. The co-ordinates were delineated on the cathode ray tube (CRT) by two green lines about four inches long, sub-divided by ticks at decimals. As Cliff recalled: 'My navigator, a Canadian, must have set up the wrong release point for the TIs and bombs fell among his own countrymen.'[45]

Harris was rightly aggrieved, having assured the generals of accurate support, and Cliff was immediately taken off marker duties and threatened with being sent back to a Main Force squadron. Bennett protested but Harris was adamant. However, the AOC 8 Group managed to find a way around it, by sending both pilot and navigator to fly Mosquitoes in PFF but without a marking role. Cliff thus became a flight commander of 128 Squadron at Wyton, and soon after, once the dust had settled, was given command of 608 Squadron at Downham Market, where he and his crews were affectionately nicknamed 'Alabaster and his 40 thieves'.

By the middle of August, the campaign in Normandy was all but finished. Paris was liberated on the 24 August. Some strongholds remained for several weeks in various ports that had been ignored or circumvented for reasons of expedience, and this situation continued for some time until Pathfinders and Bomber Command again played their parts in teasing the enemy from its lair. By that stage, they had perfected a new technique to avoid hitting their own side, by introducing a 'master' master bomber, known as a 'long stop', to prevent bombs from falling beyond a particular point. It was a system that worked well, and no other significant friendly-fire incidents were reported. The ground forces were soon ready for the assault on Germany, by which point command of the bomber force had once again reverted to its previous hierarchy, and Harris was free to pursue his passion for bringing Germany to its knees by bombing its industry, its cities and its people to destruction.

Chapter 10

The Original Multi-Taskers

B y the winter of 1944, the Handley Page Halifax had been retired from service in PFF to make way for the Avro Lancaster. Regular visits by Sir Frederick Handley Page had not been enough to dissuade Bennett from his decision to favour another design from Sir Frederick's industry archrival, Roy Chadwick.

While it is not uncommon to find Pathfinder aircrew who preferred certain marks of the Halifax over its more successful counterpart, there are many more who say they owe their lives to the performance and reliability of the Lancaster. It had few vices, many virtues and was generally loved by the crews who flew it.

Within a PFF Lancaster crew the captain of the aircraft was the pilot, regardless of rank. Good pilots could make poor captains and vice versa. Flying skill was not the principal qualifying criteria, though it helped. What made a good captain was the ability to exert enough authority, while still keeping everyone happy.[1] This was easier than it sounds, given that many captains were barely out of school and could be responsible for men who were half as old again and very occasionally older still. Flight sergeants – non-commissioned men – could also be giving orders to men of more senior rank, and who messed separately. Rank, however, meant very little in the air. One airman recalled a trip where the crew comprised a group captain, two squadron leaders, three flight lieutenants, a flying officer and a pilot officer![2] Len Judd, a sergeant flight engineer, remembered first meeting his new skipper, a squadron leader: 'Squadron leader was an exalted rank, whereas I was a mere sergeant, so when he asked me my name I said: "Sergeant 1864805 Judd, Sir!" "No," he replied, "what is your name?" I said "Len", and he said: "Len, I'm Mac." And that was that. He had no front to him and I was immediately welcomed as part of the crew.'[3]

It was the pilot who was responsible for his crew's discipline in the air and even while on the ground. Reg Cann said nothing ever fazed his skipper, Bob Cairns: 'He was an excellent pilot and skipper. I flew with some crews later who would chatter incessantly. We didn't have any of that. We flew in absolute silence and only spoke when it was necessary to do so.'[4] Several used the words 'calm' and 'authoritative' to describe their pilots. Roy Last, an air gunner, described his skipper, Paddy Finlay, an Irishman from County Wicklow, as a man who 'never panicked'.[5] Gerry Bennington, flight engineer to Ted Swales, a future VC, said the thick-set South African 'inspired confidence'.[6]

It was through the skipper that the rest of the crew took their lead, and who they looked to if their aircraft was in trouble. Norman Ashton described how his fellow flight engineers would speak of their captains with near reverence.[7] Fred Edmondson would have followed his skipper to the end of the world and back again, and there were very few duds.[8] Those that were, were weeded out long before they managed to make it into PFF. Ernie Patterson had two skippers during his time on PFF. The first, Jack Harrild, was posted after 30 ops and never made it beyond being a 'supporter'. Bennett clearly expected more from his captains.[9] No one, however, doubted Jack's bravery. His second, Alex Thorne, was someone more promising. Before the war, Thorne had been a band leader, Lloyds underwriter and, it was rumoured, a racing driver. Ernie flew at least five master bomber trips and two as deputy with his 'new' skipper. Whenever the squadron was asked to provide a master bomber, it always seemed like their names were the first on the list.[10]

Besides the skipper, the most important men in the crew were the navigators. Navigators were, in fact, probably the most important men in PFF, certainly in Bennett's eyes. In a Pathfinder crew there were two: the Nav 1, responsible for the plot, spent every trip tucked away behind a curtain, with a small lamp over his desk, not coming out unless it was to take an astral fix, which was unusual, especially over the target area. He worked in tandem with the Nav 2, who operated the two principal navigational aids – Gee and H2S – constantly feeding information into the plot. The two men would be working continuously, concentrating hard, not daring to let their minds wander for a second, and both aware that, in navigation, you can never know precisely where you are, only precisely where you have been.

In PFF, the navigation team would work to tenths of a minute and would keep three minutes in hand for every hour they were in the air. So if it was still two hours to the target, they would keep six minutes in hand so they could lose/make up time as required. To lose time was simple and would require flying a short dog leg (flying two sides of an equilateral triangle). Making up time was more difficult.[11]

Reg Cann had trained as a navigator on Main Force and took the seat as Nav 1 in PFF. Most Nav 2s, on the other hand, were almost always air bombers who had been retrained to use the sets. Air bombers had experience of navigation from their original training but learning to use new technology – and especially H2S – could be a challenge. Boris Bressloff trained on one of the original sets, which was different from the one he would later use operationally. He recalled that it was difficult at first, but he soon became an accomplished operator. The secret was concentration: 'You had to concentrate, because if your mind wandered or if you became distracted, you lost where you were. It was like a noisy office job, sat behind the curtain in the Nav's position. The only time I knew things were getting a little sticky was if someone left their intercom on and I could hear their breathing.'

Air navigation in those days was all about wind – establish the wind strength and direction and you could navigate. An accurate wind could only be found from an accurate fix. The best fix was, of course, a visual pinpoint or a clear image on the H2S set. Boris would get a fix every three minutes and pass it to the Nav 1 when he asked for it.

Sometimes the sets went u/s, and it was the Nav 2's job to fix it. Sometimes he couldn't and would be left like 'a spare tart at a dance', as Boris recounted:[12]

> The set had a modulator valve that had to be switched on below 6,000ft. One night I forgot, and the set wouldn't work. Of course, it had to be one of our longest trips, to Stettin on the Baltic, and I ended up sitting there, almost as a passenger. What was interesting is that we were routed in over Sweden, and we could see the place beautifully lit up. We were absolutely on track, a great testimony to the skill of the Nav 1.

Syd Johnson, another Nav 2 and a competent set operator, said the chief virtue of H2S was that it couldn't be jammed: 'If neither gremlins nor enemy action reduced its serviceability, you could map read your way across Germany.'[13] He also recalls the final duty of any Nav 2 in the event of being shot down – to set a small explosive device to ensure the secret technology did not fall into enemy hands.

Even the best trained navigators, however, could occasionally get lost. Reg Cann recounted his 33rd operation in which he managed, quite literally, to lose the plot. The H2S set went on the blink early into the flight, and stronger-than-forecast winds were blowing him steadily off track. On the return leg, their aircraft was coned by searchlights, obliging his pilot to take evasive action. Then the guns opened up. Although, in the event, they were only nine miles off track, those nine miles had allowed them to stray over Nuremberg, where they were singled out for special attention by the German defences. They were lucky to make it home.[14]

Ray Wilcock, a veteran of 44 ops, recalled being interviewed after the war and being asked whether he was sure he had always found the right target. His stock answer was that he was 'fairly certain' but one thing he did know for sure was, he always found his way home.[15]

Supporting the two navigators and equipped with a Marconi T1154/ R1155 transmitter/receiver set, was the wireless operator. Although arguably one of the less glamorous 'trades' – and a job that could leave the airman with little to do for large parts of a flight – the role of the wireless operator was nonetheless essential. They not only kept the aircraft in touch with the ground but also sent and received weather reports and estimates of wind speeds, which were passed to the navigation team. Weather, beyond flak and fighters, was the airman's greatest enemy.[16]

They were also there, of course, in case of emergency, to block night fighter communications, if possible, and could be the final 'voice' heard as an aircraft ditched in the icy cold waters of the North Sea. Sometimes they never got the chance to get an SOS message away, a fact borne out by the phrase 'nothing was heard from this aircraft after take-off' that appears written into squadron ORBs with alarming regularity.

Ernie Patterson remembers listening in to HQ (Huntingdon) at ten-past and twenty-to the hour: 'We would be sent the frequencies of German night fighters and tune in to listen to them. We had a microphone attached to the brushes of the generators, so if we found a transmission, we would clamp down the Morse key and in doing so drown out the communication. The fighters would then be obliged to change frequencies and so we could disrupt their attack.'

Certain Pathfinder aircraft within the stream would be tasked with measuring wind speeds and transmitting those speeds back to HQ so that HQ could, in turn, re-transmit that information to the rest of the attacking force. Ernie also recalls the routine for the return home:

When we were 50 miles from home, I would call to get the barometric pressure at base, which the skipper would then feed into his altimeter. The WAAF controllers were always spot on. They were always in control – even when you could hear other aircraft in the circuit, low on fuel or coming in on three engines or with wounded on board, there was never any panic.

Once we received a corrective call on the way back from Merseburg to divert to Ford on the south coast because of fog. It was all very orderly and when we landed, we were met by a van with a large sign on the rear that read 'follow me', which we did to our temporary dispersal. In the morning, we saw a Halifax with six feet missing from its nose. That was the abuse a Halifax could take and still make it home.

Wireless operators might also be trained air gunners, from the days when bomber aircraft had fewer crew members and a wireless operator/ air gunner (WOP/AG) was a single 'trade' fulfilling dual roles. It was only later, when the need for more air gunners became greater, that they split the two disciplines to allow more air gunners to be trained more speedily. Having twin talents meant, in Ernie's case, occasionally leaving his position to relieve one of the regular air gunners in the case of illness, injury or the need for a comfort break, even though no such 'comfort' really existed. A chemical toilet, the Elsan, was provided but rarely used, for most air gunners dared not leave their respective mid-upper or rear turret seats for fear of fighter attack. One captain was known to deliberately throw his aircraft into a tight turn any time his rear gunner was sitting on the can!

Bert Wilson was a WOP/AG with 156 Squadron who remembered on one flight being asked to check on the rear gunner. Outside temperatures could fall to below −20°C, and even though some of the aircrew wore electrically heated suits, they were far from foolproof. In this case, the air gunner's suit had failed, and he was literally freezing to death. The mid-upper therefore took over in the rear, and Bert took his place in the mid-upper.[17]

Wireless operators within master bomber aircraft had further responsibilities, their role being to record every word transmitted by their captain to his fellow Pathfinders and Main Force crews. Ernie Patterson said that after every master bomber trip, his logs were used to plot the precise details of the raid: 'Our call sign as master bomber was "Portland One" – I have never been able to look at a bag of Portland cement without being reminded of those times.'

PFF Lancasters relied on the skill of the pilots and the accuracy of the navigation teams to keep them away from known concentrations of flak and fighters. They also, of course, relied on the air gunners. In a PFF Lancaster, and indeed in all Main Force Lancasters, there were two: the mid-upper gunner occupied a position halfway down the fuselage of the aircraft and had responsibility for heading off beam attacks; the rear gunner, the 'tail-end Charlie', sat at the back of the aircraft on the look-out for night fighters creeping up from behind.

Turret manufacture and armament varied, but typically there were two Browning .303 machine guns in the mid-upper and four in the rear. Their maximum range (approximately 3,000ft) and hitting power were questionable, certainly compared to the more heavily armed night fighters with canon that packed a bigger punch from a longer range and enabled night fighters to 'stand-off' in relative safety knowing they couldn't be hit. On the plus side, the Brownings were reliable, accurate and generally liked by the air gunners who used them. If a fighter got too close, the air gunners certainly stood a chance, but most knew that this chance would only come if the fighter had missed them in the first place.[18]

A good air gunner had to be able to shoot and have a keen eye. He also had to stay alert. If ever they felt drowsy, they could take a 'wakey' pill to keep them awake. An amphetamine sulphate known by its brand name Benzedrine, the substance was a powerful stimulant that could promote both wakefulness and wellbeing and was approved for use in November 1942.[19] Some swore by it; others left well alone. It was wise not to leave them lying around. One air gunner left some tablets in his bathroom while on leave. His father mistook them for aspirin and was awake all night.[20]

While the groups would issue tactical instructions on the safe operation of an aircraft, different air gunners and different crews adopted different practices. For every pilot who would fly a constant weave so as not to be caught unawares, there were those who insisted that straight and level was best, and the only way to ensure accurate navigation. As a pilot, Stafford Harris said his secret to survival was to pass through the target after dropping his bombs and fly on for some distance before making a long looping turn. It took them away from trouble but meant he was nearly always the last to make it home.[21]

At more than 6ft tall and 15-and-a-half stone, Eric Wilkin was much larger than the average air gunner, and only just squeezed into the mid-upper position. He used the metal frame above his head, and over which the Perspex was fitted, to his advantage. 'At night we were taught never to look directly at a target, but rather either above or below it (i.e., within our peripheral vision), so the metal frame was ideal. I don't recall anything ever getting past us that I hadn't seen – either Jerry or one of our own aircraft.'

If he ever saw an enemy fighter, Eric's tactic was to direct his skipper away from danger, rather than staying to fight it out: 'There was no point in trying to take them on with your .303s when they had canon and could lay off and shoot at will. Fighters didn't bother me; you could see them.' Flak, however, was a different matter: 'I hated flak. If you were one degree off, then the flak could predict you.' On one occasion, a flak shell burst so close that a piece of shrapnel knocked the glass out of Eric's turret, went through his Mae West, ricocheted off the armour plating and back out again through his life preserver. All he remembers was a blue flash and the shatter of Perspex. On another occasion, shrapnel came through the side of the turret and into the ammunition cans, setting off half a dozen rounds, which dented the box and thumped into the side of his leg.[22]

Alf Huberman, a spare bod on 83 Squadron, remembered being trained to run and not to engage unless absolutely necessary. He saw quite a few fighters in his time – both from the rear turret and in the handful of trips he spent as a mid-upper – but only once opened up, on the last flight of his first tour. He believed he owed his life to keeping fit with PT and exercise to help him stay alert. 'On a long flight you could not afford to lose your concentration or daydream, not even for a minute. You could never relax. I always used to take my "wakey wakey" tablets just to make doubly sure.'[23]

Standard procedure in a fighter attack was the corkscrew, throwing the heavy bomber into a series of spiralling dives and climbs ascribing the shape that gave the manoeuvre its name. The air gunner would call for a corkscrew either port (left) or starboard (right), depending on where the attack was coming from, and which would give the pilot the best chance of getting away. Mid-upper Percy Cannings said discretion was always the better part of valour: 'He had a much better chance of picking you off than you had of shooting him down.'[24]

The gun turrets left little room for comfort; this was especially true when wearing full flying gear, a sheepskin coat or electrically heated suit. Even for smaller men, a long trip was uncomfortable. The seat for the mid-upper was similar to the seat on a child's swing, while the rear gunners in some Pathfinder crews sat on their parachute packs. Parachutes were provided in two forms: a 'seat' type parachute for the pilot and a two-piece clip-on chute for the rest of the crew. The latter required wearing a harness to which the parachute pack could be retrieved from its stowage point and clipped on in the event of an emergency. The pilot, of course, would not have had time to complete such an exercise, and so his parachute was already attached, and strapped across his bottom. Pathfinders realised that rear gunners were especially vulnerable: in the event of attack, they would have to leave their turret to clip on a chute, while all the time the aircraft may be on fire or out of control, leaving them little chance of making it out alive. By providing rear gunners with seat-chutes, however, all they needed to do in an emergency was to rotate their turret such that the back door was effectively outside of the aircraft and drop out. Bob Pearce, an air gunner with 582 Squadron owes his life to such forward thinking, having performed just such a trick when shot down in December 1944 and living to tell the tale.[25]

Completing a heavy bomber crew was the flight engineer. With the advent of the first four-engined bombers, and a shortage of trained men, it was determined that the Lancaster should fly with just the one rather than the regulation two pilots in the cockpit. Bennett believed the move foolhardy and unfairly blamed Cochrane directly for adding to the dangers of an already dangerous job. At that time, Cochrane was officer in charge of training. The net result of the move was to create a new category of aircrew in Bomber Command to replicate what its colleagues in Coastal Command had been doing for some time.

The flight engineer might typically be an ex-RAF apprentice, already well versed in the art of engines and airframes. He might be a former garage mechanic or have a natural empathy for machinery and moving parts. Tom Williamson, for example, had been an engine fitter in 10 Group, servicing Spitfires for pilots 'with their fancy scarves and their top buttons undone'.[26] In 1942, he was on board USS *Wasp* looking after the 50 or so Spitfires that were flown off to relieve the siege of Malta as part of Operation *Calendar*. Concerned that he might be posted overseas permanently, Tom volunteered for aircrew: 'I was asked if I wanted to be a gunner but in the event they decided that would have been a waste of an engines' man. When I completed my course at St Athan, of the 100 or so of us standing in a line, Chiefy split us in half. The left half went to Halifaxes; the right half to Lancs. I never did work out why.'

Not untypically, the flight engineer was older than many of his contemporaries, and very rarely commissioned. Doug Reed remembered his flight engineer, 'Baz' Butterfield, as having a 12-year-old son: 'Remember I was only 20 myself.' [27] There were younger men too, of course, like Harold Siddons. Siddons was an engineer leader at the age of 22 and later went on

to enjoy modest success as a film actor, often playing RAF types in the likes of *Angles One Five* and *Appointment in London*, the latter purporting to tell the story of a Pathfinder captain played by Dirk Bogarde.[28]

Regardless of age or experience, the role of the flight engineer was essential. He was the extra pair of eyes, ears and hands that the remaining pilot and captain had lost. He closely monitored and

Tom Williamson serviced Spitfires en route to Malta before joining PFF. (Sean Feast Collection)

managed the fuel, petrol supply cocks, boost regulators and engine coolers. He may also have carried out certain temporary repairs to equipment damaged by enemy action, such as a broken oxygen lead. Ted Stocker, an engineer leader, reckoned there was little physically on an aircraft that he could not repair temporarily with a piece of chewing gum.[29]

This 'jack of all trades' would also be trained as an air gunner to replace the 'regular' air gunner in an emergency. In a Pathfinder crew, he might also be expected to drop the bombs, certainly if they were in a 'supporter' role or indeed any operation in which a specialist air bomber was not required or part of the crew. Harold Kirby remembered that Bennett expected all Pathfinder aircrew to be capable of multiple roles, and that meant acting as air bomber if needed: 'We received training on the squadron that included bombing targets on a map projected onto the floor. When it came to the real thing, Jim (our original bomb aimer but now Nav 2) would make all the calculations and set the bombsight up so that all I had to do was press the button. It was all very straightforward.'[30] Gerry Bennington would also regularly alternate with his Nav 2, 'Whisky' Wheaton, in dropping the bombs: 'We shared responsibilities depending on the role. He would set up the bombsight and I would press the release. It was all very simple.'[31]

Sometimes the flight engineers enjoyed spectacular success, not only with their bombing but also with their marking. Ted Stocker flew a master bomber trip to the oil production and storage facility at Wanne-Eickel in October 1944 and was commended for the accuracy with which he marked the target and the ongoing commentary he provided to Main Force. It was his 100th trip and he received an immediate DSO, the only RAF Pathfinder flight engineer to be so recognised. His most notable flight, however, was when he broke the sea wall at Westkapelle, flooding the surrounding area and forcing the Germans who were holding out on the island of Walcheren to retreat. He specifically remembers seeing an anti-aircraft gun opening up on them and returning the compliment by lobbing a few small bombs in their general direction. It was very satisfying, he said, after seeing the Germans 'doing a runner'.[32]

Flight engineers and pilots worked in close harmony. A good PFF flight engineer could anticipate his skipper's next move. Spare bods were, therefore, not much liked. Doug Reed recalled whenever his skipper called 'flaps', his regular flight engineer would take the flaps up 5°. The spare bod didn't know this, and when he heard 'flaps', he took the flaps up completely and they very nearly went straight in. The groundcrews watched on in horror with their fingers in their ears, waiting for the bang.[33]

In an emergency, many flight engineers were also capable of flying the aircraft, or at least keeping it on the straight and level. Their understanding of the flight controls, and the role of the various switches and dials in the Lancaster cockpit, gave them something of a head start, alongside their proximity to the pilot, which enabled them to learn from their captain's actions. Len Judd did several hours in the Link Trainer, a primitive flight simulator, learning the fundamentals of flight: 'On cross-country exercises "Mac" would switch the autopilot off (he never used the autopilot on operations) and let me take the controls. I could just about keep the thing straight and level and sometimes the crew would call in and ask who's flying?!'[34]

Bill Lanning recalled a long-haul to Stettin (now Szczecin) and seeing his pilot's head begin to roll. He volunteered to take over:

It took some convincing, but he agreed. The next thing I know there was a voice from the rear gunner screaming 'get your fucking arse off the deck.' Then my pilot was struggling with me to gain the control and I thought he had gone bonkers. It then dawned on me that we were very, very low and guessed what had happened, pulled it up to a few thousand feet and swapped back. Our oxygen had been snagged by shrapnel close to the pilot's supply and was leaking like mad. The pilot had succumbed first and me next. The rear gunner, being in the open air comparatively, suffered the least and recovered first. We lived again for another chance for me to show him I could drive the thing![35]

Others might also be able to fly the Lancaster too; many of the Nav 1s and Nav 2s had started out training as pilots and been 'washed out' for failing to make the grade. Sometimes they got as far as the flying training schools in the sunshine and safety of the United States before finally being 're-mustered', perhaps for scaring their instructors half to death one too many times. Their experience may not have gone past basic take-offs and landings in single-engined aircraft, but it was better than nothing. Boris Bressloff is a good example. Initially trained as a pilot, his instructor said he never knew the meaning of fear until Boris arrived as a pupil. His meagre experience, however, was put to good use: 'My pilot knew that I was capable of flying the aircraft but not landing it. He told me that if it came to it, I was to land with the wheels up, get as close to the ground as possible and then cut everything.'[36]

To the 'standard' crew of seven in a PFF Lancaster might be added other specialists, depending on their appointed role. A third navigator, for example, was not unheard of, though more common was a specialist air bomber, specifically in those aircraft tasked with primary visual marking. Specialist air bombers received additional training in their art at Warboys, and were constantly tested and examined to ensure their worth. An 8 Group bombing shield awarded to the top-performing squadron was hotly contested.

Norman Westby, a specialist air bomber with 35 Squadron, recalled having to demonstrate a consistent bombing accuracy of within 100 yards of the target. There was a particular training exercise where a large photograph of an area of about five miles square was covered with a similarly large sheet of paper with a small hole cut in the centre. The instructor would move the hole around the photograph, and from what little Norman could see, he was expected to know where he was in relation to the target, and how long it would take to get there.

As soon as he knew the target, Norman would spend three or four hours studying the target photographs with his fellow specialists until he knew it completely, from every direction. It was very intensive work. It had to be. It was the secret of accurate bombing. The bombs of 800 or so Main Force aircraft were relying on the accuracy of Norman's markers, and although highly trained, they were all very young and the responsibility weighed heavy on his shoulders: 'If I couldn't see or identify the aiming point then I would tell the skipper to go around again. Sometimes this happened three or four times until I was certain, by which stage the pilot would be shouting at me. I did not want to be up in front of Bennett, however, for allowing my markers down with such a large error. Sometimes, also, we had to bring our TIs back with us.'

What Bennett achieved with his Pathfinder crews were men who were genuine multi-taskers. On training flights, they were encouraged to swap roles and practise one another's jobs, just in case there was an emergency and they needed to do it for real. Doug Reed recalled a fighter affiliation exercise when he asked to have a go in the mid-upper turret and promptly shot the aerial away. They didn't allow him in the turret again.[37] Doug was lucky not to have had the AOC on board at the time, for Bennett was not averse to going along for the ride and pointing out their mistakes. With only a few exceptions, Pathfinder crews were the best that Bomber Command could offer. As with any elite unit, however, there were always those who were more 'elite' than others – the difference, perhaps, between a top club player versus one who is truly world class. Both are at the top of their respective game and are on the field of play at the same time, but there are always those who impress more, and who are capable of greater things. Some made it through to PFF and never made it beyond the ranks of 'supporter', but these are few and far between. Contemporary logbooks show the variety of tasks a Pathfinder crew may be briefed to undertake: backers-up, illuminators, visual re-centerers, primary visual markers and primary blind markers. A few – a lucky and very talented few – made it to the rank of deputy master bomber. Fewer still achieved the ultimate prize.

Competition was strong. Pilot Artie Ashworth desperately wanted to make it to master bomber, or even deputy, but had to settle for being a primary visual marker. 'It would have been nice,' he said later, 'but the war ran out on us.'[38] Artie was a modest man, but his disappointment is clear. Sharing

Doug Reed shot the aerial off his Lancaster during a fighter affiliation exercise and was never allowed in a turret again. (via Doug Reed in Sean Feast Collection)

such disappointment was Andrew Maitland, who fancied his crew had the makings to go all the way. He even volunteered to stay with his crew, even though he was tour expired, for them to reach their goal: 'The squadron commander was very pleased I wanted to continue and assured me it would not be long before I could expect to carry out a master bomber attack.' The CO was no doubt honest in his intent, but while Maitland flew no fewer than nine trips as deputy master bomber, he never achieved his desired ambition. While that may have been disappointing, he was pleased that one of those deputy trips was to Essen: 'The whole crew was pleased we had reached such a standard of efficiency where our superiors thought us fit for the role.'[39]

Australian Fred Phillips, a contemporary of Andrew Maitland on 7 Squadron, had more luck, skill or maybe both. He well remembered the situation facing those crews who had completed their tours, but whose service were still much in demand: 'Very few crews finished in the normal way and as our losses continued, many of the old hands were asked to stay on.' He flew three trips as master bomber and a further 14 as a deputy, seven to Brian Frow[40] and seven to Alan Craig,[41] two of the PFF's most accomplished leaders. Prior to becoming a master bomber, Fred was allocated a specialist air bomber and remembered being called to HQ to be briefed personally by Bennett before one of his trips, because they were to bomb close to Allied positions. He was delighted when the attack was subsequently described as 'carefully controlled' and 'very successful'. He was even more delighted to celebrate his 21st birthday a few days later![42]

Stafford Harris, who spent the early part of his RAF career instructing, flew his first Pathfinder trip on 11 September 1944, the day of his formal posting to 156 Squadron. By his 14th operation he had been 'promoted' to primary visual marker. For his next trip, he was appointed deputy master bomber and flew four more operations as deputy before being given complete control of a raid on the benzol plant at Harpenerweg: 'When we were selected as master bomber it was not a big deal, it was just the job we were given. You felt an inner pride but didn't let it show. It was the same when I was awarded the DFC. I thought it was nice for my parents.'[43]

Dudley Greenaway flew as the mid-upper gunner in the crew of Brian McMillan, a master bomber with 582 Squadron. The majority of Dudley's Pathfinder tour was flying either as deputy or primary visual marker which, he said, meant flying across the target at least twice and sometimes three times, as the markers were usually dropped in small batches, and the bombs separately as their trajectory was different. The trickiest of all duties, however, was 'mastering', as this meant being first in and last out.[44] On one such occasion, over Cologne on 28 October 1944, they lost an engine to flak, and being the port inner, it was the source of electric power to the air gunners' heated suits. It was a long, slow, lonely and cold flight home.

Master bombers were extraordinary men, much respected by their Main Force peers, and feared by their enemies. Michael Renault, perhaps speaking for the majority of squadron COs at the time, said his sympathies were always with the man who led the attack: 'The master bomber told the 800-odd bomb aimers exactly what to do and what markers to bomb. We were lucky on average to be in the target area for three minutes only, whereas the master bomber was being shot at non-stop for a period of half to one-hour.'[45] The Germans were understandably less enthusiastic, describing the master bomber simply as 'the most unwelcome man in Germany'.[46]

One of the most famous master bombers was Ted Swales. He would constantly badger Dudley and his skipper for their experience, eager to learn. It was with tremendous sadness that Dudley learned, long after he had left the squadron, that Swales had been shot down and killed while controlling the attack on Pforzheim in February 1945, just a few short weeks before the end of hostilities in the West. It was only some comfort to learn that Ted won the VC that night for staying with his badly damaged aircraft long enough to enable the rest of the crew to escape by parachute.

Chapter 11

'It Was Like Watching an Execution'

S ir Arthur Harris likened a bomber operation and the courage and determination of his men to the frontline soldiers of World War One 'going over the top'.[1] Donald Bennett did much the same thing; he never doubted the bravery of the men under his command. If they failed, he argued, it was most probably down to lack of training and not a lack of moral fibre – a phrase and three letters (LMF) that provoked misgivings at the time and is still a source of hurt and ill-feeling among the survivors today.

A typical first tour of operations in Bomber Command Main Force squadrons was 30 sorties followed by a period of 'rest', typically at an OTU or similar to pass on their experience to junior crews, learning the 'gen'. After six to nine months or so, they could be called back for a second tour of not more than 20 operations, after which they could not be called back for a third, although many volunteered to do so. It is important to note that neither figure was cast in stone. Operational hours were also taken into account, at least initially, and for a few brief weeks before and after D-Day a ridiculous system was introduced of dividing operations into fractions such that a short hop to Northern France, for example, might only count as a third. The move prompted one Pathfinder, Peter Crow, to remark that he might never complete his tour![2] Another, with some justification, proposed that if a trip to France was only a third, then an op to Berlin should count as double.[3]

It is easy to see how men with little or no operational experience could have dreamed up such a scheme; on paper, how could a three-hour sortie to bomb coastal batteries in Calais compare to a nine-hour slog to Stettin on the Baltic? This was why operational hours were considered and how a tour might end at 28 or 33 ops. Squadron morale was also a factor; bomber crews were under no illusions about their chances of survival, but they had to believe that survival was possible. Seeing a crew hacked down on their last operation could quickly undo that belief, and there are documented cases where squadron COs cut short the tour of an individual to benefit all of the men under their command. Indeed, Sir Robert Saundby, SASO Bomber Command, made provision for such eventualities, stating that less than 30 completed sorties may count as a satisfactory operational tour if the group commander is satisfied the individual concerned has carried out their aircrew duties and is in a need of rest from operational flying.[4]

All the men in Bomber Command were volunteers; all the men in PFF were also volunteers, so they had, in effect, volunteered twice! They also volunteered for an extended tour of 45 operations straight off, without a break. This 'double tour' of operations had originally been set at 60, but wiser heads prevailed. As with the Main Force crews, these numbers were not an exact science. While PFF crews did indeed sign up for a tour of 45, they could, in fact, be withdrawn from ops any time after 30. Mosquito crews flew tours of 50 operations, and many heavy bomber aircrew exceeded 45 as a matter of course, especially in the later stages of the war when their expertise was in such high demand. Some remarkable souls went on to complete three or even four tours of operations – 100 trips or more – and some, like PFF flight engineer Ted Stocker, did so all in four-engined bombers.[5]

Loss of experienced crews was a constant headache; a further concern was the loss of morale.[6] Stafford Coulson had both to contend with when he took over command of 582 Squadron from Peter Cribb, who'd been promoted to 'station master', as they were amusingly called. It was the Christmas of 1944, and the squadron had just lost five crews on a raid on the Cologne/Gremberg marshalling yards. Sitting in the mess, reading a newspaper, Coulson thought he smelled burning. Then he saw a lick of flame and realised that someone had crept in without him noticing and set fire to the paper. He knew from that moment that squadron morale was not going to be a problem.[7]

Philip Patrick, a flight commander with 7 Squadron at Oakington,[8] said that maintaining morale was a constant challenge and a key part of his role. When operations were 'on', the flight commanders selected the crews to take part and their names were chalked on the board hanging outside the flight office. If a crew failed to return, the name was rubbed out, and a new name written in its place. Against that background, it was not easy to keep people's spirits up, and sometimes they failed. It was not unheard of for a skipper or even an entire crew to have had enough. The flight commander might try and persuade them otherwise, but his words would, more often than not, fall on deaf ears, as their minds were made up. Then there was nothing he could do to prevent them being labelled LMF – a coward by any other name. Then it was Sheffield, where most of the bad boys were sent, and then – who knows? Philip didn't have the time to find out nor did he particularly care.[9]

Incidences of individuals being categorised as LMF are rare in Main Force squadrons and virtually unheard of in Pathfinder Force. Precise figures are difficult to come by, but the best statistical evidence suggests that only around 900 cases of LMF were confirmed in the whole of Bomber Command across six years of war, against a total force of circa 125,000 men. An average of anything between 13 and 20 cases per month has been offered.[10] That there weren't more cases is remarkable given the odds of coming through the war in one piece. To put those odds into context, of 100 men who made it to an OTU, 51 would be killed on combat operations, 12 more would be killed or injured in non-operational accidents and 12 would become prisoners of war. Only 24 of the original 100 would make it through unscathed.[11] This does not take into account those aircrew destined for Bomber Command who never made it beyond basic training in South Africa, Rhodesia (now Zimbabwe) and Canada (and later the US) as part of the Empire Air Training Plan.

Detecting those who were losing their nerve was never easy, but there were common signs: increased excitability, restlessness, irritability or truculence or the contrasting signs of unusual quietness with a desire for solitude.[12] Ron Smith recalled a fellow air gunner, a second tour man, who had lost all confidence in his new skipper. The gunner became increasingly isolated, and Ron noticed how his drinking, when not on operations, became obsessive.[13] Reg Cann remembered his regular air bomber, an Australian, being replaced by a second tour man on account of the former becoming 'flak happy' – every time the air bomber saw an aircraft going down, he would get a little excited. So alarmed were the others that on one night the wireless operator cut off his oxygen supply to keep him quiet and offer the rest of the men some temporary respite.[14]

Being flak happy was not the same as going LMF, but the outcome could be just as serious. Judgement became impaired and men became oblivious to the dangers around them. Gerry O'Donovan, a hugely experienced Pathfinder and master bomber with 156 and 582 Squadrons in 1944, took off the wrong way down the Little Staughton runway, failed to gain sufficient height and clipped the top of a nearby church. He survived, diverting to the nearest emergency landing ground, having first given his crew the opportunity to bale out. One of the gunners, Peter Crow, was all for going but no one would jump with him.[15] Stafford Coulson cites this as a classic example of a man being flak happy and operating for too long. There was nothing of the coward in O'Donovan, far from it, as the later award of an immediate DSO would testify. He was simply losing his judgement brought about by operational strain.

Coulson admits to only ever sending one crew back that had been posted to his squadron. If he suspected something wasn't right, or a crew was reported to him by one of his flight commanders, then he would fly with them and form his own impression. He recalls one trip to the Ruhr with one such pilot who seemed totally oblivious to the dangers around him, but not in a good sense. The man was clearly at the point of cracking up. He was grounded upon landing and posted at the first opportunity.

Lack of moral fibre, and the damage it could inflict on an operational squadron, was promoted on the basis of 'fear' and 'contagion'. LMF, like a modern-day COVID-19, was a contagion that, if left unchecked, could spread; whole units could be rendered useless. Wars could be lost. Lord Balfour of Inchrye, the Under Secretary of State for Air, who'd been a pilot in World War One, was unsympathetic. He stated that, in plain language, LMF meant cowardice, and that one LMF crew member could start a rot that might spread not only through his own crew but also a whole squadron.[16]

One unnamed station commander in 1943 took the dangers so seriously that he made sure every case presented to him was punished by a court martial and, where applicable, by an exemplary prison sentence, regardless of what the psychiatrists were saying.[17] While perhaps not alone in this somewhat draconian view, it does appear to be unusual, and in sharp contrast to the view expressed by Wing Commander Coulson. Coulson believed that with any case of LMF, it was important to try and let the man down gently. No one, in his experience, went purposefully sick, although he did recall one mid-upper gunner who lost his nerve completely on the way to the target. He had to order the navigator to go aft, pull the unfortunate man down from the turret and hold him down until he'd stopped screaming and could control himself. The man was far from a novice; he was, in fact, very experienced and three German aircraft had fallen to his guns on previous tours. Coulson was bothered by the incident and wondered if he had known the man better whether he would have been able to read the warning signs and dealt with it much earlier. What he did know, however, was that no one could afford to have unstable or unreliable personalities in their crew.[18] In this view, there is agreement from Aubrey Breckon, a distinguished bomber pilot whose brother also served in PFF. One couldn't afford a 'dud' in a crew as morale could quickly be affected. Conversely, strong leadership could bring out the best in a man.[19]

The challenge for squadron commanders, and even group commanders, was in distinguishing understandable nerves that would fade with experience from something more insidious. A common occurrence, for example, was for Main Force crews to drop their bombs early or on the first sight of any markers or fires. An inexperienced crew, facing the fiery hell of flak and searchlights for the first time, with aircraft around them falling from the sky in flames, can be forgiven for wanting to bomb at the first opportunity and beat it for home. The phenomenon, known as 'creep back', was both acknowledged and planned for, the aiming point shifted north such that the heaviest weight of bombs should fall on the target area with creep back taken into account. They even had a name for such crews: 'fringe merchants'. But at the start of the Battle of Berlin, Pathfinder crews began reporting another phenomenon: seeing Main Force Lancasters deliberately jettisoning their 'cookies' over the North Sea. Was this really a matter of nerves or simply expedience? Certain group commanders prided themselves on the weight of bombs their squadron aircraft could carry, among them Edgar Rice of 1 Group. But increasing the all-up weight of the aircraft seriously impacted its performance, and a Lancaster that could ordinarily make 22,000ft might struggle to make it to 18,000ft where it became more vulnerable. Time and again, Bennett fed the news up the command chain only to be told repeatedly that he was imagining things. Experienced Pathfinder crews did not mis-identify bomb bursts, he argued, and they certainly did not mis-identify a 'cookie'. Bennett firmly believed that of all the bombs that left England, a large number never reached Berlin.[20]

There were, however, more pronounced indications that an individual or a crew may be losing their nerve. Early returns were a classic sign, a bomber returning a short time after take-off with an undiagnosed issue with an engine, for example, or one of the crew falling sick. The ORBs of the day are full of such incidents. Most, of course, were genuine. Serviceability was always a challenge, even with the Herculean efforts of the groundcrews operating in the most difficult of difficult circumstances. Novice crews might, with reasonable justification, abandon an operation should an engine fail on the way out to a target, especially if that target was 800 miles to the east. A more experienced crew might carry on; 'Tubby' Baker once had an engine fail on take-off and still carried on to the target with three.

Regardless of experience, the flight engineer's log and navigation charts were studied closely after each flight, and anyone trying to beat the system would be quickly unmasked.

Trevor Jones, an air bomber, was on his first operation with Main Force to Bockum (near Krefeld) when he experienced a problem with his bomb release mechanism. Although the basic computer suggested his bombs had been dropped, and his air gunner confirmed as much, actually they had not. It was only on visual inspection of the bomb bay that Trevor saw the ugly nose cones of the bombs and realised they were still in place. In a designated zone over the Channel, he released the bombs as 'safe' and carried on home. At debriefing, there was a suggestion he may have frozen on account of LMF, a situation made worse when ground tests the next day failed to find any fault with the bombing equipment. It was only two days later, when a different crew took the aircraft up for a bombing exercise and reported a similar issue, that Trevor was exonerated.[21]

In common with many Main Force raids, the attack on the rocket manufacturing and testing facility at Peenemünde witnessed its fair

Tubby Baker, OC 635 Squadron, was ordered to rest after 100 sorties. (RAF Wyton Pathfinder Collection)

share of unfortunate 'early returns', usually through aircrew sickness or a technical fault. A spluttering engine or a gun turret that was jammed, frozen or otherwise 'u/s' left each skipper with a dilemma and a difficult decision to make. To press on and take a chance or turn back and protect the crew, always in the knowledge that the trip would invariably not count as an 'op' if they did, and they would more than likely incur their squadron commander's displeasure. Nobody wanted to be thought of as a coward. Indeed, arguably the greatest fear to many aircrew was not the fear of being afraid, but the fear of being suspected of being frightened or, worse, lacking in moral fibre. To that extent, the policy of promoting LMF as 'shameful' appears to have worked. But it also could have the reverse effect, in unwittingly sending brave men to their deaths. Even some of the most famous Pathfinders – and most famous in Bomber Command – feared the stigma of LMF.

Ted Swales is one. His flight commander, Johnnie Clough, told of an incident early in Swales' operational career when he returned early with a faulty canopy that had blown open and couldn't be closed. He didn't fancy five or six hours sitting in a gale at −20°C but was torn off a strip by the CO, for which he felt much aggrieved. He confided to Clough that he would never return early again, and he never did.

The punishment meted out to any man 'going LMF' was also a deterrent. Beyond the shame, and being reduced to the ranks, it meant the removal of their aircrew brevet. The brevet, gained after months, and sometimes years, of training, was a symbol of intense pride to every member of Bomber Command, perhaps even more so than rank or even decoration. But whereas in the United States Air Force, a flying brevet was a symbol of completed qualification, in the RAF it was a badge of continuous training and as such it could be taken away, for it was never permanent. Under such a pretext, aircrew were robbed of their dignity, to serve out their days in the squalor of some distant posting.

Some crews had direct experience of LMF; for others, there were only stories. Jock Cassels,[22] who flew with 139 and 162 Squadrons, heard of one crew in Main Force who spent part of their tour taking off and flying around the North Sea without ever attempting to reach the target, before the pilot and the navigator ultimately had a blazing row and the matter was reported.

Reg Parissien, a wireless operator with 156 Squadron, remembered a morning when the whole squadron was asked to parade, and one of their number was accused of lacking in moral fibre. In front of everyone, the CO tore the sergeant's stripes from the man's sleeve and ripped off his aircrew brevet. The man was humiliated and degraded in a disgraceful scene that no man deserved. While it was clear the CO was making a point, it was, in Reg's mind, 'like watching an execution'.[23]

Bert Wilson, who flew 76 ops without a rest, was similarly appalled and saddened at how some LMF cases were treated. Early in his training, his pilot had been obliged to crash land after a fighter affiliation exercise. They'd lost an engine, which put the hydraulics u/s, meaning

Reg Parissien never felt fear and positively looked forward to operations. (Sheila Parissien)

they had no undercarriage and flaps. Despite their best efforts, the pilot was forced to land on the grass, with only one wheel down, and as the aircraft came to a halt, it spun around like a top, leaving the rear gunner dangling in the air. Afterwards he left to be replaced by another gunner with several trips behind him. He too decided he'd had enough and so had to go LMF.[24]

Bob Gill, a rear gunner with 35 Squadron, recounts a similar incident after a particularly hairy trip to Nuremberg on 27 August 1943: 'We bombed our target OK and were on the way home. On crossing the French coast, the navigator (Graham Walters) gave a change of course but Hardy (the pilot) for some reason, probably tiredness, went straight on. We arrived over a town that was lit up by searchlights trying to find us.'[25]

From 4,000ft, the Halifax crew could see the city's main docks, and the air bomber argued it was Portsmouth. Others disagreed, as it had no river. The flight engineer fired off the colours of the day, at which point all hell broke loose: 'We thought the world had ended. We had holes all over; the astrodome was blown off and we were circling over Cherbourg! We were nearly out of fuel and made it to Tangmere and made a Mayday request for a priority landing. Tangmere was a fighter airfield with a runway that was too short for bombers. Consequently, one wing got stuck in a tree and the plane had to be pulled out by a tractor. Our wireless op said that was enough for him, and never flew again.'

Official records talk of men being predisposed to fear, but that is, perhaps, a huge over-simplification of an issue that is now much better understood. Even at the time, however, aircrew could forgive their fellow men for losing their nerve in exceptional circumstances. Percy Cannings of 97 Squadron, who flew 47 operations, remembered practising formation flying and seeing two of the aircraft collide. There was only one survivor from the two crews. Naturally, the survivor was badly shaken by his experience and refused to fly again. He was posted LMF; the matter was all hushed up and he simply disappeared off the station.[26]

Dr Roland Winfield, who won the DFC with 7 Squadron, was similarly empathetic: he believed it was utterly wrong to think of a man as being

Percy Cannings had the harrowing experience of seeing two aircraft collide while practising formation flying. (via Percy Cannings in Sean Feast Collection)

a coward because he failed to face up to the risk of being killed if he continued to fly against the enemy.[27] Although not a PFF man, John Wainwright, who flew more than two tours in 5 Group before refusing to fly any more, avoided being labelled LMF by a whisker. He wrote of the policy: '[It is] more likely these three letters killed more men than German flak or fighters. They sent terrified men to their deaths; they forced men to operate when they were a menace to their own crew.'[28]

Experienced Pathfinder aircrew like Ernie Patterson admitted to getting the jitters. Constipation was never a problem: 'When the Battle Order went up, you couldn't get to the toilet fast enough. I used to have a code: if I said to my girlfriend, "How did work go down this morning?" she knew I was on ops that night.'[29] Harold Kirby also admitted to being frightened, especially on one particular occasion when their aircraft was struck by bombs dropped on them by another aircraft overhead: 'It was a daylight attack on a V1 storage depot and the mid-upper gunner warned that there was a Lancaster above us with its bomb doors open. It was too late to take avoiding action. Two bombs hit us, taking the port undercarriage clean off and leaving a large hole in the wing. Even though my parachute was close, I knew that if the wing came off, we wouldn't have stood a chance.' With so much damage, and only three engines, they were diverted to Wittering as it had a grass runway and was thought less of a risk. Harry's pilot, Bill Ryan, pulled off a first-class emergency landing only to be torn off a strip for damaging the airfield!

Harold admits to being frightened, especially when his aircraft was hit by two bombs from above. (Harold Kirby)

Norman Westby said that in Main Force he was scared all the time (Norman completed a tour on 101 Squadron prior to joining PFF) and that fear got the better of some crews. But it was different in PFF: 'On a Pathfinder crew, we were working so hard that I didn't have time to be frightened.'[30]

Peter Crow had great sympathy for those who couldn't go on, especially given the 'chop' rate in some Bomber Command squadrons. Towards the end of his tour, there was no doubt he was getting nervous and was not surprised that others cracked under the strain. Jeff Chapman had similar feelings. Having survived a tour of operations in the Middle East, he'd been posted to PFF as a commissioned 'spare bod' to be assimilated into an existing crew whose previous wireless operator had been badly wounded. He was starting his second tour while the rest of the crew was no more than halfway through their first, and he was not a little apprehensive.[31]

Another whose courage was beyond doubt but who was honest in the fear that he felt was David Mansel-Pleydell. Having been awarded the DFC in May 1944 as an air bomber with a Main Force squadron, he joined PFF as a retrained Nav 2 with a regular pilot, Owen Milne.[32] Mansel-Pleydell was

Joining PFF after a tour in the Middle East, Jeff Chapman was anxious about joining a new and inexperienced crew. (Peter Chapman)

not operating the day that Milne and the rest of his crew were shot down, an incident that deeply affected him. Like Jeff Chapman, Mansel-Pleydell was at best anxious about the new crew to which he was allocated, saying as much in a letter to his uncle, and admitting to 'having the screamers' so much so that he convinced himself that he wasn't going to make it and knew that he was 'for the chop'. On the night of 12 January 1945, the aircraft in which he was flying to assess the crew as a future master bomber was hit and the order given to bale out. Mansel-Pleydell needed no second bidding and was first out of the hatch, but in the interim, the pilot, Frank Lloyd, regained control of the Lancaster and made it home. Mansel-Pleydell wrote about the incident after the war, grateful to have survived but less than enamoured with the orders of his pilot.[33]

There were, of course, the extraordinary few who genuinely appeared to neither experience nor show any fear. These men had no need of the lucky scarves, girlfriends' underwear, or teddy bears that kept others sane.

David Mansel-Pleydell convinced himself he wasn't going to make it. Happily, he did. (Tom Mansel-Pleydell)

'Nick' Nicholson never felt frightened; to him it was a job, a day in the office. Even when they returned on two engines, his only thought was that he would be late home.[34] Jim Rayment was sitting in his rear turret in cloud, with clumps of ice breaking off the wings and hitting the sides but could only worry about his tomatoes.[35] Perhaps, in Jim's case, it was because he was almost a full 20 years older than the rest of the crew. Reg Parissien positively looked forward to operations. When he was on leave, he couldn't wait to get back to the squadron.

But men like Nick, Jim and Reg were the exception, not the rule. So, too, were men like Abel Mellor.

Mellor was posted to 582 Squadron at the start of October, flying his first Pathfinder operation on the 28th. Six operations in nine days followed, such was the frenetic pace of operations in the months after the break-out from Normandy. Described as something of a loner, on the morning of 11 November, the 21-year-old asked to see the CO, Peter Cribb. Cribb was every inch the airman's airman, who'd been reported once for using his service revolver to shoot the light out in his hut, rather than use the switch. Later he would take a wholly unauthorised flight across Germany to bomb Berchtesgaden, having been denied the opportunity of leading the raid on the Führer's retreat.[36]

At the meeting, Mellor asked to be transferred out of the squadron, explaining that he had no objection to flying on operations but wanted to be transferred to a unit where he would not be responsible for the lives of a crew. Cribb responded that everyone on the squadron felt fear to some degree and they all had to overcome it and get the job done regardless. Mellor's request was denied, not that Cribb had much choice in that situation. He put Mellor's crew on the battle order for that evening's operation to Dortmund, thinking it best to get him flying right away.[37]

Mellor and his crew went through the standard preparations and briefings and were taken out to the dispersal at the required time before take-off. After getting to the dispersal where his Lancaster was waiting, Mellor said he had forgotten something and had to go back to get it. He didn't return and the senior officers were livid when one Lancaster did not start up and take off with the others, even more so when they found out it was Mellor that had disappeared. They began searching the station for the missing pilot.

A few hours later, Flying Officer Mellor was found dead behind one of the huts, with his service revolver in his hand. He had killed himself because the weight of his crew's lives on his conscience was too much for him to handle. While it is easy for us to see the enthusiasm and courage displayed by the men who flew with Bomber Command, Mellor's story reminds us of the tremendous strain and pressure these men were all under and usually hid so well. Mellor is a tragic figure who, in an unusual way, sacrificed himself for his crew. Mellor's crew were assigned a new pilot; they completed their tour of operations and all survived the war.

Mellor's death troubled Peter Cribb for the rest of his life.

Chapter 12

Operations are On

It is 0700hrs and the start of a new day, but it's much like the last, and the one before that. Working on a Mosquito squadron in PFF's LNSF is not a nine-to-five job. Never is. You're up early, assuming you haven't been up with the lads through the night, in which case you're up anyway.

You have a 'trade'. Every crew has a fitter for the engines and a rigger for the airframe, and some of the old hands, the regulars, the ones who may have trained at Halton as apprentices, are skilled at both. Like you.[1] You're what's called a fitter II. You know almost everything there is to know about the aeroplane, but your preference is towards engines. You've been around Mosquitoes now for some time, since before they came to 8 Group. Alongside your general training, you've been on specific courses. Like the one at Cricklewood, to learn about hydromatic airscrews.

Home to you is a Nissen hut that you share with several others. As a Senior NCO, you're responsible for your own space but have an Aircraft Hand (ACH)[2] to clean out the hut daily. The washhouse is nearby and that's also a Nissen hut and the water is usually cold, but you might be lucky. It's only a short walk and the fresh air is good for blowing the cobwebs away. You wash – not saying much – get dressed and head for the sergeants' mess for breakfast, taking your irons with you – knife, fork, spoon – and an enamel mug, slightly chipped.

You don't march to work since this is an operational squadron, and your aircraft is at the dispersal. So you cycle. You are all issued with a bike, though of course they get pinched. You're never late, not unless there's a problem with the bike, like a puncture or it has mysteriously vanished.

At the dispersal, you check in to the flight office, again another Nissen hut, or sometimes a more robust wooden construction, and you begin to look though the Form 700 – the serviceability sheet for the aircraft. Everywhere the aircraft goes, the Form 700 goes with it. It's on this form that the pilot writes down any complaints he has about the aircraft, something he wants you to look at. It could make the aircraft u/s and you don't want that, because it will remain u/s until the fault is found and rectified. The form is then signed off by you, the relevant tradesman and, ultimately, the pilot before he flies it again. On this squadron, there is also a 'snag' sheet for reporting less serious faults, but issues nonetheless that deserve your attention.

In most cases, the lads have their own aircraft, so they know it like the back of their hands. You check on the labour available – the fitters, riggers, instrument repairers, armourers, electricians, wireless operators, photographers and radar mechanics – and then detail the airmen and corporals to specific jobs and make them aware of any issues they need to fix. Spares are in the General Stores and have to be drawn from the storeman, although it's usual to keep some spares at the dispersal, especially those parts that are most in demand. Saves the hassle.

The engineering officer tells you about the operational requirements for that night's operation. Those aircraft that require a daily service are processed, serviced and put on standby. An estimate is then made of how many of the remaining aircraft will be serviceable that day. If it's a shortage of spares, you might look to cannibalise one of the lame ducks, robbing Peter to pay Paul. The fitter inspects the engines every day. He checks the cowlings for any indication there might be an oil leak. He takes the cowlings off and checks the exhaust stubs. He checks everything – ignition system, leads, plugs, hoses and radiator. He checks to make sure no pipes are in contact with other pipes, housings or controls because anything that is not properly clipped in place is a potential hazard and could eventually cause a problem, especially electrical leads. He tops up the oil where needed and the engine coolant, rotates the propeller and listens for noises from the supercharger's bearings. When he replaces the cowling, he gives it a thorough clean, so that any subsequent oil leak can be noted and not confused with any previous leak. The cowlings can take some time to replace; some fit better than others and lining up the slots with the cowling buttons, so they are all secure, is not easy.

The rigger carries out a visual check of all parts of the exterior. He wants to make sure there are no bullet holes in the fuselage or wings and no cuts to the tyres, and that they're not flat and need more air. He checks the fairings and housings of the undercarriage and cleans them. He checks to see if the paint is cracked at the top end of the undercarriage – a possible sign of a heavy landing and abnormal pressure. He clambers into the cockpit and tests all the controls to make sure they're functioning correctly – the elevators, rudders and ailerons. He checks the brakes for any sponginess and notes the pressure. He checks the seat adjustment, the windows and the integrity of all the panels, especially the escape hatch. He centres the control column to check for a slight droop in the ailerons.

The aircraft's engines are run against the chocks at maximum revs. The groundcrew look for any drop in engine revs and oil pressure. They also do a slow running check while you look for black smoke from the exhausts – a sure sign of a rich mixture. This is during the day. In the dark, you'd note the colour of the exhaust flames.

While the engines are running, the functioning of the flaps and bomb doors are checked, and when the engines are switched off, the rigger looks for any signs of droop. If all's well, just like the fitter before him, the rigger signs his name in the relevant column on the Form 700. Indeed, each tradesman, when they have completed their work, signs their part of the form, and only when all the relevant columns are signed will you sign it yourself and list the aircraft as serviceable.

If the aircraft needs a test flight, this is arranged with the pilot. Immediately after, the aircraft is inspected again, between flights, which is why it's called a 'between flight inspection'. It's not much more than a visual check, just to be sure there isn't any damage, and then the only thing left to sign off on the Form is the petrol. If it's a long operation, drop tanks have to be fitted, tested and filled. While the aircraft is on the ground, a cover is put over the pitot head on the leading edge of the fin. Covers are also put over the tyres to prevent them from deteriorating in the sunlight. Large wooden chocks are placed in front of the wheels to stop the aircraft from moving, and a locking bar is secured on the undercarriage.

Sometimes a problem is not easily fixed, like a 'negative earth' and that could mean missing lunch. Everyone hates negative earths. They can take days to rectify. You normally split the shifts, so half go to lunch early, and half late. You remember to take your irons and mug. In the morning and in the afternoon, the NAAFI van arrives, and you purchase some well-earned char and wads.[3] It is a break to which you are entitled but it doesn't last long. There is still much to be done.

You are in A Flight but that doesn't mean you won't lend a hand elsewhere, if needed. You remember the occasion when your opposite number in B Flight asked if you could help with a mag drop problem.[4] They had changed the plugs, the harness and the magneto itself, but the problem still persisted. A mystery earth of something, probably. You asked the sergeant to run the engine for a while. You stood and watched. Slow running. Black smoke. Run it up and throttle back suddenly and petrol comes down the intake. Switch off. Check the enrichment capsule and the aneroid has failed, putting the needle in the maximum rich position. Change the aneroid. Set up. Replace. Run engine. Fault cleared. While the rev drop occurred when the magneto was switched off, it was nothing to do with the ignition.

Broken exhaust studs are another problem. The studs shear off flush with the cylinder block face. The aircraft has to be taken to an area where there is electric power so that the stud can be trepanned out, an insert fitted complete with stud and the exhaust stub refitted. The fitter has to be very, very careful. One mistake and it could mean a whole engine change. You don't say it out loud, but there have been a few occasions where you've let an aircraft go out with the exhaust held on by only three nuts and not four.

Mainly you supervise, but you always have your eye on the clock. You take pride in making sure the necessary number of aircraft are ready. When the lads are really up against it, and you know you can do the job quicker than them, nothing pleases you more than getting your hands dirty. They respect you for it. Some of the lads even ask for your help. Rank doesn't matter much at the dispersal when you're all working together.

Around the station, a small army of groundcrew are completing their checks until, one by one, the Mosquitoes are serviced and declared serviceable and on standby. Now it depends on the operation to determine what bombs or markers are loaded. If you are in the Main Force LNSF, like you are, there are no markers, just bombs. The LNSF marker squadron is different. Its payload will be a mix of bombs and TIs. All of the munitions need to be treated with respect. The Mosquito you are responsible for usually carries four 500-pounders, although that's a pretty hefty payload for a small wooden aeroplane. Some – the 'pregnant ducks' as they are called – have been modified to carry a single 4,000lb 'cookie', and that's a dangerous beast. On the ground and in the air. You've heard of men who have broken fingers and even wrists in the usual flap to get an aircraft bombed up. You've also heard of explosions on other PFF stations, caused by faulty arming pistols. In one case, a year or so ago, seven groundcrew were killed in one such explosion, not that there was anything left of the men to bury. The chop rate of armourers is second only to aircrew; it is a trade where there is no second chance.[5] A trade where there is no funeral, only a memorial service.

You can recall another example of an electrician who did his best to blow himself and his chums to kingdom come. It was on one of the heavy squadrons. He was working on a Lanc that had returned with one of its bombs still on board. He'd noted a short in one of the bomb circuits and a second earth could cause the bomb to drop. He needed to sort it and sort it fast. He found the cause of the problem quite quickly: below each of the bomb selector switches was a tiny screw, and one of these had come loose and dropped among the connections. It was an easy fix, he thought, as long as he used his magnetic screwdriver to lift the screw out of harm's way. However, his screwdriver proved not to be magnetic and, long story short, he heard a dull thud and a metal clanking sound as the bomb fell to the floor. He was lucky. It was a 2,000-pounder and they were more forgiving than many of the smaller bombs.[6]

You try not to think about any of this and focus on the task in hand. The bombs are loaded, and the oxygen checked (and signed for) and now you and the lads can relax, kick a ball around in the hangar, using the door as a goal, obviously well away from any aircraft. One of the lads is reading a book, a 'hot' one and a little tattered, having been passed from hand to hand.

You're told to report back to the dispersal half an hour before your aircraft is due to take off. Take-off times can be a bit iffy, depending on the weather, and sometimes you and the lads can be hanging around for a little while. Then at last the crew arrives. The first part of your job is almost done.

✳ ✳ ✳ ✳ ✳

You are part of a squadron comprising people with widely different levels of experience, temperaments and backgrounds. You're also sharing a station with a 'heavy' Pathfinder squadron, and accommodation is somewhat stretched. In fact, there is so little room that you actually sleep in an old house, just outside the main entrance. It's where all the new boys are put.

The relationship with your 'heavy' friends is an amicable one… mostly. There is a fair amount of leg pulling on both sides. They resent you, perhaps, ever so slightly for having an easier life. But they rarely, if ever, show it. Not unless you shoot too many lines. Your chances of survival are much greater than theirs. You can fly faster and higher. If two or three Lancasters are lost in a single night, there are more than 20 empty chairs at breakfast. You hear of a feud on one station between the two commanding officers and of a 'raid' mounted by the Lancaster boys on the Mosquito CO's office. A flare was dropped down the man's chimney and caused all sorts of mayhem. It's all rather childish, but then many of them are not that long out of school and it does them good to let off steam occasionally.

You were a trainee accountant in more peaceful times, a Londoner who'd enlisted at the age of 18, determined to do your bit. You're one of three boys; one of your brothers is in the Royal Naval Reserve, the other in the Army, so there's one of you in each service. Before joining the squadron, many had operational experience behind them, normally from a tour on heavy aircraft. You are the same. You trained as a navigator and spent some time as an instructor with 106 Squadron and were even loaned to the Americans for a period to lead numbers of Liberators and Fortresses from Prestwick to their bases in East Anglia. It was only for a month, but you ate like a king. Then at last you are posted to Lissett in Yorkshire, and a tour of operations flying Halifax Mk IIs with 158 Squadron, for which you and your skipper were awarded the DFC.[7]

You talk to the others and learn that many have suffered personal injuries or seen members of their crew killed. Many have encountered aircraft failure from enemy action or from mechanical faults and have survived bad crashes. This kind of experience always leaves its mark, sometimes in the form of a particular dislike of one aspect of operational flying or more commonly in the form of a 'twitch'. It doesn't stop them operating and everyone else ignores it.

You've had a close shave yourself. Early on in your career and before you started ops, you joined a crew at your OTU that had lost its navigator. You were flying your last night-time circuits and bumps, and on the third go the starboard engine caught fire just after becoming airborne. The aircraft crashed and only you and the rear gunner survived.

Aircrew on the station can show logbooks with more than 100 operational trips to their credit and DSOs and DFCs are not uncommon. The thought of coming off operations does not seem to occur to them. One navigator here has an artificial leg, another an artificial hand. If there is a limit to the number of operations for a tour on Mosquitoes, you have certainly not heard of it and are not aware of any aircrew asking for a release from operations.[8] Perhaps it's because of the performance of the aircraft, and because your loss rate is so low – certainly much lower than operating in heavy aircraft.

You've trained to operate Mosquitoes at Wyton, where individual pilots and navigators are formed into crews. You were lucky to know one of the pilots already. You worked in the same office before the war and agreed to team up. After such a build-up, your posting to your new squadron is almost an anti-climax. The CO is friendly enough but admits he wasn't really expecting you and so you're told to push off and take some leave.

Your squadron is part of the LNSF. It's not an Oboe squadron but you are the unofficial marker squadron for the rest of the 'Ghost Raiders,' marking blind with H2S. Your working day starts at 0900hrs in the Flight Office, presided over by the flight commander. Only crews who flew the previous night are excused. At these meetings you are given the latest gen on all kinds of things related to operational flying. Target photographs of the previous night's operations are displayed and, where possible, the accuracy of the bombing in relation to the aiming point is identified by the intelligence officer. During the morning, you may do a flight test or your pilot may get in some additional time on the Link Trainer.

Around midday, instructions are received from Bomber Command via 8 Group HQ, detailing operations for that night. At this stage the target is only known by a handful of senior officers, but the number of aircraft required, fuel load and bomb load are known and acted upon, and a battle order drawn up with the names of each crew posted on the mess noticeboard around lunchtime.

Any remaining night flying tests are carried out during the afternoon, and any problems are disclosed to the ground crews, who deal with them as a matter of priority. You've had a couple of early returns. Once when you had an engine fail on take-off, and it happened again three days later on your way to Magdeburg. It was eventually found to be a petrol feed problem: some foreign body had got into the system. You also had a shaky do over Berlin one night when you were not only hit by flak but also set upon by a German night fighter. You were lucky to make it back.

Later that afternoon you are called for a navigators' briefing, the time of the briefing relative to the time you need to take off. The navigation officer provides details of the route to and from the target, marking of turning points for the Main Force of LNSF Mosquitoes that will follow behind, target-marking details, meteorological forecasts and ToT. You use this information to create your flight plan, a meticulous and neat piece of work in direct contrast to the navigational work you will do in flight (on a piece of board on one knee). You establish your take-off time and wait.

The main briefing follows, and you assemble with the other navigators and their pilots. The CO shows you a large map of Europe, which you've seen many times before, and on it is a coloured tape showing you the route in and out of the target. Your navigation officer goes next, followed by the met officer and intelligence officer with any special points to look out for. Your briefing on a Mosquito squadron tends not to be a lengthy affair; the station master usually likes to add a few words of encouragement at the end and with his words ringing in your ear you look forward to your operational meal of eggs and bacon or variations on a theme. Sometimes there's steak. In wartime Britain, this is a real treat and jealously guarded so that only those crews actually flying on operations get it.

Not all of you eat with much gusto. Some prefer to eat nothing at all and say their reactions are much better if they go hungry. They take some chocolate along to eat on the trip home. Men stand around smoking and wondering – wondering if any of you will go missing tonight, remembering the two fellas who went missing last time.[9]

Take-off time approaches and you return to your flights to don your flying gear. You wear battledress: a thick sweater, flying boots and helmet. Many of you are superstitious, and there is an order with which you dress. Get that order wrong, and you may have to start all over again. You empty your pockets and unbutton your collar and remove your tie, if you're wearing one, and wonder whether anyone has actually ever been strangled in the water by their own tie?

Escape aids and torches are collected. Parachutes are drawn from the parachute store in flights and issued to you by WAAFs whose job it is to look after them and periodically re-pack them. Their job is perhaps the most responsible, for the only way to test a parachute is if you use it. Then you clamber into a waiting bus or lorry, driven by another WAAF from the

Motorised Transport section, to be taken to the aircraft on the dispersal. One is called Cinders, and she's been driving the boys out to their aircraft for almost two years. She is about the only WAAF the boys really like and don't try any funny business with.

At the dispersal the groundcrew are waiting for you, with the battery trolleys ready for starting up, and you exchange some friendly words. The armourer approaches and asks for a signature on a sheet to sign for the payload. It makes you chuckle every time. You look in the bomb bay and there they are. Because you are leading this attack, you have one 500-pounder and three different types of TI. They haven't tried to fob you off with one short. You and your pilot have a good look around the aircraft to ensure all the locks and covers have been removed before signing the Form 700 and note that your aircraft has only done ten hours so far. She's beautiful, brand new and sleek. The boys have been polishing her all day.

Then you settle into the cockpit and run through your pre-take-off routine. There's not much room in a Mossie and you need a hand with your parachute. You clip the strap from your dinghy to your Mae West and then help each other to strap in. You plug in the intercom. Start-up and take-off times have been clearly laid down and now only a red flare from Flying Control can cancel the operation. No such flare appears.

The pilot goes through his routine – trim set for take-off, revs fully fine, throttles open half an inch, etc., and you check the instruments, radar and other gadgetry. It is start-up time. The pilot opens the starter buttons and yells to the groundcrew, 'Petrol on, ready to start.' Then, 'Contact Port.' He repeats the instruction. He puts up the port switches and presses the starter buttons. The engine thunders into life, and he repeats the exercise for the starboard engine. The trolly accumulator is disconnected, and the pilot opens the revs to 1,500 to warm the engines. The engine temperature creeps up and then the pilot opens the engines to full bore – 4,000 revs – then throttles back to 2,000 revs ready to taxi. There are a few more small checks and you're almost ready. The pilot uncages the gyro and waves the chocks away. Now you can go and taxi to the runway in use. You've gone over the route with your skipper. He's got the basics on a card tucked into his boot just in case you cop a packet and he's left to find his own way home.

From the control caravan, a green light blinks at you from an Aldis lamp and you set off, knowing that in four hours or so you will be back again, hopefully, safe and sound.

Your Mosquito surges ahead in its natural element. Farms and woods, cattle and corn pass by in a flash. You're like a great horse striding at full gallop. Fully loaded, your Mosquito climbs to an operational height at an indicated airspeed of between 155 and 160 knots, and it takes you 25 minutes to reach 25,000ft. Winds are invariably from west to north-west at altitude and often above 75 knots. Temperatures at operational height are very low, sometimes 50° to 60° below zero.

Unlike your time on heavies, no time is lost forming up or heading for an assembly point. You head straight out, on your course, to the English coast. It takes you about 17 minutes and you concentrate on keeping the aircraft on track to the point of the coast using Gee. With normal climbing boost settings, you cross the coast at around 17,000ft and it's possible from the Gee fixes to work out the actual strength of the wind.

The Merlin Packard engines in your Mk XX Mosquito are equipped with a two-stage supercharger and these are designed to keep the rate of climb going at the higher altitudes. You take a Gee fix every three minutes from the coast, and from this data you calculate the wind speed and direction every six minutes and revise the time for the next turning point accordingly. Establishing the correct wind velocities is essential, and Gee is flogged to death until enemy jamming makes it inoperable, usually around 4.5–6° east longitude. You write the times and mark the chart on your knee board for the H2S chart. This is a very busy time, with alterations of course being made to ensure you arrive as precisely as possible to the turning point in the North Sea. Coloured flares appear for the Main Force of 60 or so Mosquitoes of the LNSF following behind.[10] They are a potent weapon in their own right.

If you're heading for Berlin (or 'Whitebait' as it is known, for the cities are all named after fish), you normally take the northern route.

You fly across the North Sea, past Heligoland island to the enemy coast north of the river Elbe, across the German plains with Hamburg on your starboard and on to the great lakes north-west of the capital as the final turning point before the run-in to the city itself. H2S is invaluable for this kind of track, for the coastlines are well defined as are the rivers, large towns and lakes. For the leg to the lakes, there is plenty of information for the navigator to interpret and ensure he is on an accurate track.

Now you are on the final run to the target. It's a distance of 60 miles, the most dangerous part of the operation. For H2S to be functioning properly, you need to be straight and level. At 25,000ft, your aircraft streams contrails and you know there is a night fighter beacon at the lakes. It takes ten minutes to reach the target. You await the reception committee. The pilot lowers his seat and stares at his instruments rather than outside the cockpit. You keep your head in the H2S screen visor. The target comes steadily into the centre of your radar screen and onto the ten-mile line. You adjust the set for even greater definition and start your timed run to the aiming point.

You recall the detailed instructions you've been given by the radar officer for the final moments of your run-in to the aiming point. You have them written down: with the target aiming point on the eight-mile circle, you alter course 25° to port with a timed run on the stopwatch of 73 seconds for three carriers in the bomb bay (carrier one: photo-flash red bursting at 5,000ft; carrier two: TI green with yellow stars bursting at 9,800ft; and carrier three: a 500lb bomb), and four seconds later for carrier four (a TI green with red drip bursting at 3,000ft). As the target markers are released, you announce your letter and transmit to Main Force on VHF. You've done your bit and successfully marked the target. It's now up to the Main Force of LNSF to do their worst.

The route home from the Big City is a long-haul right across central Germany to the Dutch coast, a distance of 320 miles. With a strong headwind, of anything up to 70 knots, that's a flying time of 85 minutes. H2S is of little use. There are no large towns or lakes. Time seems to stand still until H2S, at last, begins to show the outline of the Ijsselmeer, and Gee begins to show signals in the mush as the coast draws near. Gee now comes back strongly, and you make a straight line for home.

What a wonderful site it is to see England again as you return from a successful sortie. There are searchlights on the east coast, lighting up the skies. Then you can see the familiar beacon flashing its two letters in Morse code and you know you are home. The only words you speak to Flying Control are the letters of your aircraft and 'funnel' to indicate you are on finals to land. Then you are down safely and clear of the runway to be met at the dispersal by the groundcrew and a vehicle to take you back for debriefing.

✳ ✳ ✳ ✳ ✳

It is only after the aircraft have taken off, and you are given their time of return, that you have any idea where they might be going. Depending on that time, a skeleton staff is maintained at the dispersal, in case any of the aircraft return early because of some kind of technical failure. The rest of you go to the cookhouse for supper, returning to the dispersal at an arranged time. Should there be an abort, and all of the aircraft are obliged to return, you won't need to be told because the sound of so many Merlin engines overhead is unmistakable and acts like a siren.

You recall an occasion when a pilot did return early, complaining there was no power in the port engine and it would only give him 2,000rpm. You run the engine yourself to check and it's true; it's only giving you 2,000rpm, but the boost is all OK. The CO arrives. He asks for your opinion, and you give it. The upper ranges of the rev counter are registering 1,000rpm short. He asks if you would have abandoned an op because of it. You don't answer – it's a hypothetical question. He asks if you would fly in it. You would. The next thing you know, he's throwing the navigator's parachute at you and soon after you're at 20,000ft and all's well with the world. You land and change the rev counter. The aircraft is now serviceable again.

Of course, your work involves much more than just daily inspections. The RAF has the best preventative maintenance system you know, and scheduled inspections are very important. Scheduled inspections mean an aircraft is grounded and taken from the dispersal to a repair and inspection hangar, usually closer to the main buildings and workshops. Parts that need to be changed or inspected are carefully listed and itemised on cards and, again, each item has to be accounted for by the relevant tradesman. There are 20-hour inspections and 40-hour checks, and then considerably more work involved in an 80-hour check. The most time-consuming inspection is the 240-hour check: cam covers come off, valve springs are inspected, the camshaft is removed, the engine is re-timed, tappets are set and adjusted, and the engine is given a general overhaul.

The night shift is back at the dispersal half an hour before the aircraft are due back. Again, you can hear the unmistakable sound of a Merlin overhead as the first one comes home, and then the count begins to ensure all the aircraft have returned safely. Maybe one is missing, but there's always the chance it has landed elsewhere, at another aerodrome.

You're there to greet the aircrews as they return, and you enquire as to any faults. These are discussed immediately upon landing and any snags are recorded on the Form 700, which could put the aircraft u/s. Then the night crews are given their tasks. Perhaps they are servicing their own aircraft, but if their aircraft is damaged, they could be assigned to another.

Every operational squadron is different. The night shift works through until relieved by the day shift at 0800hrs. They then go and have their breakfast and return to do another four hours' work. Then they are free until 0800hrs two days later. It is not a standard RAF operating procedure, but it suits you all.

Life at the dispersal is a happy one. You rarely come across any aggro. Arguments, yes, but never fisticuffs. If you get chance to relieve the night shift early, you take it and they will love you for it. The lads will work all hours to get those aircraft off the ground on ops. The airmen are not allowed in the SNCOs' mess, so you all meet at a local pub. You have to find the one with the most beer, for while there are plenty of spirits, beer is in short supply. You have rules about what you can/cannot discuss: politics, religion and work are all off limits.

＊ ＊ ＊ ＊ ＊

You're being debriefed, and the WAAF officer on duty asks whether you want your hot drink 'with or without?' It's a lovely touch on your squadron, since there is a ready supply of rum. Then it's off to bed, unless it's your day off, in which case you can push off, providing you're back by 0900hrs the next morning. There are no excuses for being late. Perhaps the next operation will be scrubbed anyway, and there'll be a spontaneous party in the mess. You have an infinite capacity for enjoyment whenever the opportunity presents itself.

Chapter 13

Special Operations – 'Not Even a Rowboat was Allowed to Risk the Passage'

In 1938, the anonymous authors of the world's most famous encyclopaedia wrote that the Kiel Canal was 'the safest, most convenient, shortest and cheapest route from the North Sea to the Baltic'.[1] Both the British and the Germans understood its military importance as a supply route and it was a convenient short-cut for German warships to be released into the North Sea without being obliged to navigate a 250-mile voyage around the Jutland peninsula.

Opened in 1895 as the Kaiser Wilhelm Kanal, the 53-nautical mile waterway ran from Brunsbüttelkoog at the mouth of the river Elbe to Kiel-Holtenhau in Kiel Harbour and was described on its completion as one of the most outstanding achievements of modern Germany.[2] Certainly it represented a strategic threat; no less a vessel than the world's most powerful battleship at that time, the *Bismarck*, had passed through the canal on its way to sea trials in the Baltic after leaving the Blohm und Voss shipyard in Hamburg.[3]

As soon as war was declared, the canal was under near-constant observation from RAF reconnaissance aircraft, and within 24 hours, a small group of Wellington bombers had attacked shipping at Brunsbüttel, with little or no effect. Further attacks were made throughout 1941, not only on shipping but also on the oil storage facilities at either end of the canal, but only limited damage was reported, and a number of RAF aircraft were lost.

It was not until the spring of 1944 that the Kiel Canal once again became a focus for a planned attack. This time, the objective to block the canal was the same but the tactics were different. Rather than attacking and sinking ships directly, the aircraft would drop mines that should, in theory, do the job for them. And responsibility for the attack was given to Steve Watts, a wing commander with the LNSF.

Watts, a doughty New Zealander, had flown a tour of operations in the winter of 1941/42 with 77 Squadron from RAF Leeming when his CO had been none other than Don Bennett, then a wing commander. Watts' tour with 4 Group was not without excitement. On an attack on Wilhelmshaven on the night of 27/28 February 1942, his aircraft was hit by flak. It limped back to Leeming, landing shortly after midnight. Happily, no one was hurt.

Almost two years later, on 1 April 1944, he'd taken over command of 692 Squadron at Graveley from Guy Lockhart. Watts was summoned to see the AOC and was shocked to find his former squadron commander looking much older and thinner than the last time they'd seen each other at Leeming.[4] The strain of four long years of war was beginning to tell. He wondered if he himself would age as Bennett had done, with the tremendous responsibility now being placed upon him. He was determined not to let the side down.

Not that Watts had done anything but his level best throughout his operational career. Six weeks earlier, on 23 February, Watts had claimed plaudits for becoming the first Mosquito pilot to drop a 4,000lb cookie on an enemy target, beating his close friend and fellow Kiwi Val Moore[5] to the prize by a mere 60 seconds. No doubt Bennett had been pleased for his protégé and even more delighted with the performance of the Wooden Wonder. Throughout the flight, Watts had been amazed at how the Mosquito had handled, and how it had climbed easily to 25,000ft in 25 minutes.[6]

The significance of such an achievement is best explained by the story of the visit to Pathfinder Headquarters by an influential American journalist from the *New York Herald Tribune*, Mrs Helen Rogers Reid. Accompanied by Bennett to see a Mosquito take off for a raid on Berlin, she asked how many bombs it could carry. When Bennett replied that it was carrying a 4,000-pounder she did not appear particularly impressed. Bennett, never one to shirk from an opportunity of embarrassing a guest, compared the performance of the Mosquito to the much-promoted B-17 Flying Fortress: 'At present, with the routing which they use and with the larger load of ammunition necessary for daylight operations, they are carrying 3,500lb.' He added, 'In any case, they cannot carry a Blockbuster as it is too big for their bomb bays.' Mrs Reid looked serious. 'I only hope,' she replied, 'that the American public never realises those facts.'[7]

The first week of May had been taken up with a series of attacks by the squadron on the chemical works at Leverkusen and Ludwigshafen and on 9 May 1944 they went to Berlin. On the 10th, Val Moore chalked up his 100th operation and with it the end of a remarkable third tour. A great party in the mess was followed, mercifully, by a stand-down the next day, which Watts spent on the golf course with his great pal John 'Sandy' Saunderson, one of the flight commanders.

Watts had wind that a special operation was in the offing and an early morning phone call on 12 May from the AOC confirmed his suspicions that the operation that night was to be a radical departure from the norm. As was the case with all such secret trips, the squadron was not immediately told the target, nor was the RAF public relations department informed that anything was afoot, rather the crews were to spend the morning practising low flying. More specifically, they were to practise losing height from 10,000ft to 300ft over a 13-mile track, finishing their descents over the Great Ouse river. In the afternoon they practised again, by which time a rumour had gone around that it was a suicide job, and some were beginning to get the jitters.[8] Even Graveley's station commander, 'Paddy' Menaul, a man not prone to exaggeration or unnecessary emotion, was concerned.

At 1730hrs a staff car arrived, and the AOC stepped out to be greeted by a somewhat anxious wing commander. The job, Watts was told, was a simple 'gardening' trip to lay mines. The mines themselves were known as 'vegetables'. The target was the Kiel Canal. That explained the low-level flying over water, albeit the canal was a very different prospect to the Great Ouse, and they would be over enemy territory and vulnerable to flak. The canal was known to be defended by 25 searchlights and almost four times as many guns. The intelligence bods had thought of that, however, and identified a three-mile stretch of the canal that they assured would be undefended, or at least not as heavily defended as it might otherwise have been. The armaments boys had also done their thinking: rather than the standard mine, they'd developed their own 'special' device that could be fitted into a Mosquito bomb bay, and they were not to be wasted.

In all, 13 crews were listed on the battle order, including both squadron and flight commanders. Some spent the rest of the day writing letters home and looking a serious,[9] with justifiable cause. Take-off was scheduled for 0155hrs and the crews retired in the early evening to be woken again not long before midnight. Few were able to get much sleep, and most were kept awake, thinking about the job in hand. A pre-op meal was followed by a final briefing. As well as merchant vessels, it was said the canal was being used to transport vital heavy submarine parts from the east to Wilhelmshaven, Bremen and Hamburg in the west, and the canal was also being used by the submarines themselves. There was talk that enemy E-boats were also being kept out of harm's way in the Baltic but could rapidly be out into the North Sea and down into the Channel where they could play havoc with a potential invasion fleet. All in all, and for whatever the reason, the canal had to be blocked.

The crews took a final opportunity to pour over every map and photograph of the area and possible gun positions, which had been kindly provided by the intelligence section. A 'brown job' (army officer) was there to advise on flak. Not all the crews were happy. Terry Goodwin, a former NCO bomber captain, was concerned that the attack should take place at almanac dawn; to a night bomber, he said, this was 'like being in Piccadilly with your pants down'.[10]

Watts calculated it would take slightly less than three minutes to make the descent from 10,000ft to 300ft and felt reassured. He was also reassured that a 'spoof' raid was being made at the mouth of the Elbe to occupy any potential night fighters in the area and give them a clear run. He was further pleased that fellow Mosquitoes from 139 (Jamaica) Squadron would drop route markers at the appropriate turning point and then further red spot flares at the beginning of the final run-in to the target. The squadron was to be split into two waves: the first wave would attack with only the light of the moon to guide them; the second wave would have the help of further flares dropped by the markers.

The recently appointed wing commander was the first to get away, bang on the allotted time. Within the space of 13 minutes, all the aircraft were safely off the ground and disappearing into the gloom. Climbing to 8,000ft in the bright moonlight, and with only a slight wind, the navigators set course for a route that would take them to the north of Heligoland. They would then turn south-east to the point where they would start their final run. For once they were able to get a decent Gee fix to keep them on track. The marker boys from 139 Squadron played their part, dropping green Very cartridges at the first turning point, though one crew failed to spot them and went slightly off track.

Watts was unaware and as he reached the coast, he was happy that everything was going according to plan. As he began his descent, he and his navigator could clearly see the river off to the port side of their aircraft as they started their run, the Mosquito picking up speed in its shallow dive. There may not have been any flak, but they had been warned to also look out for barrage balloons covering a bridge not far from the release point, and Watts was determined not to get caught out.

Then he saw it, the canal itself, glinting in the moonlight. Sleepy cottages flashed by beneath them, whisps of smoke drifting from chimneys, a peace soon to be shattered by war and the roar of 26 Rolls-Royce Merlins screaming in to attack. In the cockpit of Mosquito DZ599, everything was deathly quiet, the eyes of the pilot and his navigator, Cyril Hassall, firmly focused on the target ahead and the dials that showed their exact height and speed. At 300ft and travelling at 200kts, the first of the mines was successfully released, Watts banking sharply to port just as a stream of tracer zipped over his tail. So much for this part of the canal being undefended, he thought. Hassall thought the same: 'All hell seemed to break loose,' he said afterwards.[11]

Then he was away, just as the whole countryside appeared to light up with flares as the second wave came in to attack before the first wave had fully completed its run.

Ian MacDonald in DZ649 levelled off a little below 300ft and raced across the now illuminated countryside, cursing the markers but amused to see someone below in their pyjamas – a farmer, perhaps, or a German soldier – desperately trying to extinguish one of the flares. Concerned he had overshot the canal, and doubtful of the forecasted winds, the Australian was all for turning around, but his navigator, Ted Chatfield, said otherwise and assured him the canal was straight ahead. He was right. Directly in front of them lay the expanse of the canal, with a number of ships moored nose to tail.[12]

Within the space of seven minutes, six mines were successfully laid, most without opposition, the first going down at 0348hrs. At least one of their number had to make two runs to be sure. More mines went down over the next 20 minutes until the last was recorded at 0415hrs. Two of the crews in the second wave had a few problems with their approaches – one on account of having crossed the coast north of the correct point and failing to spot the markers. Undeterred, they map read cross-country, though had some trouble finding the canal.

The last of the aircraft, flown by Sandy Saunderson and his navigator, Richard Clarkson, encountered more than a little light flak from both sides of the canal, firing at them at near point-blank range. They had to make four attempts before they could be sure of a successful drop.[13] At first, they overshot the target and were in danger of running into the balloon barrage but Saunderson realised his mistake just in time and executed the steepest of steep turns before any harm was done. At last, they located the canal and dropped their mine, opened up the taps and headed for home, skimming the deck until they reached the coast when they, again, climbed sharply out to sea in time for the coming dawn that was already breaking in the sky.

The CO was among the first to make it home, landing at 0530hrs, fully relieved to have made it back in one piece. He was even more relieved when, over the course of the next half an hour, 11 more Mosquitoes landed and taxied to the dispersal. Terry Goodwin and his navigator, Hugh Hay (Hay was on his third tour), were the last to land at 0606hrs, their engines falling silent just short of four hours after leaving Graveley.

The excited chatter at the debrief suggested a highly successful operation. Of the 13 crews taking part, 11 reported they had dropped their mines fair and square in the canal;[14] one crew failed to find the target, on account of their windscreen misting up and being covered in glycol, and had brought their mine home as instructed. One of their number, Canadian David Burnett, and his navigator, George Hume, were missing; nothing had been heard or seen of their aircraft since take-off. Later it was learned their Mosquito had crashed and broken apart. Given that Steve Watts feared he might lose anything up to three-quarters of his force, they had emerged remarkably unscathed.[15] Indeed it was said that, just prior to take off, Bennett had remarked, 'Well good luck, Steve. If you pull it off, you should be in line for a VC.'[16]

As the only squadron operating that night, the AOC, his SASO, the group intelligence officer and the station commander were all at debriefing to welcome the boys home and congratulate them on their success. It was a tired but elated squadron commander who flopped into bed two hours later.

The parallel with other special operations was not lost on Bennett. He justifiably held the operation up as a shining example of the spirit and intensity with which the LNSF approached operations without the fuss and bother to which some others of Bomber Command were prone. Neither did it require an intense period of training. He bemoaned, however, that the raid did not receive the recognition it deserved. He claimed the episode was not mentioned to the British public, neither were any awards or recognition given in relation to it.[17]

It is in such comments that Bennett lets his obvious dislike of Cochrane and 5 Group get in the way of better judgement and the truth. Steve Watts, in his diary, recorded that he was called the next day and told to put up ten of his officers for awards. He was also told that both he and Sandy Saunderson were to be recommended for an immediate DSO. The success of the operation was also widely publicised in the press, albeit many weeks after the events they described. That is not unusual. A report in *The Times* heaped praise on the bravery and skill of the crews involved and gave credit to the careful planning and preparation essential to the raid's success. It talked about the mines being specially adapted for the purpose and how through 'perfect navigation there can be no doubt that the mines were laid right in the middle of the canal'.[18]

Of the success of the attack, accounts differ, though most appear to agree that the canal was closed for at least seven days and only partially re-opened thereafter for a further week. *The Times* estimated that at a critical time, when it was important to block every possible route for German supplies (remembering the attack took place three weeks prior to D-Day, the invasion of Europe), approximately one million metric tons of cargo was held up – cargo that included iron ore from Sweden, coal with which to pay for the ore and military supplies to Norway. And all this achieved by a single Mosquito squadron.

A contemporary *Daily Telegraph* report quoted one of its special correspondents and an interview with a deckhand on a German freighter: 'Not even a rowboat was allowed to risk the passage of the canal from 13 May to the evening of 19 May when the ban was lifted… Shipping was piled higgledy-piggledy at both sides; there were about 70 of us lying at Brunsbüttel and probably the same number at Kiel.'

John Page, a student who enlisted at the age of 18, had flown ops with three previous squadrons and skippered Hampdens and Halifaxes prior to joining 692, was one of those to receive the DFC, along with his navigator, Sidney Ainsworth. He was in no doubt of the raid's success: it was the only raid out of 71 where he was absolutely certain that he got the target![19]

* * * * *

The attack in the early hours of 13 May was not the only special trip by the LNSF on the Kiel Canal. They went again on the night of 5 October, a small force of nine Mosquitoes from 692 and 571 Squadrons. It was an operation that lived long in the memory of the OC 571, Jerry Gosnell.[20] He had only been with the squadron a few days when he was called upon to lead this special op: 'I was lucky and came home unscathed, but "Johnnie" Greenleaf was wounded and his navigator killed beside him by a direct hit from a 37mm light AA shell that shattered the Perspex and filled Greenleaf's face and eyes with splinters. He did well to fly home and land successfully on the emergency runway at Woodbridge with no instruments.'

Gosnell's recollection tells only half the story.[21] Greenleaf had just released his mine when the flak shell exploded, killing his navigator outright and severely wounding the pilot in the face and arm, such that he could only fly one handed. It was in this condition, without navigation aids or his erstwhile crew member to guide him, that he limped the 400 miles home to Woodbridge. Greenleaf, a former Halton apprentice who later joined PFF HQ staff in the closing stages of the war, was awarded an immediate DSO, as he was the raid leader. Goswell had the melancholy duty of attending the navigator's funeral and meeting the grieving parents. The raid closed the canal for several weeks.

* * * * *

As special operations go, Bennett had one more 'spectacular' up his sleeve and, once again, it was in direct support of land forces at a critical point in the war.

When German panzers and elite troops broke through the Ardennes one winter morning in December 1944, the Allies were taken completely by surprise and were soon in full retreat. For a few brief weeks, the Allies' complacency was rocked to its very foundation as a serious bulge appeared in its lines that would ultimately give the battle its name. German forces were helped, and the Allies hindered, by the weather, which momentarily negated the RAF's and USAAF's air superiority.

But whereas the weather on the battlefront enabled the German divisions to advance unmolested from the skies, the planners turned their attention to other targets that would directly support their troops on the ground by stopping the flow of men and materiel to the front line. Railway marshalling yards were pinpointed, and attacked, and as a new year dawned, another new target was found, and another special operation was briefed. In much the same way as the movement of shipping could be halted by dropping mines in the canal, railway engines could be stopped dead in their tracks by blocking the tunnels through which they must pass.

Aircraft from three squadrons were detailed for the attack: 128 Squadron put up six crews on the battle order; 571 mustered four; and 692 a further six, with take-off set for the early hours of New Year's Day. Tommy Broom[22] of 128 was merrily downing pints at the New Year's Eve mess party when his skipper, Ivor Broom,[23] tapped him on the shoulder and suggested an early night. Tommy agreed but sneaked in a couple or three more before finally retiring to bed.[24] It was as well that he did, for the attack would require all his skills in navigation to find and destroy the target – one of 15 tunnels nestling in the woods and hills of the Eifel, between the Rhine and the Ardennes battle area.

The method of attack was brutal in its simplicity: Mosquitoes would approach at very low level along the length of the railway track and 'skip' a bomb into the tunnel entrance. Rather than a 'standard' 4,000lb cookie, a more 'traditional' bomb was loaded with a thinner casing and timed to explode 11 seconds after being dropped, to ensure the aircraft was clear of the blast area.

The raid did not get off to an auspicious start. As the first Mosquito roared down the 2,000-yard runway at Wyton, with Leo Wellstead[25] at the controls, a connecting rod in the port engine fractured, causing the Merlin to seize.[26] Both Wellstead and his navigator, George Mullan,[27] were killed in the subsequent crash and fire that resulted. Mercifully, the five remaining aircraft got off the ground without mishap and set course for Belgium. Among them were the 'Flying Brooms', as they were known, and the squadron CO, Richard Burrough, with his experienced navigator, Ernest Saunders.

A similar scene was being played out at Oakington, home to 571 Squadron. Bill Ball, navigator to Norman 'Griff' Griffiths, was keen to get going. They'd been shaken by their batman at 0430hrs and, after briefing, spent a considerable amount of time studying the route, paying particular attention to the height and contours of the surrounding area.[28] There was little margin for error at 50ft.

It was cold and dark, with a thick frost on the ground, as they made their way out to their aircraft. It was a crisp, clear morning, free from the mist and fog that had restricted flying for the last few nights. One of the first to take off, shortly after 0700hrs, Bill set course for Orford Ness. As they crossed the English coast at 5,000ft, daylight was just coming up on the eastern horizon.

At Graveley, Frederick Hill of 692 Squadron had thought it strange when he'd been sent off to the bombing range to practise low flying 24 hour earlier. No explanations had been given, but he knew that, whatever the target, they would be attacking at first light.[29]

In the cockpit of Mosquito MM220, Tommy Broom expertly navigated his pilot to their target, the Kaiserslautern tunnel, and while they were untroubled by flak, they both kept a keen eye out for any telegraph poles or similar obstacles that could spell disaster. The pilot decided to attack from east to west, so if they should be attacked, they were pointing in the right direction for home! Just as they turned in for the attack, they had the tremendous luck of seeing a goods train enter the tunnel, with its clear white smoke from the engine rising up into the sharp winter's morning air. It was the pilot, rather than the navigator, who pressed the bomb release in such instances and Ivor Broom was delighted to see the bomb skip into the tunnel entrance. It was with even greater pleasure that they saw the bomb explode a few short moments later. Looking around for enemy fighters and confident they were alone, Ivor circled back to see black smoke billowing from the tunnel's mouth. A camera fitted to the aircraft for the purpose turned over to capture the scene as they sped away at low level, hedge hopping their way to the coast.[30]

Bill Ball and Griff Griffiths, meanwhile, were having similar success. At Charleville, they found themselves in bright sunshine as they cruised across the countryside at 500ft, keeping a watchful eye out for enemy fighters. Despite concentrating hard, Bill still had time to notice the tiny villages huddled around a church in the wooded country of the Ardennes. The rooftops of the houses and chalets were covered in snow. They raced on at 300mph, lower and lower, and swept over a high railway/road bridge with only feet to spare. An old man driving his horse and cart below them had kittens when he saw the RAF roundels on the Mosquito racing straight for him. He dived head-first over the side of the cart, doubtless convinced that his number was up.

From the big railway junction, dead on the ETA, the tunnel came up in a flash and they overshot. Calmly, Griffiths went round again, and this time ran up, dead in line, astonished that the ack-ack batteries had not been alerted. Rapidly, they reached the target, dropped the bomb and soared up, almost vertically, to get away from the blast. As they gained height, they looked back and saw a column of brown-black smoke amid sizeable debris rumbling upwards – a mixture of bricks, shattered masonry and jagged keystone, rising, falling and scattering. Both agreed it would be some time before that tunnel would ever be used again. They headed for home, hurried on their way by some heavy flak.[31]

Frederick Hill's flight out had been momentarily interrupted by the sight of another aircraft on a convergent course – though this 'aircraft' turned out to be a V1 flying bomb. Hill had neither the time nor the equipment (the bomber version of the Mosquito had no canon or machine guns) to deal with it, and he wondered what misery the weapon would go on to cause. Some of his squadron had been briefed to attack their designated targets in pairs, and Hill and his navigator, Jack Simkin, had been 'teamed' with Geoffrey Crow and his nav, Charles Earl. All went well and the target was easily found and identified. As Crow finished his run at one end of the track, he noted a large flash under the port wing, and thick smoke was seen wafting from the tunnel entrance. Hill came next and, as he approached, he had the fright of his life as he stared down at a machine-gun post on the embankment directly beneath them. Luckily it wasn't manned, either that or the crew were asleep. Either way, he was able to make his run unmolested, and similarly had the satisfaction of seeing his bomb explode and smoke now pouring from either end of the tunnel. Still a good distance inside enemy territory, and further from home, Hill climbed to 5,000ft and put on maximum speed until they were over the front line and in comparative safety. Usually, they would have the comfort of the dark, and it was an odd sensation to be operating in daylight.[32]

Bennett was at Graveley to welcome the 692 Squadron crews home and was delighted to hear the raid had been a complete success. Robert Wadsworth, a squadron leader who'd been tasked with blowing up the Mayen tunnel, dropped his bomb from 100ft at one end and saw it explode at the other, palls of black smoke and dirt rising into the air. One of the 692 crews was missing, however, and George Nairn and his navigator, Daniel Lunn, were posted missing. Both were, in fact, dead. The first aircraft of their pair (flown by Cyril Burbridge) had made a good run and a successful attack, but in doing so had woken up the defences who were now intent on revenge. As Nairn sped down, he was caught in withering crossfire from four or five different flak positions, setting both engines on fire. The Mosquito crashed almost immediately, giving pilot and navigator no chance to bale out.

At Oakington, there was jubilation at a job well done and much excited chatter at the debriefing. Douglas Tucker was particularly pleased to have seen the roof of his tunnel erupt and all but cave in. It had taken him three runs to achieve the perfect result. Hugh Dawlish was similarly pleased, having sped for home leaving a column of brown smoke in his wake.[33]

At Wyton, the squadron CO, Burroughs, saw his bomb clearly strike the top corner of the tunnel entrance and explode; similar successes were claimed by all the remaining crews. Archibald Robinson had seen the end of his tunnel collapsing, enveloped in dusk and smoke. In his opinion, the bomb had gone right up the spout – a claim also made by Allan Heitman.

In keeping with the other 'special' operations, a number of 'immediate' gallantry awards were forthcoming. These included a DSO for Ernest Saunders of 128 and Robert Wadsworth of 692, a second bar and a bar to the DFC respectively for Ivor Broom and Tommy Broom. Ten other DFCs were awarded and a single DFM to Flight Sergeant Ian Ramage, navigator to Cyril Burbridge. A group citation was issued describing the 'difficult and dangerous' operation as requiring 'a high degree of skill'.[34]

In any operation, there is an element of luck in terms of who lives and who dies. When Ivor Broom was invited to join the AOC later that day for dinner, he was shown a photograph of the attack – a photograph taken from Broom's aircraft. The photograph had been interpreted by experts and confirmed that Broom's bomb had indeed been right on the money. Bennett also pointed out two specks in the background of the print – specks that the photographic interpreters had confirmed as two Focke-Wulf Fw 190 fighters.[35] It seemed the Flying Brooms had not been alone after all.

Perhaps even luckier had been a man who had not flown on the raid, Derek Smith.[36] His name and the name of his skipper had been on the battle order for the attack. However, prior to briefing, their place was taken by a more experienced captain, George Nairn, who had just returned from leave.[37] Such are the fates.

Chapter 14

Towards Annihilation

In the small city of St Vith on the eastern border of Belgium, the local inhabitants had become used to the ebb and flow of war and looked forward to the end of the conflict that had caused so much destruction around them. With the winter of 1944 and the approach of the Allied armies, it seemed that peace had come at last, and they might escape some of the devastation that had befallen similar cities caught up in the maelstrom of war. Unfortunately for the 2,000 people of St Vith, their city was strategically important to both Allied and German armies alike. It was the site of a vital road junction and situated close to an area known as the Losheim Gap, a critical valley through the densely forested ridges of the Ardennes. It was also to be the axis of a massive German counter-offensive to drive the Allies back to the coast and recapture the port of Antwerp. The codeword for the attack was *Wacht am Rhein* – Operation *Watch on the Rhine* – from a patriotic German song designed to inspire those taking part. More commonly, it is known as the Battle of the Bulge.

The attack began in the freezing early hours of 16 December 1944, catching the Allied commanders almost completely unawares. One of Bennett's Oboe controllers, now on mainland Europe and close to the action, telephoned his boss to say the Germans were on the move, and they'd had to retreat post-haste. Bennett informed his superiors; none appeared interested.[1]

St Vith was an early objective of the German's 5th Panzer Army, but stubborn resistance by US troops kept the Germans at bay for a full five days, and the American defenders only fell back when ordered to do so on 21 December, and only then reluctantly. The doughty defence offered by the infantry and armoured divisions of the US VIII Corps under General Bruce Clarke seriously disrupted the German's timetable, ultimately contributing to its failure. German troops poured into the town and began looting US supplies, but their presence partially blocked the flow of men and armour to feed the advance, and the initial satisfaction of taking the city fast turned into doubt over its real significance – by now the inclement weather, which had been on the side of the attackers, began to improve and the thick fog that had covered much of the German's advance began to drift away.

Until that moment, the PFF's only significant contribution to the battle had been to attack railway marshalling yards to the rear around Cologne and hamper the resupply of the German panzers. One, on the marshalling yards at Cologne-Gremberg, had been an all-8 Group affair comprising 27 Lancasters and three Mosquitoes in a heavy Oboe in daylight. While the marking was a success, the raid went very badly on account of very accurately predicted flak, clear blue skies and the chance arrival of a squadron of expert German fighter pilots who stumbled upon the raid by accident, having failed to intercept a force of American bombers. The aircraft should have scattered but many didn't and held formation. Six of the Pathfinders were shot down in the melee, including one flown by Bob Palmer, a squadron leader, who was subsequently awarded the VC for 'heroic endeavour beyond praise'. It was his 110th bomber operation.

Now, at last, the Allied air forces, and PFF in particular, were able to attack the German troops more directly.

The Americans started first with an attack by B-26 Marauders on Christmas Day, with the tactic of 'putting the city into the street' – effectively filling the roads with rubble so the German supply convoys could not get through.[2] Then it was Bomber Command's turn, and an opportunity for the Pathfinders – who, by now, were at the height of their powers – to demonstrate just how great their skills had become.[3]

The inhabitants of St Vith were still cowering in their cellars when the first of 12 Oboe Mosquitoes from 109 and 105 Squadrons commenced their attack in the early afternoon. It had not been a happy Christmas in St Vith, and Boxing Day looked to be heading much the same way. Even from 22,000ft, Tony Farrell had a clear view of the city beneath him as he dropped the first of his target indicators dead on time and with remarkable precision. Tony had only recently returned to 105 Squadron from 692 Squadron, and this was one of his first Oboe operations.[4] (Later he would visit one of the Oboe ground tracking stations at Kingsdown and watch a raid from a different viewpoint. It gave him more respect for the hard work and technical ingenuity of the Oboe controllers.) Five more from the Oboe force also successfully attacked the primary throughout the course of the raid while the master bomber – Tubby Baker with the callsign 'Plato' – confirmed the accuracy of the marking and instructed Main Force to aim for the centre of the red and green TIs that lay directly on top of the aiming point.

Tubby was happy that he could see the target so clearly, sticking out like a sore thumb in the snow-covered landscape.[5] He was annoyed, however, that some of Main Force had already started to bomb before being ordered to do so. He swiftly took charge and kept the bombing concentrated and well under control throughout the attack, even as the markers began to become obscured by huge columns of smoke and dust rising many thousands of feet into the air. Emile Mange, the longstop – a 'master' master bomber and present to prevent any bombs falling too close to the Allied positions that lay ten miles to the north – was not obliged to interfere and the young flight commander was most satisfied with the result.[6]

Almost 300 aircraft from every group in Bomber Command (except 100 Group) including 12 PFF from 635 and 35 Squadrons dropped some 1,140 tons of heavy explosives and incendiaries in the raid and only three of their number were lost. An escort of Spitfires and Mustangs were there to keep the German fighters at bay, and the only real danger was flak. What looked like a successful attack from the air was even more devastatingly obvious on the ground. The blast effect created shockwaves that could be felt in villages several kilometres away, terrorising the local people, consumed as they were with the asphyxiating smoke and soot. It prompted one German soldier to write, 'The whole countryside is covered by one big cloud of smoke and fire.'[7]

The raid is little talked about in reference books and warrants only a few lines in the *Bomber Command War Diaries*. Bennett may have felt similarly disenfranchised a few days later when his men laid on something of a 'spectacular' of their own, bombing a series of railway tunnels with extreme precision to prevent further German reinforcements from being rushed to the front. Bennett describes the attack on St Vith as a major contributing factor in finally bringing a halt to the German's Ardennes offensive. It was a vital choke point – impossible to go from east to west without passing through it – and therefore of vital importance in bringing supplies to the German spearhead. After the attack, according to first-hand reports received at Bennett's headquarters by his own Oboe controllers who were now well-established on the continent, the German tanks had to dig themselves in at the tip of the spearhead and try and fight without any fuel and with little ammunition.[8] The heavy support to the army, he wrote later, was one of the things he thought was seldom appreciated and yet of vital importance. If the attack on St Vith is anything to go by, he was right. Thanks to the accuracy of the marking, and the bombing of Main Force controlled by a highly skilled master bomber, all roads in and out of St Vith were blocked for three days and some for as long as a week, while German engineers were obliged to construct bypasses around the town. The cost to civilian life was indeed high – perhaps as many as 250 according to some reports[9] – but in purely military terms, the raid was a success.

The attack on St Vith was one of several in which the skill and accuracy of the Pathfinders was called upon to support ground operations following the break-out from Normandy and in the latter stages of the war. The strategy of the Allied advance had meant certain pockets of German resistance – for examples those in Boulogne, Calais and Le Havre – were ignored in the short term to be dealt with at a later date. An all-out assault on a strongly fortified position was not an attractive proposition, at least not without softening up the defences first. Seven daylight attacks mounted by PFF and Bomber Command on Le Havre in the first and second weeks of September caused such destruction that the German commander, a bank director in civilian life, cashed up and surrendered within 24 hours of the last bomb falling. One of his subordinates was later to testify that nothing, even in Russia, had been so unnerving as the bombing of their positions.[10] The Allied bombing of Boulogne prompted a similar response, the German garrison surrendering soon after a massive attack on 17 September, in which more than 3,000 tons of bombs were dropped on German positions. 'Can anyone,' a German soldier wrote afterwards, 'survive after a carpet of bombs has fallen?'[11]

Calais was the next on the list and quickly went the same way. Thus, before the month of September was out, the RAF had played a prominent part in the extensive mopping up of operations carried out along the French coast. The Pathfinder aircrews' experiences of such raids tended to focus not so much on the dangers, but more on the spectacles. Some of the attacks were made from heights of 3,000ft or less, and on one raid in particular, a PFF navigator in a master bomber aircraft recalled almost coming face to face with a German gunner perched on a hill: 'We were below 2,000ft and he was on top of a hill less than 500ft away. He couldn't miss. We had so many hits to the main spar that the wings started to droop.'[12] A similar fate befell 'Howie' Morrison, a wing commander with 405 Squadron: he was controlling the third of five aiming points at Le Havre on 8 September and was on his fourth run over the target when he was hit by light flak and his aircraft shot down. Happily, he evaded capture and returned to eventually take command of the squadron.[13]

The Main Force in such attacks, as at St Vith, did not always do as it was told, a cause of constant frustration to the PFF master bomber who faced dangers enough without having to spend any more time over the target area than was strictly necessary. The master bombers were clearly being stretched, as evidenced by the attacks on Le Havre and Boulogne, which invariably involved multiple aiming points.

A case in point was an attack on Calais on 24 September, a relatively small affair comprising a high number (25) of Mosquitoes to mark five aiming points, requiring a master bomber, deputy master bomber and backers-up on *each*. On one of these aiming points, the Lancaster of the master bomber, Douglas Murray of 35 Squadron, was hit by light flak, sustaining damage to his starboard outer, which began to vibrate alarmingly. The vibrations became so bad that Murray was forced to hand over to his deputy, Roy Roberts. On his run-up to the target, Roberts' aircraft was also hit in the nose, and he too was forced to pass the baton to the next in command, Sven Hausvik, one of the squadron's Norwegian pilots and the son of a wealthy shipping owner. Since bad luck always comes in threes, Hausvik's aircraft was also hit, losing one engine on his first run over the target and a second on his return visit. It is a testimony both to the strength of the Lancaster, and the skill of a PFF pilot, that both managed to make it home in one piece. Seven aircraft were shot down that afternoon, and it might have been many more. Among the missing and the dead was the longstop, Ken Doyle of 156 Squadron.

The increasingly low-level nature of attacks in support of ground operations exposed PFF to even greater dangers. Another master bomber, Charles Palmer, OC 405 Squadron, was shot down on 26 September, and the CO of 7 Squadron, Reg Cox, was lucky not to go the same way when his aircraft was hit and badly damaged on the same day.

One of the most spectacular attacks during this period was against the sea wall at Westkapelle, the most western point of the island of Walcheren. Walcheren held the key to the effective use of the port of Antwerp, which, in turn, held the key to the Allies' success in northern Europe. Antwerp could handle more than 40,000 tons per day of urgently needed supplies, assuming the cargo vessels could negotiate the heavy coastal batteries on Walcheren that threatened to sink them. The navy called in the RAF, and the RAF called in the Pathfinders.

The plan was for an attack by eight waves of bombers, with 30 aircraft in each wave. Initial marking was by Mosquitoes, with the crews of Peter Cribb, Dickie Walbourn, Gerry O'Donovan and Bill Spooner – possibly the four most expert of all experts on 582 Squadron at that time – in charge of the show. Cribb was master bomber.

The attack started well, the first TIs going down on time and a succession of 1,000 and 4,000-pounders hitting the target over the course of a two-hour period, causing a breach 100-yards across. The seawater came flooding in as many of the German defenders became flooded out. Eight Lancasters of 617 Squadron, the Dambusters, had been on standby, circling off the coast with their massive 12,000lb Tallboy bombs, but the Pathfinders – with whom there was an intense rivalry – had tremendous pleasure in telling them their 'special' weapons would not be needed. As Ted Stocker, flight engineer in the master bomber aircraft later recounted, it was one up for the Pathfinders![14]

Some in Bomber Command, Harris being among them, were becoming frustrated with the perceived lack of urgency by ground commanders in exploiting the many advantages that he believed his men had secured, often at considerable cost. It was a view that Bennett was inclined to share. But such views did not endear them to their peers. When ordered to attack Walcheren, Harris reportedly told the generals at SHAEF that when the bombing was over, 'I shall send my batman to occupy the island.' In the event, it proved to be one of the harder fought battles of the war.

As a man of action, Bennett respected action in others. He admired Montgomery's audacious *Market Garden* plan to smash through into Germany by capturing a series of bridges, describing the famous British general as 'a soldier of far more brilliance than any of the Americans'.[15] A little matter of the weather, and the presence of a whole unit of German panzers refitting in the area, did for the brave Red Berets holding out on the bridge at Arnhem and surrounding town against impossible odds. Because of thick fog over the target, desperately needed supplies were not getting through to the troops. Bennett pleaded with Harris' deputy, Saundby, to be allowed to intercede and use Oboe to drop supplies 'blind', but he was continually denied. 'I do not know whether Bomber Command ever offered our services to the Army, but whether they did or not, it was a deplorable thing that we were not allowed to help.' Bennett felt sure that a timely drop of anti-tank weapons and additional ammunition may have made all the difference: 'The gallantry of our troops was magnificent; the support from behind was pathetic.'[16]

Besides the support given to the army, one other target dominated in the last few months of 1944, in a period described in the history books[17] as 'the sunset over the Reich': oil.

Harris had, of course, objected to bombing yet another 'panacea' target but was left with no choice, and Bennett was obliged to follow. In the official directive published in the equally official *Official History*, a clear first priority was given to destroying the enemy's petroleum industry, with particular emphasis on petrol, including storage. Rail transportation, tank production and motor vehicle production ranked close behind. Harris firmly believed his force would be better directed attacking German cities and the Nazi's industrial might, and said so forcibly, challenging his commander to sack him. Of course, no such event unfolded; Harris had called the Chief of the Air Staff's bluff.

Pathfinders had no love for targets involving oil. They were dangerous places to hang around – heavily defended with the latest weaponry and industrial smoke screens. Wanne-Eickel, Castrop-Rauxel, Bottrop, Scholven and Sterkrade became names to respect and even fear.

The Germans did everything they could to defend their oil production and storage facilities, moving badly needed guns from other areas including Berlin and the Ruhr. By way of example, Leuna, a district where the Germans also made fixed nitrogen, explosives and synthetic rubber – all of which were dependent on oil, was protected by no fewer than 374 guns. These numbers were continuously strengthened throughout the summer months of 1944, such that the number of heavy guns defending Leuna eventually exceeded 460 but left many cities – Dresden included – virtually undefended.

John Smith remembers Castrop as 'a real stinker' and with good reason. 'As the nav said ten minutes to go, all I could see was a thick layer of flak and thought we would never get through it. We were hit several times in the fuselage, tail plane and port wing, and I could hear [the shrapnel] rattling around like peas in a tin.'[18]

A raid on Castrop-Rauxel in the late afternoon/early evening of 11 September serves to illustrate the dangers involved. Three synthetic oil plants were targeted – Castrop-Rauxel, Kamen and Gelsenkirchen (Nordstern) – with the attack on Castrop-Rauxel being led by a force of 16 heavy bombers from 582 Squadron. On the route in and out, they had little-to-no fear, thanks to a huge escort comprising three of the RAF's finest fighters: Spitfires, Mustangs and Tempests. Over the target, however, they faced fierce opposition from the enemy ground defences. In the brilliant sunshine, the German anti-aircraft defences were at the very top of their game.

Dickie Walbourn, the master bomber, was hit by heavy flak in the port wing, starboard wing and port outer engine. Philip Williams, flying to Dickie's stern, had his DR compass damaged by flak, and took hits to the tail plane, with one hole in the starboard inner engine, eight holes in the bomb bay, two holes in the main plane between the starboard inner and outer and five holes in the fuselage. George Hall was hit by heavy flak, causing two small holes in the fuselage, and one small hole in the bomb doors. Graham Nixon was hit by heavy predicted flak in the petrol tank (starboard side) and had his pneumatic pressure line severed. Johnnie Clough was also hit, putting his starboard engine out of action.

Indeed, not a single aircraft or crew from 582 Squadron came through unscathed or without incident. Bob Cairns' Lancaster suffered hits to its starboard wing, while an American pilot, Walt Reif, was hit by heavy flak in both wings, the fuselage, the mid-upper turret and nose. For good measure his hydraulics were also pierced. Jimmy Brown received several small holes in the fuselage, tail plane and port wing. 'Baz' Nathan was similarly hit in the port wing, while another pilot was heavily engaged to such a degree that he had no opportunity of identifying the aiming point visually, so he pottered off and bombed Dortmund (the approved secondary target) instead. Hit by heavy flak, his starboard outer radiator and mid-upper turret Perspex were both damaged. Similarly, Owen Milne took flak in both wings and the fuselage.

Inevitably, there were casualties. One aircraft made it home with damage to its starboard wing, fuselage and bomb doors, and an injured navigator. 'Tiny' Shurlock wasn't so lucky. Tiny, a massive South African, was not in his usual aircraft 'T' Tommy that day, but rather 'N' Nuts, the 'regular' aircraft of their flight commander. Coming in to attack, flak began to explode all around them, and one of the gunners, Haydn 'Taffy' Jacobs, suggested they should weave. Tiny was having none of it, as it would upset their bombing run. In the nose was the flight engineer, Victor 'Davy' Davis, waiting to toggle off the bombs. He was on his 97th trip. Just then they took three direct hits, shattering the front of the aircraft and fatally wounding Davis. Jack Gorman, one of the navigators, went forward to give

As he baled out and his parachute opened, 'Taffy' Jacobs remembers seeing his Lancaster in flames, falling to earth. (via Vera Jacobs in Sean Feast Collection)

first aid but his crewmate died in his arms. The aircraft had been fatally hit, its starboard outer engine literally blown off and the inner engine on fire; the skipper gave the order to bale out. Somehow, Tiny managed to keep the Lancaster stable enough for a few precious seconds to enable the rest of the crew to escape, before he too left through the hatch. The last thing Taffy remembered seeing was the inverted Lancaster going down in flames.[19]

The experiences of 582 Squadron that day were far from unique. In another daylight attack, this time on Scholven Buer, all six aircraft taking part from 635 Squadron were hit; one was so badly damaged it had to make a crash landing at the emergency airfield at Woodbridge, which had been set up for just such an eventuality. On the same day and over another oil target, Sterkrade Holten, several PFF aircraft from 35 and 156 Squadrons were hit, one seriously. Lindsay Cann, a young flying officer, was wounded in the arm and the shoulder when his aircraft took a direct hit, shattering the pilot's windscreen. Seeing Cann's body slumped over the controls, the flight engineer and Nav 2 assumed their skipper was dead and baled out. However, Cann recovered and, although bleeding profusely, pressed on to the target and dropped his bombs. Piloting the Lancaster away from the target and by now exhausted, he had to be dragged from his seat by the wireless operator and Nav 1 and taken to the rest bed. The navigator, Raymond Fisher, took the controls and flew the aircraft back to base, whereupon Cann – who was still very weak from loss of blood – was helped back into his seat to make a perfect landing. The skipper was awarded an immediate DFC; Fisher received the DFM and was also granted an immediate field commission for an outstanding display of leadership.

Despite the stubborn resistance of the German defenders, their guns failed to inflict the level of destruction needed to meaningfully protect their oil infrastructure. While numerous Allied aircraft were damaged, the number actually destroyed was wholly disproportionate to the effort involved. It also led to an acute shortage of ammunition, just at the time it was needed the most to fend off attacks on the ground and in the air on multiple fronts.

But where the German defenders failed, so – perhaps – did the Allies. While the destruction caused by the bombing on Germany's oil production and storage facilities was extensive, some believe that in failing to direct sufficient force to bring Germany's oil production to a complete standstill, the Allies missed a huge opportunity. In the last three months of 1944, only 14 per cent of Harris' effort fell on oil targets compared to 53 per cent on cities and 15 per cent on transportation; between January and May 1945, and during the cessation of hostilities, still only a quarter (26 per cent) of his effort was directed against oil, compared to 37 per cent against German cities.[20] Harris argued that even in attacking German towns, he was hitting targets associated with the oil industry, but it is something of a disingenuous argument.

Several German cities that had, up to that point, defied all of Bomber Command's efforts were now destroyed,[21] including Brunswick and Nuremberg, the scene of such tragic losses at the zenith of the Battle of Berlin. A second Battle of the Ruhr commenced, and as Bomber Command ran out of larger cities to attack, it turned its attention to smaller, less industrial communities like Bonn, Darmstadt and Ulm. Daylights became commonplace; PFF aircrew logbooks for the period were filled with green ink.[22]

In the last three months of 1944, PFF flew more than 8,000 sorties; in December alone, its crews flew almost three times as many sorites as they had flown in the corresponding month of 1943. As demands for the PFF's time and skills increased, so too did its operational strength. Bennett's 'little group', as he called it,[23] ultimately comprised eight 'heavy' squadrons and 12 of his 'light brigade' (including the two Lancaster and one Mosquito squadrons detached to 5 Group for the duration). Pathfinders maintained its policy throughout of rotating its Air Staff with operationally experienced men, one of the last being Douglas Cracknell. A veteran of three tours and the penultimate wartime commander of 7 Squadron, Cracknell started his operational career in the Middle East. He completed no fewer than 75 operations including 18 as a master bomber.[24]

During those dying days, some among PFF began to question, although not too forcefully, what was left to bomb. After a particularly heavy raid on Essen, Andrew Maitland remarked that it was sometimes difficult to see what more destruction they could cause in an already bombed-out city, and that it could be little more than 'slum clearance'. That said, 'if Sir Arthur and his intelligence service felt that some place needed the attention of the bombers, this was good enough for his aircrews'.[25] So long as Germany kept fighting, Harris, with a bigger bomber force than ever, would ensure they were not left idle, and PFF would continue to lead the way.

Pforzheim, a city in the south-west of Germany and one of the centres of the country's watch-making trade, was on the list of targets earlier in the war. Watches translated into 'precision instruments' and, more importantly, required skilled workers. That said, it was far from a high-priority target, until such time as it became a hub through which German forces were being transported, and then it took on new significance. An attack on the night of 23/24 February 1945 on 'Yellowfin', the RAF's codename for the city, proved devastatingly efficient. Although comprising only a comparatively modest force of 380 aircraft, the devastation caused was almost total. Not only was the target accurately marked, but the raid was also superbly controlled by the master bomber, Ted Swales SAAF. Main Force also behaved itself in a fine piece of bombing described later as the best ever achieved.[26] More than 80 per cent of the city's buildings were destroyed by over 1,800 tons of bombs dropped in a little over 20 minutes. More than 17,000 people met their deaths in the fires and explosions that were comparable to the terrible raid on Hamburg. Ted Swales, however, was also killed, his aircraft being attacked by a night fighter and severely crippled over the target. Swales was transmitting instructions at the time over VHF and, as such, did not hear the warning cry from his gunner. It was this momentary delay that inevitably did it for him. Down to two engines, but managing to make it to friendly territory, he ordered his crew to bale out. This they all managed safely but by now Swales was too low to make it out himself and so attempted a crash landing. The Lancaster smashed into the ground and burst into flames. The next morning, Swales' charred remains were still at the controls, a booted foot jammed in the rudder pedal. The citation for his VC referenced his 'total disregard for his own safety and his acceptance of certain death for himself'.[27]

Just a few days earlier, Swales had been the master bomber for an attack on Chemnitz as part of Operation *Thunderclap* and ended up bringing his own bombs back. He saw nothing of the Main Force after rendezvousing over the town of Reading and the raid was not a success. *Thunderclap* was the codename for a plan devised by the Air Ministry to smash the Germans into submission once and for all and, very specifically, to support the Russian armies advancing from the east. Dresden was among the cities selected and enthusiastically endorsed by the Prime Minister, Winston Churchill. The bombing of Dresden has since become a subject of much soul searching and emotional debate, but in strictly Pathfinding terms it was a well-conducted operation.

The attack was in two parts: the first was carried out entirely by 5 Group using its own low-level marking methods; it achieved only modest success. The second part was an all-Lancaster affair led by Charles de Wesselow with Hugh 'Speed' Le Good as his deputy – an excellent example of how a junior officer (de Wesselow – a squadron leader) on the ground could lead his superior (Le Good – a wing commander) in the air, such was the all-inclusive culture of PFF. Many of the Pathfinders retained their TI, as they were unable to confidently identify the target, and de Wesselow called for blind marking. This proved more successful, and with TIs close to the aiming point, the master bomber instructed Main Force to aim for these with a two-second overshoot. For the inhabitants and peripatetics in Dresden, it proved catastrophic. No one has ever been able to determine just how many people died while the city burned, but even a conservative estimate puts the total at 50,000.

As well as supporting the Russian advance in the east, Pathfinders also supported the advance of US troops from the south and the west after the final phase of the land war opened towards the end of March 1945 with the crossing of the Rhine on 24 March. This had been preceded the previous night with a raid on Wesel that destroyed 97 per cent of the town and left the defenders too shocked or too dead to offer any further resistance.

Among the many other small cities to receive the unwelcome attention of Bomber Command in the last few weeks of the war was Paderborn, a city that could trace its roots to the time of Charlemagne and the great Carolingian Empire. It had the misfortune, on 27 March, to be in the way of the advancing US Army in its quest to encircle the Ruhr, and so Bomber Command was called in to lend a hand. It was, in many respects, a quiet day for PFF; while 5 Group was busy attacking an oil depot at Farge, and 3 Group was also on its own, attacking Hamm, Harris detailed 268 Lancasters and eight Mosquitoes to hit Paderborn in daylight. Stafford Coulson was master bomber, taking with him Ted Swales' surviving crew. A Met Flight Mosquito flew ahead and reported ten-tenths cloud over the target, and so Stafford called for a Wanganui: 'Sky marking was the least most satisfactory [method],' Stafford recalls, 'but in this instance accounted for one of my most successful attacks. We coolly wrote off a German town in less than a quarter of an hour. We razed the town to the ground and boy did it burn.'[28]

Pathfinder casualties fell significantly during this time and comparisons are interesting: in January 1945, they lost 18 aircraft in 1,964 sorties; for the corresponding period a year earlier, they lost 69 aircraft in 1,383 sorties, although this was, of course, at the height of the Battle of Berlin. But even in those later battles, several very senior or experienced aircrew were lost. On the last night of 1944, the OC 156 Squadron, Donald Falconer,[29] was killed when his aircraft received a direct hit over Cologne. He was an experienced master bomber and longstop, who had only been in charge of the squadron for a few weeks. Doug Reed remembered how the event put them all off their New Year beer.[30] Kenny Lawson, Bennett's former group navigation officer, was lost on 2/3 January, along with his crew. Kenny had re-qualified as a pilot and, at the time of his death, had at least 90 operations to his name.[31] The larger-than-life station commander at Coningsby, 43-year-old Anthony Evans-Evans – known as 'Tiny', a nickname inspired by his height and girth – was killed on the night of 22/23 February while marking the

Mittelland Canal near Gravenhorst. His navigator that day, by contrast, was 22-year-old William Wishart, a man who had won three decorations for gallantry in a remarkable 12-month period.[32] Thus, one of the oldest and more senior officers to be lost on operations went down with one of the youngest of squadron leader rank.

Without doubt, one of the saddest losses was that of a true Pathfinding legend and master bomber, Danny Everett. Quiet, yet with a steely determination, Everett's operational career had started as a sergeant pilot in early 1943 with 158 Squadron, but it was with 35 Squadron PFF and as a commissioned officer that he made his name. He was thrice awarded the DFC (the third was originally a DSO – why this was 'reduced' to a lesser award is difficult to fathom) and survived an extraordinary incident when his aircraft returned without a rear gunner, and without the rear gunner's turret. The turret had been severed by a bomb dropped from above, taking the unfortunate air gunner with it.[33] Described as a brilliant captain of aircraft, possessing the greatest determination and utmost thoroughness in all manners of airmanship,[34] outside of flying he was a popular figure who liked to share a beer with his crews.[35] But Danny was impatient to get on with the war, and when he was ordered to take a rest after clocking up 98 operations, he couldn't resist the temptation to get one more in. On 7 March, while testing aircraft at a group maintenance unit, he heard there was a spare aircraft going begging at his old squadron. Gathering a scratch crew of very experienced airmen, he took off to attack the Deutsche Erdöl-Aktiengesellschaft oil refinery at Hemmingstedt. Captain and crew failed to return, shot down by flak over the target area.

As the war accelerated to its close, the number of Pathfinder sorties peaked in March when some 4,258 were recorded.[36] A large proportion of these were siren raids, Bennett detailing three dozen Mosquitoes or so to raid Berlin twice a night. In the last year of the war, the LNSF evolved from being a mere 'nuisance', to becoming an effective bombing force in its own right. Contemporary newspaper articles attested to the damage the LNSF could cause: 'They are not just nuisance raids carried out by two or three planes. They are junior blitzes, and more!'[37]

As the Allies continued to advance, Pathfinders also began to drop leaflets and food in support of Operation *Manna*, notably to the starving Dutch. In one of the more conciliatory acts of the war, the German commander in charge of the pocket in western Holland, still in Wehrmacht hands, agreed a truce with local Allied commanders, allowing the Allied air forces to fly unmolested through a dedicated 'corridor'. Pathfinders still marked the relevant aiming points, and Bomber Command dropped some 6,672 tons of food during the operation. It required flying at less than 100ft. 'It was a very emotional time for all of us,' Gwynne Price recalled, 'helping the Dutch people who had suffered years of German occupation and enforced starvation. They came out in joyous force, despite the frightening sight of bomber aircraft coming in at low level and the last remaining fully armed German sentries standing by.'[38]

With the end of the war in Europe, eyes turned towards the east and Japan and the role of the Pathfinders as part of 'Tiger Force' then being assembled. Happy times were also spent on *Exodus* operations, bringing prisoners of war back from Germany, where some had been incarcerated for five years or more. The British Army and the Royal Navy had devised a ponderous plan[39] to repatriate POWs over several months until Bennett took things into his own hands and demonstrated how his bomber force could be used in a transport role. Twenty or so former captives could be accommodated on every flight, and soon the full weight of Bomber Command was thrown into the enterprise. 'We packed them in,' Harold Kirby remembered. 'They were enormously grateful.'[40] Bennett flew the first trip himself and 8 Group played its part in transporting nearly 3,000 of the 75,000 men that would eventually be brought home before the war was over.

Where once again PFF had led, others were to follow as the curtain began to fall on the biggest conflict in world history.

Chapter 15

Tales from the Archives

Pathfinder Force comprised many different nationalities. Whereas those from Canada, Australia, New Zealand and South Africa tended to dominate, outside of the UK at least, several smaller nations were also represented. Chas Lockyer, an articled clerk before the war who enlisted at 18, was delighted upon arriving at 608 Squadron to find a mixture of nationalities to add to the usual complement of English, Scottish and Welsh:

There was Henk, the Dutchman, who'd previously escaped from the Germans and joined the RAF, only to be shot down over Magdeburg, escape again and make his way back to England, having on the way called in to say 'hello' to his wife in Holland.

There was Doc the Irishman, whose main claim to fame was the ability to down a pint of beer in five seconds flat. Having performed this trick several times one night in Kings Lynn, he was finally carried out of the pub, loudly proclaiming that 'ops in a Mossie are a piece of cake'. He went missing two nights later.

There was Dobby the Englishman, caught one night in the act of milking a petrol bowser in an effort to supplement his petrol ration and thus depriving us of the opportunity of witnessing the effect of 100 octane aviation fuel in his clapped-out Austin-7.

There was Twitcher, the short, rotund New Zealander who, at every function or dance where a band was playing, would insist on conducting it through the Spike Jones version of 'Cocktails for Two'. To do this he always stood on a chair from which, overcome by his exertions, he invariably fell off before the end of the number.

There was Pop the Welshman, who hitched a flight in an Oxford one day when Jock (Bart 'Jock' Sherry, my navigator) and I were taking some Air Training Corps (ATC) cadets for short flips around the area and persuaded us to make a minor diversion to Cardiff where he wanted to watch a rugby international. The ATC cadet was sick both ways.

There was Henderson, a Canadian, always moaning about 'this goddam climate' and who dressed to go to bed in full flying gear with a balaclava replacing the helmet and socks instead of flying boots. He invariably borrowed the blankets off the bed of anyone who happened to be on leave and would create a cocoon, sealed at one end. He would then burrow in, complete with hot water bottle, and by prior arrangement someone would seal the open end. We called him Captain Oates, but Jock once observed that if Oates had worn what Hendy was wearing, he probably would have survived.

And there was my pal Jock, the Scot, who navigated me accurately, impeccably, and spot on time to targets all over Germany, but seemed to experience unaccountable difficulty in performing the same service in order to get us back at night to Downham Market from Kings Lynn or Wisbech. In fairness to Jock, the thick mists that so often came off the river and blanketed the roads often made the drive back to Downham more dicey than a trip to Berlin.

The international nature of 608 Squadron at Downham Market was replicated at other stations across the UK. Among the aircrews and groundcrews were those from the occupied territories who, by hook or by crook, had found their way to England and were given a chance to have another crack at the Germans.

Johan Rad, for example, fled to Britain to fly with the RAF as a member of the Royal Norwegian Air Force. He flew twin-engined Bristol Beaufighters with 604 Squadron from Middle Wallop in November 1941 prior to joining 85 Squadron in the spring of 1943. The squadron operated Mosquitoes under the command of the doyen of night fighters, John 'Cat's Eyes' Cunningham, a famous post-war test pilot.

On the night of 17/18 June, Johan claimed a Focke-Wulf Fw 190 'hit and run' raider as a 'probable', a claim subsequently confirmed as a 'kill'. He recalled the incident after the war:

> It was actually a lucky shot, the distance being at least 1,200ft. The reason for this was that I could not get any closer; it was running away. It was diving with full engine and so was I and I thought I'd have a go. There was a rather big flash and then some smaller flashes before it disappeared. It was a shame I did not get to see it before it dropped its bomb, which I saw hit a post office and I believe killed quite a few people.[1]

Johan was 'rested' as a sector controller at Biggin Hill after completing a tour of operations and then volunteered for PFF, successfully completing his training on 1655 MTU at Warboys in July 1944. Posted to 139 Squadron, he flew his first PFF operation on the night of 24 August, with Douglas Martin as his navigator. He flew 18 trips altogether until disaster struck on the way to Berlin.

With a full load of markers, Johan's Mosquito was at the point of take-off when he lost an engine at the critical moment. Unable to stop, he pulled up the undercarriage and slew across the runway and into a pile of empty fuel containers and bomb casings before finally coming to a halt. Quick as a flash and fearing the aircraft might explode, Johan jettisoned the escape hatch and climbed out through the roof before scrambling clear, his navigator close behind.

Slightly injured, Johan was sent to hospital to be checked over. An unrelated stomach ulcer was diagnosed, which put paid to any future flying. Douglas Martin found himself another pilot and completed his tour. At the war's end, Johan returned to Norway to become station commander at Tromsø, the former Luftwaffe seaplane base.

'We Norwegians who escaped from Norway were extremely happy and, I think, did a reasonably good job. We got on very well with the English, in and out of uniform.'

* * * * *

Wars are sad repositories of hard-luck stories, men who went along as a spare bod, absented from their usual crew, and failed to come back, or whole crews who flew with a new captain, never to return. Hamish Mahaddie's crew, for example, was lost on their first operation without their skipper. There are stories also of men with a huge number of ops under their belts who perhaps went along for one last trip and similarly never made it home. Experience mattered to a very large degree, but luck mattered even more.

One of the unluckiest was Bill Porteous. Porteous, from Portree on the Isle of Skye, was a hugely popular local figure, much loved and respected by his island community. He was described by his local newspaper as a

boy who was 'quietly humorous and at ease with young or old, but bringing to every task, mental or physical, his contribution of quick appreciation and complete reliability'.

Bill joined the RAF and, as an air bomber in the 7 Squadron crew of Granville Wilson, won an immediate DFM for great courage, skill and tenacity in the most trying circumstances. It was

Bill Porteous, one of only a very few Bomber Command aircrew to win the DSO, DFM and Bar. (Peter Scales and Sally Barber)

during an attack on Hannover that his Lancaster was coned and hit on the run-up to the target. Four members of the crew were wounded, including the second dickey, and much essential equipment rendered u/s. Despite the damage and the faltering controls, Wilson managed to keep the aircraft straight and level long enough for Bill to drop his bombs on the target. On heading for home, they were intercepted by an enemy fighter, the mid-upper gunner and pilot doing sterling work to avoid any fatal damage while Bill took over the wounded navigator's table to plot a course for base. It was touch and go but they made it back, Bill writing later in his logbook: 'Navigated home by guess and by God.' He was awarded the DFM along with the air gunner, Bernard Mulholland, while Wilson received an immediate DSO.

Awarded a bar to his DFM and commissioned shortly after, Bill continued flying when many others might have taken the easy way out. Such was his skill that he was often chosen to fly with the CO or senior flight commanders, including Fraser Baron and John Dennis. It was with the latter that he met his fate.

It was the night of 11/12 May 1944, and the target was the railway yards at Le Mans. Fraser Baron was the designated master bomber and John Dennis his deputy. Baron was last heard issuing instructions to Main Force and was mid-sentence when he was cut off. In the silence that followed, Dennis could be heard attempting to contact his CO before assuming responsibility for the raid himself. He too was heard on the airwaves before silence again prevailed and it was apparent that both master and deputy were lost.

How they came to be lost is something of a mystery. It has been suggested they collided. That is entirely plausible, given the immediacy of the two occurrences. It has also been suggested they were shot down by flak. They may also have been the victim of a night fighter: a 115 Squadron Lancaster crewman reported seeing an Fw 190 in the combat area, raking a Lancaster in its belly while almost standing on its tail. Whatever the reason, the outcome was the same. Two hugely experienced captains and their crews were lost within moments of one another, and Bill Porteous, a veteran of more than 80 operations was killed. He was 23. The citation for a third award for gallantry, the DSO, appeared shortly after, stating that his achievements and the precision of his bombing had achieved 'the greatest praise'. He was one of only a very few Bomber Command aircrew to win the DSO, DFM and Bar.

An obituary piece appeared in memory of Bill in the *Oban Times* dated 2 September 1944. In it, the author describes a talk Bill had once given reluctantly to the senior pupils at his old school. He finished by saying, 'Well, that's all. And now I'm going to ask if I may do something I often longed to do when cramming in this study – sit back in my chair and smoke.'

✳ ✳ ✳ ✳ ✳

Danny Everett's story is possibly the best known in Pathfinder circles as one in which a man gambled with his life once too often and finally, and inevitably, lost. Guy Lockhart was another. Bennett himself said of Lockhart that he never met, throughout the entire war, anybody 'so fanatically

courageous and press-on at all times an in all circumstances'.[2] It is not surprising, for there was scarcely a moment in the war that Lockhart was not flying operationally, and not always in Bomber Command.

William Guy Lockhart was a pre-war regular, originally trained as a fighter pilot. His short-service

Guy Lockhart, who Bennett described as fanatically courageous and press-on at all times. (via Kelvin Youngs, Aircrew Remembered website)

commission ended up being shorter than he originally envisaged, when he was court martialled for a low-flying incident at the Empire Air Day flying display and dismissed from the service. It appears that his antics caused a visiting AOC to fall flat on his face, and the AOC demanded his head. With the outbreak of war, however, Lockhart was allowed to re-enlist with the VR as a sergeant pilot.

Flying defensive sorties and then offensive sweeps with 74 Squadron as part of the Biggin Hill Wing in the summer of 1941, Lockhart accounted for the loss of a Bf 109 on 2 July, flying as wingman to the great fighter ace and wing leader 'Sailor' Malan. Escorting 12 Blenheim light bombers on a 'circus' – an operation to lure enemy fighters into combat – Malan and Lockhart found themselves in a dogfight, Malan taking a shot at a Messerschmitt as it dived through the bomber formation and into a steep climb. Lockhart fired too, a two-second burst, and had the satisfaction of seeing the enemy fighter spin onto its back, trailing smoke. He lost sight of it as it disappeared below 8,000ft and was rewarded with a half share in a 'kill'.[3] A few days later he had even greater success, accounting for two Bf 109s before himself being shot down. He baled out over France from 16,000ft, landing unconscious in the top of a tree in Ergny, while his aircraft – a brand new Spitfire – crashed at Avesnes. Despite being captured for a short spell, he managed to get away and, on 9 August, crossed into Spain after several adventures along the way. Held by the Spanish authorities, it was not until the end of October that he arrived back in the UK via Gibraltar and was posted to fly Whitleys with 138 (Special Duties) Squadron. Almost immediately he asked to be transferred to the squadron's Lysander flight, to be trained in the hazardous role of landing enemy agents (called 'Joes') in France.

The 'Moonshine' Squadron, as it was called, was not for the faint-hearted and involved incredibly dangerous work. Lockhart never knew the real identities of the men and women he dropped off or picked up from the hastily arranged landing strips in the French countryside, but he recognised their work was vital to the war as part of the Special Operations Executive with a brief to 'set Europe ablaze'. Posted to 161 Squadron upon its formation for similar duties, Lockhart had a heart-in-the-mouth moment on one of his first trips (Operation *Baccarat II*) when his aircraft became bogged down in a field. The reception party helped with turning the aircraft around and Lockhart managed to make good his escape, with his two agents safely on board. He had been on the ground for 17 long minutes and was a relieved man to make it back to Tangmere in the small hours of the morning.

By now commissioned, Lockhart was awarded the DFC in June 1942 – the citation noting his 'great skill and initiative' – and given command of A Flight. With the French underground networks in turmoil following a number of betrayals, 161 Squadron was given a cameo role as a light bomber force until pick-up operations could resume, dropping 250lb bombs on the marshalling yards at Serqueux and the chemical works at Oissel.

On the night of 31 August/1 September, and with normal service resumed, Lockhart took off for Operation *Boreas II* but, upon landing, crashed into a grass covered ditch, taking out the landing gear. The field had been poorly chosen and the error thoroughly avoidable. Lockhart attempted to make contact with a second Lysander overhead by signalling the letters of his name but the pilot, fearing it to be a trap, left the area soon after. Lockhart destroyed the Lysander's identification friend or foe device and hacked at the auxiliary fuel tank with an axe before setting the aircraft on fire with an incendiary bomb. He made his way to the south coast with two French agents to a pre-arranged rendezvous with a Polish-crewed Felucca from Gibraltar that would take them to safety. An altercation with the coast guard led to the two Frenchmen being arrested, but Lockhart was taken off safely and again returned to the UK via the Rock. He was awarded an immediate DSO, this time being praised for his 'careful organisation and planning'.

Now a squadron leader, Lockhart's promotion had been little short of meteoric, given only a few months earlier he had still been an NCO. He flew another hairy operation on 18 November when his Lysander was intercepted by seven Fw 190s near Jersey and he was obliged to take violent evasive action, with his passengers still on board. The high manoeuvrability of the Lysander and Lockhart's undoubted flying skills saved the day, along with an embracing blanket of cloud, but they were now far from home and partly lost over the Channel. Despite briefly considering the option to bale out, pilot and 'Joes' agreed to attempt to make it home. It was a brave decision. When they landed, they had just five gallons left in the tanks.

Tour-expired and posted to the Deputy Directorate of Intelligence as an acting wing commander, Lockhart was not flying a desk for long before he wangled a posting to 627 Squadron, one of the LNSF squadrons, as a flight commander. This was followed soon after with his first operational command, as CO of the newly formed 692 Squadron, and the award of a bar to his DFC (gazetted after his death).

Lockhart was only in charge of 692 for a few weeks but he made a lasting impression, both on the authorities and Bennett himself. The citation for his second DFC credited him for the fine record of the squadron and his own willingness to take on the enemy with 'unremitting keenness and zeal'.

With the loss of Kenneth Rampling on the night of 22 March 1944, Lockhart was asked to swap two engines for four and take command of 7 Squadron. He arrived on 24 March and nearly came to grief on his first familiarisation trip a few days later. This was the night of the infamous raid on Nuremberg, Lockhart choosing to fly as second pilot to an inexperienced NCO, Robert Banks.[4] Homeward bound, their Lancaster was attacked by an Fw 190, Banks throwing the heavy bomber into a starboard corkscrew. The German fighter, however, was no novice and stayed with them throughout the manoeuvre, latching onto their tail. The rear gunner let fly with a long burst, whereupon the fighter seemed to break away and into the sights of the mid-upper gunner, who also fired. Their actions were enough. Hits were registered and the fighter disappeared.[5]

Four weeks later, Lockhart's extraordinary luck finally ran out when he was shot down and killed on operations over Friederichshafen, taking with him a vastly experienced crew. They included a 35-year-old former postman, George Ryle, who had taken part in the first ever raid on Berlin and whose wife, Peggy, kept a moving diary while her husband was missing.

She had to wait until September before final confirmation that her 'darling Georgie' was dead.[6]

It was said that Lockhart's personal hatred for the Nazi regime was what motivated him to press home attacks in circumstances that might have deterred other pilots.[7] There was certainly one occasion when he lost an engine on the outward leg to bomb Berlin and continued on to the target. And there were many others when he braved flak and fighters, undertaking 'spoof' raids to draw the enemy defenders away from their real objective. Whatever his motivation, Wing Commander W G Lockhart DSO, DFC and Bar, Croix de Guerre is surely more deserving of recognition, and there can be very few, if any, who matched his phenomenal operational achievement as a fighter pilot, Moonshine pilot, Mosquito pilot and PFF pilot extraordinaire.

＊ ＊ ＊ ＊ ＊

Loss was often difficult to take. Many PFF aircrew have stories to tell of empty beds in the Nissen huts they shared, or empty chairs in the mess. Gerry Bennington remembered that sometimes, after a particularly difficult trip, he would know that others had been shot down but their loss did not immediately register in his mind. 'We were too caught up in our own battles for survival,' he said.[8] Tom Williamson recalled that if it was a bad trip, the padre would be round.[9]

Gordon Green, a New Zealander, flew 52 operations over the winter of 1944/45 with 608 Squadron. He remembered losing one of his great pals:

> Tommy Long, a big jovial fellow from Northern Ireland, would demonstrate his ability to drink a tankard of ale in approximately three seconds. His throat never moved as the ale disappeared and we all applauded his act. One of my most poignant memories is the night when we all trouped into the bar and Mine Hostess [the landlady] filled his big tankard. She placed it on the counter and with a smile on her face asked: 'Where's Tommy?' A deep

silence reigned for three or four seconds. Nobody answered. She turned pale and then emptied the tankard, placing it high on the top shelf. Tommy and his navigator had failed to return from operations the previous night. The party carried on.

* * * * *

It was occasionally said that the Mosquito boys had it easy. It was certainly true that their chances of survival were far greater than those on the heavy squadrons. Peter Hobbs certainly thought so. Many, like Peter, had flown tours on heavy bomber squadrons prior to flying Mossies. After 25 ops with 620 Squadron on Stirlings, Peter, like 'Doc' the Irishman, said Mosquitoes were 'a piece of cake'.[10] He admitted, however, that 50 ops in six months was 'a long slog'.

Jack Currie, who in the latter stages of the war flew with 1409 Met Flight, said the greatest threat to the Mosquito was not enemy action but existed 'either in the weather, in the aeroplane itself, or in some failure by the crew to fly it right'.[11]

It would be wholly wrong, however, to assume that Mosquito operations were a cakewalk. The 'met men', for example, were particularly brave. Carrying neither bombs nor armament, but long-range fuel tanks and cameras, they flew straight to where they had to go and back: 'No circling for height above the base; no zig-zag route to dodge the hot spots along the way; no safety in numbers; just down the sky and up again to check the temperature and humidity, take shots of anything interesting, and then back to base like a boomerang'.[12]

Joe Patient considered his time on Met Flight to be more dangerous than his time on 139 Squadron:

Weather fronts obviously moved, so our role was to bring back information on the weather our bomber crews could expect when they got to the target. This meant flying to where the weather was 'then', on the basis of where it would be 'later'. We reported on cloud levels, temperatures, icing conditions, etc. The latter could be especially dangerous, as it meant deliberately flying into the thickest CuNimb cloud and measuring the icing index – in short, timing how long it took before ice began appearing on the wings and the windscreen, and then getting out before things became really hairy.

Then we would get home as fast as possible to report what we had found. Norry (my Nav) would jump out of the aircraft and get straight on the phone to HQ. The call was scrambled, and other Groups would be listening in. There was the occasional question but that was all. We once were obliged to land at RAF Pershore, some way from home, and Norry was in a hurry to get the weather report to HQ. A senior officer (I think it was the station commander) called after Norry and said: 'I have you know that junior officers salute senior officers on this station.' To which, Norry shook the officer's hand and replied: 'Glad to hear it.'[13]

Notwithstanding Patient's claim, his time with 139 was not without its adventures. On one occasion over enemy territory, he was hit by flak and lost an engine. Then he was set upon by two enemy fighters, sustaining significant damage and only just making it home to a wheels-up landing. He was awarded an immediate DFC.

Others had similar experiences. Doug Wilkinson was over Berlin one night in September 1944 when someone broke radio silence to warn him – not that he hadn't noticed – that he was being 'coned':

A night fighter came in from astern and fired a burst which clipped the starboard wing. At that point 'Titch' Dale (the navigator) let go the bombs and I closed the bomb doors. Still in the searchlight the Hun came in on his second run just as Dale came out of the nose. This time the fighter's aim was dead on, and he raked us from the tail to the nose, shattering the nose of the aircraft and the rear part of the cockpit canopy. The starboard engine caught fire and Dale was struck in the eye with shattered Perspex.

I also collected some particles in my right cheek (this I discovered the next day when I shaved, and my cheek became covered in blood).

I thereupon flipped the aircraft on its back and made a vertical 180-degree turn which took me out of the searchlight cone. The speed built up with this manoeuvre was terrific and on pulling back on the control column we shot back up to 20,000ft. I feathered the burning engine and on pressing the fire extinguisher buttons was delighted to see the flames disappear.

Doug then faced a dilemma: whether to continue eastwards and head for Russia, or try and make it back to base. Even though the crews had been issued with paperwork to prove to their Russian comrades that they were friendly, he opted for the latter.

It was now very cold and noisy, and we had no electrics. The battery had been shattered, the side hatch blown off and the generator was on the closed-down engine. I trimmed the aircraft to fly on one engine, but it still required a steady and constant pressure on the rudder bar to hold it straight. We set course for home. I set the throttle as low as possible to conserve fuel and gradually lost height as we reached the Dutch coast.

Picking their way through storm clouds, the battered Mosquito made landfall with the English coast at 2,500ft. Doug fired off the colours of the day (to identify themselves as friendly) and was rewarded with a 'Sandra' searchlight to help guide them home:

Dead ahead a 'drome turned on its lights. What a sight! A green Aldis winked at us. We had no hydraulics, no flaps, no wheels and no fuel. Did I have a tail? Take her in to the left of the runway. Speed 130 knots. No time for a circuit. Straight in. Feel for the deck. Switch off engine, props touch. And there you are watching the fire truck probing with his spotlight looking for us. My heel felt tender. No wonder. A bullet had passed through the heel of my escape boot.

Pilot and navigator were taken to the airfield sick bay where they spent the night. In the morning, Dale was taken to the hospital at Halton where he was eventually fitted with a false eye. Doug was awarded the DFC for setting 'a fine example of courage and determination'. Wallace Dale was similarly awarded the DFM.[14]

* * * * *

Some of the men in the Oboe and LNSF squadrons of PFF flew an almost superhuman number of sorties, challenging the odds. Men like navigator Ron Curtis, for example, flew 139 ops; Ernest 'Benny' Benson flew 145. Even if the 'chop' rate on Mossies was circa 1 per cent, by the law of probability, both men were lucky to have survived the war.

Benny Benson enlisted in the RAF a month after the war began and was commissioned into the RAFVR. By the spring of 1941, he was operational with 99 Squadron, completing a tour of 27 ops on Wellingtons from Waterbeach before being rested as a navigation instructor on 23 OTU in Pershore. While at Pershore, he took part in two of Harris' showpiece thousand-bomber raids and stayed in a training role until the summer of 1943, when he joined 109 Squadron.

With 109 at Marham and then Little Staughton, Benson flew a large number (66) of operations, with Hugh Arnott as his regular skipper – after Arnott's original nav had been killed when he baled out into the sea. With Arnott tour-expired, Benson was content to fly with a number of different pilots, especially those whose performance was not yet considered up to the mark.

When Benson was awarded a thoroughly deserved DSO to add to the DFC and Bar he had been awarded earlier, he was credited with 490 operational flying hours and had flown 73 Oboe sorties. The draft submission for the award, which still survives, mentions one particular sortie on the afternoon of 29 November 1944, returning from a marking trip to Dortmund. While on the climb, Benson began to suffer the effects of 'the bends' at 28,000ft, the cabin pressurisation system having gone u/s, but he made no mention of the pain he was in to his pilot, Arthur Buckland, pain that became almost unbearable as they topped 34,000ft. 'He carried on,' the citation records, 'and with great devotion to duty succeeded in navigating the aircraft, working the special equipment and dropping the markers with great accuracy.'

At the time he was taken off operations, he was the flight navigation officer and deputy squadron navigation officer. 'He is still keen to fight on,' the citation adds. And the perils he faced 'seem only to have served to strengthen his desire and determination to fly against the enemy'.[15] The station commander called him 'an ideal leader of men'.

Benson had a number of hairy trips, including one to Essen from which they returned on one engine, and another when the aircraft pranged on landing. His aircraft was often subjected to intense anti-aircraft fire and on at least two occasions his Mosquito returned with battle damage.

The stress of 145 operations is clearly illustrated in these two photographs of 'Benny' Benson, taken five years apart. (Mike Benson)

During and after Benny's time on 109 Squadron, a further 30 pilots and navigators flew 100+ trips, a remarkable achievement by any measure. Photographs of Benson (on the previous page), showing him in 1940, when he gained his pilot's wings, and at the end of the war in 1945 are enough to show the stresses and strains such men were under. They did not have it easy.

*****

Cyril Hassall, who had flown with Steve Watts on the Kiel Canal raid, continued to fly after Watts was killed, volunteering for a third tour. He had completed his first as a navigator with 18 Squadron in the winter of 1940/41, surviving 38 sorties, many at low level and in daylight.

For his third tour he was posted as navigation officer to the newly formed 142 Squadron at Gransden Lodge, under the command of Bernard 'Baz' Nathan, who was comparatively new to operational flying. A trip with Nathan to Berlin on 22 March 1945 took Cyril's total to 100 operational flights, at which point he was urged to stop. Cyril wouldn't hear of it, but his next trip was very nearly his last. On returning from Berlin, with Baz at the controls, they lost an engine and so headed for Manston. Just as they were coming in to land, and at a little more than 300ft, Baz spotted an aircraft ahead of them that had just landed but not cleared the runway:

To my horror he elected to go around again! We continued at full throttle on our one over-burdened engine for three miles before we gradually started to gain height. Hanging on by our props I feared the worst. We finally made it, to my intense relief. By the time we were able to get on the phone and through to Gransden to report our landing, we were told that the Group controller had reported us as "missing" and the word had gone around the Group that Hassall had bought it at last!

Cyril flew one more trip before finally bowing to pressure and calling it a day. He was invested with the DSO, DFC and Bar at Buckingham Palace on 11 November 1947 by King George VI.

✳ ✳ ✳ ✳ ✳

Ted Dunford flew 55 operations with 608 Squadron, a comparatively modest total for a Mosquito boy, but these included 27 to Berlin. Ted enlisted at the age of 19, two weeks before the outbreak of war. After the usual initial introduction to service life and grading in the UK, he was shipped overseas to South Africa and southern Rhodesia to complete his service flying training. He stayed in Africa as an instructor for more than three years before returning to the UK and converting to the Mosquito at 1655 MTU. He began operating with 608 Squadron at Downham Market in October 1944, with almost 2,000 hours flying time in his logbook:

> Despite carrying TIs, 608 was not a marking squadron. The LNSF was occasionally used to mount spoof raids a few minutes before the 'heavies' came in, to bring up the fighters and render them out of position or out of fuel, before the main raid went to a different target. The spoof raid comprised a couple of marker aircraft who marked the target, followed by others with Window, target indicators and bombs to stimulate a much more important raid than it was.
>
> On 24 December, a spoof raid was planned on Munster to protect a heavy raid on Cologne. Two aircraft were to be provided from each of the four squadrons. On arrival over the target, there was no marking or any activity, although my navigator (Bill Read[16]) was positive that we were in the right place. After a few minutes circling, feeling more and more naked in the bright moonlight, I turned south, dumped the bombs into the fires at Cologne, and returned.
>
> At debriefing, the squadron CO was less than pleased with the evening's performance. One of his aircraft had turned back with engine failure and the other had failed to find the target!

Later I went to the mess to salvage what was left of Christmas Eve, and was offered a drink by a suddenly affable CO. He now knew that the raid had been cancelled. The other three squadrons involved had received the cancellation before take-off, so my navigator and I were the sole representatives of the LNSF at Munster that Christmas Eve!

Ted always marvelled at the accuracy of PFF navigation – aircraft making their own lonely journey in the dark to a common destination. Only rarely did he see another aircraft, and then unintentionally: 'One night as the raid went out over the North Sea, one Mossie stood out in the blackness. The pilot had forgotten to switch off his navigation lights on leaving the English coast. I waited until I felt sure we were on German radar before breaking radio silence to transmit one word: "Lights". They snapped off immediately. Someone somewhere owes me a drink!'[17]

On 14 March 1945, he nearly came to grief when his Mosquito was hit by flak over the German capital: 'I lost all aileron control (as well as having a hole in the wing and the petrol tank) and lateral level could only be maintained by heavy rudder applications. It took me three approaches to make a night landing at Woodbridge (the emergency runway). No training course had covered this procedure!'

For his efforts that night, Ted was awarded the DFC, the official citation making reference to the 'severe damage' sustained by his aircraft (a Mosquito XX) and the 'superb skill, great coolness and determination' shown by the pilot in the face of great difficulty.

After the war, Ted converted to Lancasters and subsequently flew with BOAC and then as a Trident captain with British Airways.

* * * * *

Group Captain 'Fatty' Collings was another of PFF's great personalities who led from the front. On one occasion, he was present when a crew returned early, claiming their aircraft would not reach operational height and that the controls were sluggish. Collings got the crew together and piloted the aircraft himself. He managed to make 13,000ft but no higher and so the crew were exonerated on that point. But what the groundcrew watching from the ground remembered next was the aerobatic display they were treated to as Collings threw the Lancaster around the sky as though it was a fighter. Apart from looping the loop, he did just about everything that was possible with an aircraft of that size. He was given a round of applause upon landing, followed by seven men with green faces, shaken by their experience. Collings had proven there was nothing much wrong with the Lancaster's controls.[18]

✳ ✳ ✳ ✳ ✳

PFF pilots had their quirks. Some would weave all the way to the target. Others believed resolutely in flying straight and level, but not many. Their attitude to 'George', the automatic pilot, was another mystery. Some ignored it altogether, never once wanting to give up control of their aircraft; others exploited it for all that it was worth. Dennis Hughes, a flight engineer, remembered his skipper, Harry Manley, never used George unless he could help it, but he would let Dennis fly the aircraft if he promised to keep it straight and level.[19] Laurence Deane took a different line. As he became increasingly (and some might say dangerously) fatigued by operational command, he'd use George to do more and more of the flying while he took a little snooze, though never in the target area.[20]

Colin Bell was much the same. He was studying to become a chartered surveyor before the war and had gained his wings in Georgia, US, staying on as a flying instructor on attachment to the USAAF. Returning to the UK in 1943, he wanted first to become a night fighter, but on hearing that 8 Group was looking for pilots with 1,000 hours or more to convert to Mosquitoes, he applied for a transfer to Bomber Command. At 608 Squadron he teamed up with a RCAF navigator, Doug Redmond: 'Doug was acknowledged as the best navigator in the squadron, and I was lucky to have him. When

Doug said you were at a particular point somewhere in Europe, you were there. No argument – he was right – every time.'

Such was the trust between the two men, that Colin, like Laurence Deane, was not averse to taking the occasional nap once clear of the target:

> I did take a number of naps but only after I had trimmed the aircraft to fly straight and level and on the correct course for Downham Market. Doug's job was to wake me up if the aircraft commenced straying off course or if anything untoward needed my attention. That, after all, is recognised as being part of the duties of a navigator. Doug always woke me in good time as we approached the airfield, enabling me to land the plane safely. The system never failed and neither of us ever needed counselling![21]

✳ ✳ ✳ ✳ ✳

Sitting alone in the 35 Squadron mess, Nick Nicholson was quietly minding his own business when he was approached by the squadron gunnery leader, Cedric Fraser-Petherbidge, and asked if he'd fly with the CO, Speed Le Good. They were to be the master bomber for an attack on Potsdam, the last raid of the war by a major Bomber Command force on a German city. Heading out to the aircraft, Nick was making for the rear turret when the other air gunner, Jim Simpson,[22] asked if he'd have a go in the mid-upper instead. Nick wasn't fussed and so agreed. Also, he was an NCO, whereas Simpson was a flight lieutenant. On their way to the target, Nick was disturbed by an intermittent glow coming from the rear of the aircraft. Concerned that there could be a problem, and perhaps the start of a fire, he reported it to the pilot and asked him to check. The pilot laughed and told him not to worry; the rear gunner was taking a pipe.

✳ ✳ ✳ ✳ ✳

The bombing campaign against Germany was characterised by the Nazi propaganda machine under Joseph Goebbels as a 'campaign of terror' and the airman were, by definition, 'terror flyers'. As the war progressed, and the destruction became more terrible, civilians were not discouraged by Nazi authorities in taking the law into their own hands should an evading airman be captured. Lynchings, which were initially unheard of, became alarmingly common, and among the victims were a number of PFF aircrew.

When 21-year-old Ronald Walker was shot down in June 1944, he was fortunate to find himself taken in by loyal Dutchmen and part of an escape line in the home of Jacoba Pulskens, known as Tante (Auntie) Coba. Hidden with two other pilots, their safety was compromised when a car containing two other airmen was stopped by the Germans, and the pair taken in for questioning. The very next morning, six Germans arrived and forced their way into Tante Coba's home, beat the three pilots to the floor and machine-gunned them to death in cold blood. Tante Coba was herself arrested and sent to a concentration camp, where she died.

Another incident in the winter of 1944, is even more brutal in the telling. On the morning of 13 December, three airmen were being detained in a former school in the city. They had been captured overnight. After a series of disagreements between their captors (including the police and a Home Guard-style unit), the three airmen were eventually led from their sanctuary and marched through the city on their way to the Luftwaffe base at Mülheim. The officer in charge of the escort had made it known, publicly and loudly, that his soldiers were not to intervene if the men in their charge were attacked.

By the time the prisoners came to the Wickenburg bridge, a short distance from their starting point, a large mob (some reports quote well in excess of 100 people, including many women) had gathered and set upon kicking and beating the defenceless men. Although there were some expressions of disapproval, in very short order the level of violence became out of control, and the three men were thrown from the bridge into the water below. One, who was still alive and desperately trying to crawl away, was then shot in the face and killed by one of the escorting guards, and all three bodies were then looted for anything of value.

Among the dead were two PFF aircrew from 582 Squadron, Michael Gisby and Harry Mawson. Only Mawson's body was ever recovered; Gisby has no known grave, and it was not until 2018 and the publication of *Missing Presumed Murdered* that their murders were discovered. The city council in Essen agreed magnanimously to a memorial being erected at the site where the men died.[23]

Ten days later, the squadron had the great misfortune of losing another of its aircrew to a baying mob. On 23 December 1944, navigator Ken Hewitt found himself one of three surviving aircrew from a Lancaster shot down while attacking the marshalling yards at Cologne-Gremberg. Coming down in a built-up area in broad daylight, he was unable to make good his escape and was quickly surrounded. Three gunshots rang out and he fell, mortally wounded. It appears he had been shot by a party official. When a local policeman arrived to take order, he found the airman on the ground, shot in the stomach. No one offered to help, and no one volunteered who had done it. Hewitt was still alive at this point and the policeman drove him away to the nearest hospital where the young airman died shortly afterwards.

In another incident in early January 1945, Jimmy Rowland of 635 Squadron was obliged to take to his parachute when his aircraft was in a head-on collision with a Lancaster of 431 Squadron, the impact severing the port wing and rear fuselage and probably killing both gunners. The four remaining crew members made it out. Rowlands landed largely unscathed, save for a few cuts and grazes, and was picked up a day later. By then, however, the four others who had made it out had been rounded up and summarily shot.

In the case of Ronald Walker, after the war, the six Germans responsible were found, tried and hanged. Gisby's and Mawson's killers were also found and hanged, and others who stood by and watched given lengthy prison sentences. Hewitt's murderer was identified but killed before the war ended and so never brought to trial. The killers of Jimmy Rowland's crew, however, were never punished. Although the identity of the unit that carried out the atrocity was known (Ersatz Battalion 36), reports of the crime became confused with others, and those responsible escaped justice.

* * * * *

Not every aircrew who came down on foreign soil shared such a horrific fate. Not all aircrew landed in hostile territory. Some, like 'Jock' Cassels and his navigator, Alan Woollard, found themselves on neutral ground, in this case, Sweden.

Jock and Alan had plenty of experience behind them. Both had flown with 106 Squadron (Manchesters and Lancasters) earlier in the war before joining 139 Squadron at Wyton and then Upwood. It was then being used as a marker squadron for the LNSF.

It was the night of 11 June 1944 and Woollard had just dropped their TIs and bombs on Berlin when they were subjected to intense and accurate predicted flak. Feeling hits on their aircraft, Jock decided to fly the Mosquito directly across the city to clear the defences as quickly as possible and take advantage of a good following wind. He could then turn north to get back on track. Despite the plan, their aircraft was hit again, the cabin began to overheat, and fill with smoke. Oil and coolant

Jock Cassels made for Sweden when his Mosquito was badly mauled and was interned for three months. (The Pathfinder Archive)

temperatures on the port engine were seen to be off the clock, and the oil pressure had fallen to virtually zero. Jock feathered the engine and continued to head north.

Fifty miles beyond Berlin, they set course for Lübeck and reduced their height. The starboard engine then began playing up and the critical temperatures increased. The whole of the aircraft now began to vibrate, and their speed began to fall dangerously low. Jock unfeathered the port engine to enable his navigator to get a fix (the equipment he needed relied on the power of the engine) and the prognosis was not good. Realising they were now in serious trouble, they had choices to make. They could not make it home; they could not even get close enough to the English coast to ditch. It would soon be daylight, and their chances over enemy territory were not good. The only option, therefore, was to head for neutral Sweden.

Limping onwards, Woollard attempted to smash the special equipment (in this case, H2S) to prevent its capture while his skipper fought to maintain height. In his struggles, however, Woollard's parachute harness became loose, further convincing his pilot that it was no longer worth the risk to bale out. Finally, they reached the coast of Sweden, only to be fired upon twice by the coastal defences. Jock headed out to sea again, to cross at a different point. He was obliged to fly further along the coast before putting the aircraft down in a field near Ystad. Pilot and navigator made good their escape, shortly before the aircraft caught fire (the result of a rogue incendiary). The Mosquito was a total write-off.

The two men were swiftly captured and held at the Falun internment camp where they were soon after interrogated by a local Swedish officer and officials from the British Air Attaché's office in Stockholm. The Swedish officer noted that the two airmen appeared 'well brought up and made a nice impression'.[24] Cassels and Woollard spent three months in Sweden before being repatriated.

Just a few weeks before, another Mosquito had been fired upon by the Swedish coastal defences and the aircraft lost at sea. As a result, it was recommended that new instructions be issued to aircrew that, in future, should anyone find it necessary to land in Sweden, they should show some signs of obvious distress and fire a red Very light as soon as the anti-aircraft defences open fire.

A few weeks after Jock's crash landing, John Robins, a New Zealander from the same squadron, found himself in a similar fix. For whatever reason, the correct procedure for a forced landing in Sweden was not observed, Robins being convinced he had been briefed to make it appear as though on a training flight and, crucially, not war operations. He wrote a stinging report, which concluded: 'If we had baled out or ditched three miles off the Swedish coast, which we could quite easily have done, we would definitely have come under the heading of "distressed mariner" and thus been eligible for repatriation. The practice flight story, we are given to understand, is not and has never been recognised by the Swedish authorities.'

His report caused quite a stir. By way of context, at the time there were circa 1,000 Allied airmen interned in Sweden. The intelligence officer at Upwood denied that any such advice had ever been given. Robins, it was concluded, was confusing instructions given to airmen should they find themselves forced to land in Eire. Whoever was at fault, a clarification notice was issued which read:

> Whenever the conditions are favourable the aircraft should be landed at sea outside of territorial waters. The crew should then use their dinghy to reach the shore and claim release as shipwrecked airmen. An alternative would be to land at sea in daylight alongside a Swedish ship if it appeared to be making for a Swedish port. Aircrew who land in Swedish territory or with Swedish territorial waters will be interned, whether they claim to have been on a training flight or not.[25]

* * * * *

Jock Cassels had several near misses, both before and after his internment. One of his navigators had a tin leg: 'I was very lucky not to have had to abandon the aircraft during the time he flew with me. It took him somewhere in the region of five minutes to get through the hole in the floor when we returned from an operation. This was the same hole I would have to get through in an emergency, only I would have had to wait for him to get out first.'

Another of his navigators had a close call: 'He used to stick his pencil behind his ear when not using it. On one trip we were hit by shrapnel and one piece came through the windscreen. When he next went to use his pencil, he discovered there was nothing there. The pencil had been clean chopped in half.'[26]

* * * * *

Jack Maclennan, a Canadian mid-upper gunner, remembers a trip as a spare bod to bomb a V2 site near The Hague in September 1944. His pilot was the appointed deputy master bomber:

> After we dropped our TIs, the pilot dove down a few thousand feet and began to circle the target. It got pretty hot with all the flak coming up and bombs coming down and after what seemed like hours the rear gunner yelled 'Tally Ho! Enemy fighter etc.' The pilot dove and headed out across the North Sea. It was daylight and I looked all over for the fighter but failed to see one. When we got back, I told the rear gunner I hadn't seen any fighter and he said: 'There was no fighter, mate. If I hadn't said that we'd still be circling the fucking target!'[27]

* * * * *

One day, a General Post Office (GPO) vehicle arrived to install a new telegraph pole by the perimeter track of Downham Market and left it by the roadside. When the workers came back the next morning, it had gone. Someone had been out in the middle of the night with a two-handed saw (from whence it came, nobody knew) and chopped it into logs for the fire. Cleverly, they had dispersed the tell-tale signs of sawdust, so its disappearance was still a mystery. A few days later, the GPO delivered another pole, and the same thing happened. On the third occasion, the GPO not only delivered the pole but also erected it and wired it up on the same day, leaving no time for the night-time thieves to do their worst. The store of logs, however, kept the aircrew warm in their beds for several weeks after.[28]

✳ ✳ ✳ ✳ ✳

Des Lewis, an Australian navigator with 571 Squadron, was about to take off on a night flying test and was on the runway when they were recalled and ordered to report to briefing. One of the other navs had gone sick and Des and his pilot, Bill Wagener, another Australian, were needed as a replacement crew. It would be their first op. Des raced to get the rest of his flying kit and nav gear and arrived at the briefing room to find the nav's briefing was already over. The legs for the op, however, were clearly marked out on the wall map and Des asked the nav sitting next to him for the name of the target. The nav demurred and um'd and ah'd before announcing finally, 'Essen'. With the details of each leg, Des hurriedly plotted them on his chart, but try as he might, he couldn't get them to arrive at Essen. He was about to query the helpful nav again when the main briefing started, and the CO took the stage and proclaimed: 'the target for tonight… is Gelsenkirchen'. Des immediately looked to the man beside him and said, 'You bastard, you gave me all the wrong gen.' To which the nav replied, 'Sorry chum. I couldn't pronounce it. And anyway, you'll be able to see it from Essen.'

Des' response is not recorded.

Chapter 16

Bitter Victory and Legacy

W hen the plaudits were offered to the senior commanders at the end of World War Two, beneath a thin layer of perfunctory goodwill it was soon apparent that, in the safety of peace, the bombers' part in the war was one that many politicians and civilians would prefer to forget.[1] The men of the army of occupation were at first awed and increasingly dismayed by the devastation wreaked on a defeated enemy. Sir Arthur Harris was denied a peerage, despite his loyal and fervent service and Bomber Command's undoubted contribution to Allied victory. While that anomaly was rectified some years later, by then it was too late and a narrative of shame and embarrassment towards the achievements of the bomber boys had already been established and, to some extent, continues to this day.

Bennett also found himself guilty by association, and the achievements of the Pathfinders quickly forgotten. There was little need or demand for PFF in Tiger Force, which only served to hasten its end. John Whitley briefly took over as AOC 8 Group in the third week of May 1945, but only until the group was disbanded in the final weeks of the year, by which time a war-weary nation wanted to forget. Bennett was the only bomber group commander not to receive a knighthood, though the genesis of this decision lay undoubtedly in the snobbery of the times towards a mere colonial officer and was surely not helped by his deep antipathy towards his opposite number in 5 Group, Ralph Cochrane.

The rivalry between Cochrane and Bennett was one of equals and opposites, both men believing firmly and earnestly that their way was the right way. While the relationship was cordial at the beginning, it soon became considerably less so, despite Bennett's protestations to the end of his days that the two remained personal friends.

Cochrane was a Scottish aristocrat who had started life in the Royal Navy and piloted airships in World War One. Transferring to the RAF, he first came across Harris when the latter was OC 45 Squadron, and Cochrane was one of his flight commanders. The mutual respect between the two men was immediate, Harris describing Cochrane as 'outstanding' and Harris was one of the only officers to address Cochrane as 'Cocky', except on formal business.[2] Their relationship crossed the boundary, therefore, from being professional to one of sound personal friendship. Marked out early for high command, Cochrane played a key role in establishing the RNZAF as a staff officer of some note, and on his return, and the start of the war, he began his long association with Bomber Command. It was his appointment as AOC 5 Group in early 1943 that led him to an early confrontation with Bennett.

Until that point, Bennett had enjoyed a comparatively free hand in establishing PFF and developing new marking techniques. With Cochrane in charge of 5 Group, and with the ear of Harris, what started as an irritation to Bennett fast descended into open hostility. Cochrane was a tremendous self-publicist, something Bennett abhorred, so much so that he refused to have a publicity officer as part of his HQ staff.[3] In hindsight, this was a poor decision and allowed 5 Group to trumpet its achievements at every turn, while the role of PFF went largely unreported and certainly uncelebrated. The success of the Dams Raid – the incredible low-level attack on the Möhne, Eder and Sorpe dams in May 1943 – only served to widen the cracks that were beginning to show. Few, if any, could deny the phenomenal bravery of the men taking part, and even if the attack has subsequently been shown not to have achieved the results intended, the raid captured the imagination of the public then and now. It was helped by a slick PR machine that leapt into action within moments of the first aircraft landing.

Bennett, in his biography, acknowledges the raid, somewhat ungraciously, by comparing the defences confronting a later attack by low-flying PFF

Mosquitoes on the Kiel Canal – 97 guns and 25 searchlights – to those on 'other pieces of water in which things were dropped'. The inference is clear: that the skill and nerve required by the men of PFF on the Kiel raid were at least equal to, and perhaps even greater than, that demonstrated by the Dambusters. And it was undertaken not after weeks of training ('in comparison to some others in Bomber Command who had to go in for intense training for a considerable period before they undertook any special duty'[4]), but within 24 hours of being ordered.

Bennett's comments do Cochrane, 617 Squadron and even his own men a gross disservice, and it is not true – as he goes on to assert – that none of his men received gallantry awards for their night's work. Rather than strengthening his position, Bennett's comments serve to weaken it and allow his detractors to dismiss them as coming from one who sought to trumpet his own men's achievements by denigrating the efforts of others. His disparaging remarks about Leonard Cheshire at the time and after the war were also misjudged and made him look petty, to the extent that even his most ardent supporters, Mahaddie among them, distanced themselves from them.

The success of the Dams Raid, the publicity around it and the mythology it created, enabled Cochrane to retain 617 Squadron as one earmarked for 'special' operations. It is strange, and wholly incongruous, that in allowing 617 to be separate from Main Force and 8 Group, Harris was allowing an elite corps of men to exist that he claimed he was so against. The irony was not lost on Bennett, who now competed not only with Coastal Command and the Royal Navy for the latest innovations and thinking but also a squadron in a neighbouring group. For example, when Bennett requested the use of VHF to control future bombing raids, he was denied; however, those very same VHF sets were made available to his rivals, without any note or explanation.

The attack on Peenemünde was the first in which Cochrane appears to have got his way and put one of his pet marking theories into practice. This was the 'time and distance run' – effectively a countdown to an aiming point from an easily identifiable landmark (a datum point) – which he believed would offer greater accuracy than PFF's existing methods. Cochrane had been advocating time and distance for some time. He'd tested his theory as part of Operation *Bellicose*, a long-range attack on the Zeppelin works at Friedrichshafen in June 1943, which combined 'traditional' Pathfinder marking with the time and distance method, but Harris had appeared to take little notice. He'd also been openly critical of Bennett's marking techniques, following a less than satisfactory attack on Stuttgart two months earlier.

The attack on Stuttgart, marking blindly using H2S, started to go wrong when Main Force bombed the red TIs almost immediately after they were dropped rather than wait for the following green TIs at which they were supposed to aim. The trouble was compounded when a single green TI went astray, and which again attracted a disproportionate weight of bombs in spite of the presence of a far greater concentration of greens closer to the correct aiming point. In Cochrane's mind, the failure was all down to poor marking; for Bennett, it illustrated the tendency of Main Force bomb aimers to drop their bombs on the first marker they saw. Cochrane wrote to Harris and copied in Bennett, asking for comment. Bennett agreed with Cochrane that some TIs had fallen short, but the worst placed marker was a red four miles from the target and Main Force had been ordered to bomb the greens. 'If all bomb aimers had been punctilious and conscientious as the importance of their job warrants,' Bennett wrote, 'then the raid would not have failed.'[5]

The AOC 5 Group had sowed a seed of doubt and repeated that a timed-run bomb release technique would have offered greater accuracy. Bennett responded on this point too, noting that it was one of his own original ideas, but that time and distance was a method that was only any use in avoiding completely stupid mistakes, such as bombing a dummy target or, indeed, the wrong town. Regardless, many crews, he insisted, had no idea whatsoever of how to make a timed run.[6]

The honour of PFF had been impinged, although Bennett was honest in PFF's shortcomings. He felt sure that even in PFF there were those who regarded exhortations to bomb with more precision as being 'the hot air of somebody who does not know operations'.[7] He also reminded Cochrane and Harris that only a few months earlier the very best of Bomber Command were perfectly happy and satisfied if they were getting 3 per cent of their bombs on a built-up area!

The third wave in the Peenemünde raid was made up completely of 5 Group aircraft and all were instructed to make a timed run from the datum point, the island of Rügen, or bomb the PFF TIs if they could see them. It was not a particular success. There was some confusion over the target and in the event, 5 Group aircraft suffered a very high number of casualties, although this had everything to do with the late arrival of the German night fighter force that had previously been 'spoofed' onto another raid. This may have been the reason that Cochrane was so piqued, for he wrote yet another letter in which he was, again, highly critical of the Pathfinders' marking and suggested the case for time and distance had been incontrovertibly proven.[8] He pointed to analysis that appeared to show those who had bombed blind at the end of their timed run had achieved greater accuracy than those who had bombed the nearest visual marker. Bennett, of course, disagreed; the Peenemünde raid, which necessitated three separate aiming points, was incredibly complex, and a time and distance approach on all three could not have worked. More to the point, it would never be as accurate as being able to see and bomb a target visually. He did agree, however, and repeated that a timed run had its place in overcoming gross inaccuracies and should be used as a matter of habit on every attack to ensure 'no stupid bomb aimer mistakes occur'.[9]

Peenemünde, it turned out, was the thin end of the wedge and, little by little, Cochrane chipped away at Harris to allow him to experiment further with his ideas. Harris, of course, was a willing listener, for although he supported Bennett personally, he behaved in a way that suggested he still only viewed PFF as a temporary expedience until such time as he could upskill other groups to lead their own squadrons into battle. This had always been his original intention and was what eventually happened.

The denouement came over Berlin. By now Cochrane had a new hobby horse in which he was supported by his co-conspirator-in-chief, Cheshire.

Both believed that very low-level marking, at rooftop height, was the only way to ensure an aiming point was accurately marked. A precision attack on the aero-engine factory at Limoges on 8/9 February 1944 had proved the point. Cheshire had achieved incredible accuracy – and displayed superlative bravery – by flying low over the target at around 50ft, first to provide time for the French factory workers to take cover and then to mark the target for a small force of 617 Squadron Lancasters to bomb. It was a tremendous success with even greater tactical importance. It appeared to show that precision targets could be successfully hit if marked at low level, and with greater accuracy than even Oboe allowed. Whether it could achieve similar success against more heavily defended targets was a point both Cochrane and Cheshire were wanting to prove.

Cochrane made his case to Harris who, in turn, asked Bennett to comment. Bennett dismissed the idea for the folly he thought it was. Theory was one thing, and, in perfect conditions, there was a case for low-level marking. But flying over a densely packed city like Berlin at night, with flak and searchlights your constant companion, did not lend itself to a successful outcome. Bennett undoubtedly thought the idea would be dropped and his comments appreciated, however bluntly they were expressed. He was wrong. Badly so. He was sent for and told in no uncertain terms that Cochrane was to be allowed his experiment. Worse than this, Bennett was to return two heavy and one Mosquito squadrons to Cochrane with immediate effect.

It was a bitter blow and, to some at least, a sad day for Bomber Command. Bennett lost his squadrons as a direct result of his blunt dismissal of an idea that Harris himself may have dismissed with further thought. Harris had immense faith in Bennett's abilities but doubtless felt his subordinate had over-stepped the mark. He actively encouraged fresh thinking from his group commanders, Cochrane especially, and was clearly irritated by Bennett's opinion, which he appears to have thought churlish. John Searby, PFF's first master bomber, thought Harris' actions 'abrupt and indeed unfair'.[10] Bennett had borne the heat and burden of the day from the moment PFF was created and had literally plucked success from a ground-bed of mediocre attempts to get the bombs on target. But some considered the Australian both conceited and intolerant, and it was this intolerance that resulted in what Bennett himself described as a tremendous slap in the face to a force that had turned Harris' Bomber Command from a wasteful and ineffective force into a mighty and successful one. 'It meant in the eyes of the rest of the Command that, in the opinion of the Commander-in-Chief, the Pathfinders had apparently failed.'[11]

Searby and more recent commentators, including Cochrane's own biographer, dismissed Bennett's assertion strongly. The destruction of Krupps, the devastation of Hamburg and the continual slogging away at every heavily defended target in the Reich tell their own story.[12] Harris too, in an oblique reference to Cochrane and 5 Group, wrote in his memoire: 'I continued to entrust the Pathfinder Force with the identification of the target in nearly all our principal attacks until the end of the war.' This was indeed the case; every major assault remained Bennett's responsibility.

Bennett fought a fierce rearguard action to make Harris change his mind but was warned to desist by Harris' deputy, Saundby. The three squadrons moved to 5 Group on 6 April 1944, never to return, although nominally still on the 8 Group roster. The fact that Bennett was expected to train and supply replacement crews to the lost squadrons rubbed salt into the soon-festering wound. Sidney Bufton, the man who had done so much to bring a target-marking force about, wrote that while the detachment was temporary, there was a real risk the transfer could become permanent should the 5 Group marking methods prove a success. This, he decided, could lead to the disintegration of the PFF which, he added, 'would be contrary to Air Staff policy'.[13]

The depth of despair was not limited to the senior commander and his staff, nor their supporters like Bufton. Searby recalled the 83 Squadron farewell party as 'not the happiest occasion', where some, like Bufton, gloomily predicted the eclipse of PFF.[14] Many in 97 Squadron felt the same and their mood was not improved by the crass actions of the base commander, Air Commodore Bobby Sharp, on their arrival at Coningsby. Sharp was described as the kind of officer who masked his lack of any operational experience by his pomposity.[15] He took the crews into the station cinema where they were subjected to a lecture on how they should now give up their 8 Group ways as they were now 5 Group men. This was deeply resented by the PFF crews, many of whom were highly experienced and understandably proud of PFF's achievements, their 'eagle' and their rank. Some rated the eagle – unofficially at least – ahead of the DFC in terms of prestige.[16] While it was true that 83 and 97 had both been 5 Group squadrons in the past, there were few, if any, aircrew who existed from those days, and another generation of aircrew would be required before the 5 Group spirit predominated.

Cochrane was not sure who was more surprised by Harris' decision – him or Bennett? However, it was to have far-reaching consequences for both men and deepen the rift between them. It meant Cochrane had his own train set with which to play, and in the spirit of childishness it was quickly dubbed (at its most polite) 'Cochrane's Independent Air Force'. There were other names given to it that left no doubt as to the anger and betrayal that many Pathfinders felt at the time. One joker, while discussing the future partner of Princess Elizabeth, was said to have remarked gloomily that whoever it was, it was likely to be a 5 Group man![17]

Some of the squadron and station commanders, men like John Searby, Laurence Deane and Peter Johnson, served both masters and had similar memories. Johnson recalled not only being surprised but indeed shocked by the depth of hostility felt by Bennett towards Cochrane and 5 Group marking methods, which the Pathfinder AOC believed could lose the war.[18] While he made sure to remain detached from the in-fighting between the two groups, Johnson believed Bomber Command owed an enormous debt of gratitude to Bennett, and that as a Pathfinder CO he was still bound to Bennett by a considerable degree of loyalty. Laurence Deane found himself caught in a tug of war between the two men when, in the autumn of 1944, Bennett requested his return to 8 Group (at the time, Deane was OC 83 Squadron in 5 Group) and Cochrane refused. Deane was exhausted, not just by the many sorties he had flown but by having to suffer the over-enthusiasm of his CO, which included the dangers of flying in a full moon and which Deane blamed for his squadron's mounting losses. As he said, 'Cochrane may have mellowed a little had he dropped the odd bomb in anger.'[19]

Cochrane's lack of current operational experience was a point Bennett raised on many an occasion. It was, he believed, Cochrane's Achilles' heel, and therefore rendered many of his opinions irrelevant. Conversely, Bennett's flying experience was his strength, and despite being told categorically by Harris that he was not to fly any further operations – an order given to all group AOCs within Bomber Command – there is plenty of evidence to suggest that the C-in-C's orders were ignored. He is known to have told Howard Lees, the photographic genius, that he had flown a reconnaissance sortie in a 1409 Met Flight Mosquito ahead of the attack on Peenemünde. It had been recorded in his logbook as 'bombing practice'.[20] Boris Bressloff recalled working on his radar plot on the way to Leipzig and being conscious of someone looking over his shoulder: 'I told him that if he had nothing better to do, he could bugger off, but just at that point an arm appeared with the clear rank of an air commodore on its sleeve. It was Bennett.'[21] Others distinctly recalled seeing Bennett at debriefings in flying overalls, when he had almost certainly gone along for the ride. Nick Nicholson remembered coming back from a raid and was about to be debriefed when Bennett put his arm around him and said, 'Be careful what you say, I was just above you over the target!'[22]

The freedom afforded to 5 Group's Independent Air Force enabled Cochrane and Cheshire to further experiment with their own brand of low-level visual ground marking. It produced attacks that were materially better than those achieved in the high-level blind Oboe marking attacks that had preceded them. Bomb wastage was reduced, and accuracy improved to a level described as 'brilliant' by the authors of the *Official History*.[23] It enabled certain bomber commanders, Jack Slessor among them, to claim that Cochrane had proved that a separate Pathfinding force had never been necessary:[24] 'There was a better way of getting the result, which we all agreed was essential, than forming a special Pathfinder Group.' Harris himself said much the same thing. In a letter to Portal on 14 April 1944, Harris wrote,

'I am still not satisfied that the institution of the PFF as a single entity has proved in the outcome to be either the right or the best solution.'[25] It is understandable, in this context, why Bennett felt the way he did.

The ORS at Bomber Command credited the use of a master bomber (often Cheshire), a single point at which to aim with a common wind value on the bombsight, and the experience of the crews in attacking precision targets for the 'superiority of the 5 Group technique.'[26] The history questions whether the crews actually had that much experience on precision targets, and thinks the success more likely to be down to the skill of the markers. Leaving Cheshire and his 617 Squadron crews aside, many of these were of course former 8 Group men!

But while the 5 Group technique undoubtedly resulted in some stunningly accurate attacks, not least a raid on the railway marshalling yards at Juvisy on 18 April, which left the place a virtual ruin, it was far from foolproof. Cochrane discovered, as Bennett had always made clear, that all operations were at the mercy of the weather. Apart from the use of PFF Oboe Mosquitoes, which were still deployed for what is described as 'proximity marking', the whole of each operation first turned on the visual identification and marking of the target, and secondly upon a clear view of the markers from the bombing aircraft.[27] It meant they could not be carried out in poor visibility or cloud. And there was another weakness: by their very nature, some aircraft were obliged to be in the target area for some time, and when difficulties were encountered, the whole of the main attacking force could find themselves standing off while they awaited further instructions. This allowed time for the German night fighters to gather, with inevitable consequences. Bomber Command suffered terrible losses over Mailly-le-Camp and Lille on the nights of 3 May and 10 May 1944, respectively, and both were as a result of a hitch in the marking technique and poor communication that left the bombing force in the target area for much longer than was intended. Thus, even against lightly defended targets of shallow penetration, Cochrane's new methods were liable to expose the bombing force to more than the usual hazards of night operations.

Bennett and Cochrane continued to champion their own marking methods, and both believed passionately in their respective position, despite neither truly having the monopoly on which technique was best. Both enjoyed successes and failures, triumphs and defeats. On the night of 26/27 April, for example, a 5 Group attack on Schweinfurt was a total failure and the bombing wholly inaccurate. Losses (at 9.3 per cent of the attacking force) were also disproportionately heavy. By comparison, an 8 Group-led raid on Friederichshafen the following night was described as 'an outstandingly successful attack based on good Pathfinder marking'.[28] Bomber Command later estimated that 99 acres of the town – including two-thirds of the town's built-up areas – were totally devastated. German officials confirmed this was the most devastating raid on tank production during the war.

Further attacks by 8 Group on Bremen (18/19 August) and Rüsselsheim (25/26 August) were wholly successful, the former being described as the most destructive raid of the war (on the city) thanks to perfect marking throughout. On the same night that 8 Group went to Rüsselsheim and laid waste the Opel motor factory in ten minutes, 5 Group went to Darmstadt and its low-flying Mosquitoes failed to find the target. The master bomber had to return early, and his two deputies were shot down. They went back to Darmstadt less than a month later, however, and produced an outstandingly accurate and concentrated raid that caused extensive fires and was promoted by the Germans as being an extreme example of RAF 'terror bombing'.

The point is a simple one: comparisons are almost always invidious, not always helpful and can easily be selected to support a particular narrative. It is interesting, however, that when Bomber Command tried an experimental raid without the use of Pathfinding aircraft from either 5 Group or 8 Group, it was a total failure. Despite all the Main Force aircraft being equipped with H2S, and told to find the target themselves, they couldn't, and other towns up to 20 miles away were mistaken for the target and bombed. Raids had to be led by experienced and highly skilled crews, regardless of what marking technique they ultimately deployed, or which Group they followed.

Bennett's sense of betrayal continued to the war's end and for many years after. It probably irked him to his dying day. He complained bitterly that his men were never given the recognition or accolades they deserved, and that although men like Alec Cranswick had flown possibly more operations than any other Bomber Command pilot, the public had never heard of him.[29] This is true, but it is also for reasons that Bennett must himself take personal responsibility – shunning publicity and encouraging his men to do the same. Cochrane, conversely, used PR brilliantly and was tremendous at promoting the success of his group.

Bennett may have had legitimate grounds for avoiding publicity. Harris said as much in his own autobiography. While he saw value in publicity, not least to aid with recruitment, the role of PFF and its men also needed to be kept secret. He feared what would happen to PFF aircrew if they fell into enemy hands.[30] But because Bennett discouraged boasting in his own group, he especially disliked it in others. When Leonard Cheshire was awarded the VC, it referenced a particularly successful attack on Munich that Cheshire had taken part in. The master bomber (or 'controller' in more typical 5 Group parlance) was Laurence Deane. Deane recounted that on that particular trip, Cheshire had to return soon after marking the aiming point, as he was short on fuel. As the raid progressed, however, a 617 Squadron Lancaster dropped a replacement marker some distance from the aiming point that Deane was obliged to correct. In the event he spent more than half an hour over the target and was lucky to make it back in one piece. Deane does not suggest Cheshire was not deserving of a VC for his undoubted bravery over an extended period of time, but rather that it should really have been awarded for one explicit act of bravery, and the attack on Munich, where he was only around for a few minutes, was not – in his opinion – a good example. He appears to suggest that the medal was as much recommended as an opportunity to promote Cochrane and his independent bombing force, as it was to recognise the specific bravery of Cheshire. This is undoubtedly unfair; Cheshire flew more than 100 bomber operations and was on his third tour of operations when Cochrane decided to call time on his protégé's career. On the raid on Munich, Cheshire displayed exemplary bravery, flying through a hail of flak at low level and high speed to accurately mark the target. On reading the raid report, however, Bennett is said to have phoned Deane and congratulated him on 'his' VC, which he firmly believed had been given to the wrong man!

Bennett's disinclination towards publicity is evidenced in many ways, not least the fact that very few wartime photographs of the man exist. There are also very few contemporary articles, besides one by Victor Lewis, the *Daily Sketch*'s air correspondent, written in the winter of 1943 and for which he was given access to Bennett and some of his men. But unlike the famous pictures of the Dams, or the sinking of the *Tirpitz*, there is no equivalent 8 Group publicity or iconic imagery for any of its stunning successes, neither was there a challenge at the time to the 5 Group assertion that it had 'invented' the master bomber concept – a claim reinforced by Slessor[31] – and certainly little or no mention of the two men who should really be given credit, John Searby and Pat Daniels.[32] Daniels controlled an operation to Frankfurt on 2 December 1942 – a full five months before the Dams raid for those inclined to suggest it was Gibson who was first to use the technique.[33]

Indeed, very few PFF aircrew achieved true recognition in the same way many 5 Group men were feted. Names like Guy Gibson and Leonard Cheshire are the eponymous heroes of Bomber Command, 'the bravest of the brave', and 617 the only 'crack' squadron. Noble and Frankland, in their mighty study, *The Strategic Air Offensive against Germany*, constantly reference Gibson, Cheshire and Mickey Martin as 'the greatest bomber pilots of the war'. There appears no place for any of the Pathfinder 'greats' – men like Guy Lockhart, for example, or Tubby Baker, who was ordered to rest after 100 sorties, or Alec Cranswick, who made the ultimate sacrifice. And what about Johnny Fauquier, described as Canada's greatest bomber pilot, who flew three tours in an operational career that spanned both 8 and 5 Groups, including a later spell as OC 617 Squadron? Perhaps it is true that giants appear as tall men when all men are tall.[34]

The antipathy between 5 Group and 8 Group continued even after the fighting was over. Just after the war, Frank Leatherdale was one of two service representatives to the court of the Guild of Air Pilots and Air Navigators. A committee had been established to discuss RAF uniform, and various recommendations were made and agreed on that included removing the coveted Pathfinder eagle. Somewhat concerned about this, Frank sought out Sir John Salmond:

> When I told him [what was being proposed], he immediately said: 'Trenchard will want to hear about this', and led me over to meet the great man. When Trenchard learned that it was none other than Sir Ralph Cochrane who was chairman of the committee and had made the recommendation, he blurted out: 'I never could stand that man. Leave it with us.' I am not quite sure what happened after that but suffice to say it was the only recommendation that was not ultimately taken up.[35]

Frank's story is not unusual. Even as recently as 2012, ahead of the official opening of the Bomber Command Memorial, the author witnessed some very real attempts by certain parties to promote the role of 5 Group ahead of any other part of Bomber Command. Some memories are long, and some rivalries are never friendly, no matter what the protagonists might subsequently say to the contrary. Despite claiming friendship with Cochrane, for example, Bennett couldn't even be bothered to spell his rival's name correctly in his autobiography!

Pathfinders should join the pantheon of military greats. They did not turn the tide of the war as has recently been asserted; that can only be true if it assumes the war was effectively won by Bomber Command, which it clearly wasn't. But PFF's contribution to victory should certainly be better recognised than it is. It is a view shared across the surviving Pathfinder community. Their achievements were legion and their sacrifice immense. PFF lost at least 3,618 men, but the credit column showed they had flown some 50,490 sorties and dealt with 3,440 targets.[36]

Its marking expertise was also adopted by air forces in other theatres of war. The men of 614 Squadron RAF (formerly 462 Squadron RAAF), for example, were trained in Pathfinding and target marking for the entire 205 Group night bombing force of Wellingtons and Liberators for raids on Italy and the Balkans. By 1944, they had the benefit of Gee, H2S and the Mk XIV bombsight, but like their counterparts in western Europe, suffered similar issues with equipment serviceability. They also had the further challenge of the mountainous terrain, a hurdle that was eventually overcome by using Gee for most of the outward track, and H2S when it was beneficial to do so. Their success in finding and marking targets increased rapidly throughout 1944, and in October of that year, 614's role as a Pathfinder squadron was officially recognised when selected crews were authorised to wear the coveted Pathfinder eagle. They flew their final Pathfinder operation in southern Europe on 3 March 1945. Fittingly, the target was oil.[37]

In his victory message, Bennett praised the men and women of Pathfinder Force for their unrelenting spirit and energy and on the results they achieved. 'Path Finder Force [*sic*] has shouldered a grave responsibility,' he wrote. 'It has led Bomber Command, the greatest striking force ever known.

'Happiness to you all – always. Keep pressing on along the Path of Peace.'

References and Sources

Chapter 1

1. Interviews with the author, 2010. John retired as an air commodore with the DFC, AFC and an LVO from The King. His autobiography, *Churchill's Navigator*, was published by Grub Street.
2. *Bomber Command*, HMSO (1941)
3. Quoted in John Terraine, *The Right of the Line*, Hodder & Stoughton (1985), p. 260
4. *The Central Blue*, Cassell (1956), p. 371. Air Vice Marshal John 'Jack' Slessor, who succeeded Norman Bottomley to command 5 Group in 1941–42, had not flown a night operation since the end of World War One and subsequently confessed to being over-optimistic about his crews' capacity to find and hit targets at night.
5. Ibid., p. 368
6. Martin Middlebrook, *Bomber Command War Diaries*, Viking (1985), p. 93
7. Slessor, op. cit., p. 385
8. Ibid., p. 366
9. *The Strategic Air Offensive Against Germany (SAOAG)*, Vol. 1., Noble & Frankland, p. 219
10. Ibid., p. 227. Bottomley was AOC 5 Group prior to John Slessor and succeeding Arthur Harris. Coningham was 4 Group AOC until the summer of 1941.
11. Ibid., p. 228
12. Ibid., p. 156

13. Terraine, op. cit., p. 275
14. SAOAG, op. cit., p. 229
15. Ibid., p. 245
16. Ibid., p. 246
17. Middlebrook, op. cit., p. 220
18. W J Lawrence, *No. 5 Bomber Group*, Faber (1951), p. 48
19. Terraine, op. cit., p. 293
20. SAOAG, op. cit., p. 183
21. Ibid. The minute is reproduced in full.
22. Middlebrook, op. cit., p. 221
23. Ibid., p. 218
24. Terraine, op. cit., p. 460
25. Taken from Churchill's history of World War Two, *The Grand Alliance*, Vol. 111, p. 748
26. SAOAG, op. cit., Vol. 1, pp. 180–81

Chapter 2

1. Dudley Sward, *Bomber Harris*, Buchan and Enright (1984), p. 154
2. Dennis Richards, *Royal Air Force 1939–1945*, Vol. 1: 'The Fight at Odds', p. 383
3. Jamming was first suspected on the night of 6–7 August 1942.
4. Arthur Harris, *Bomber Offensive*, Collins (1947), p. 128
5. SAOAG, op. cit., p. 389
6. Ibid., p. 391
7. Oboe
8. Obituary, *The Daily Telegraph*, 3 April 1993
9. These included Group Captain Gus Walker, Group Captain Hugh Constantine, Wing Commander Wille Tait, Wing Commander Don Bennett, Wing Commander Trevor Freeman and Wing Commander Jimmy Marks.
10. Letter from Trevor Freeman, OC 115 Squadron, to Arthur Morley at the Air Ministry in AIR20/4782
11. Letter from Charles Whitworth to Sidney Bufton in AIR20/4782

12. Letter from Gus Walker to Bufton in AIR20/4782
13. Letter from Willie Tate to Ken Smith at the Air Ministry in AIR20/4782
14. Slessor, op. cit., p. 373
15. Obituary, op.cit.
16. Report by Wing Commander Marwood Elton of Bomber Command Operations Branch as quoted in SAOAG p. 423 fn.
17. Harris., op. cit., p. 128
18. SAOAG, op. cit., p. 422; letter to Bufton from Harris, 17 April 1942
19. As cited in Alan Cooper, *We Act with One Accord* (1998)
20. Nigel Walker, *Strike to Defend*, Neville Spearman (1963), p. 85
21. Group Captain Laurence Deane DSO DFC, *A Pathfinder's War and Peace*, Merlin Books (1993), p. 60
22. Interview with the author, 2012. Gwynne retired as Squadron Leader Gwynne Price AFM.
23. Diary entry for C A P Noble, the author's great uncle. 'Peter' Noble was killed on his 24th operation on the night of 12 December 1944.
24. AIR 14/3523
25. Harris insisted that he was never against the formation of a target marking force, describing the suggestion in an interview in 1977 for the Centre for Air Power Studies that this was a 'half truth' and that his real desire for a target marking force in each group was subsequently vindicated.
26. From the Portal Papers as quoted in Anthony Furse, *Wilfred Freeman*, Spellmount (2000), p. 207
27. Ibid., p. 207
28. Private correspondence between Bufton and Browne, 15 June 1942.
29. Harris, op. cit., p. 128
30. Ibid., p. 129

Chapter 3

1. As recounted in a letter to the author from Squadron Leader Ian Hewitt, DFC and Bar. Hewitt and four other members of his crew, including the pilot, Don MacIntyre, evaded capture after their aircraft

was shot down in the same attack on the *Tirpitz*. Skilfully crash landing on the ice of a lake near Hocklingham in Norway, it is their Halifax that was subsequently recovered and is now exhibited at the RAF Museum, Hendon.

2. Donald Bennett, *Pathfinder*, Muller (1958), pp. 158–9
3. Ibid., p. 158
4. Bennett was wearing a chest parachute as opposed to a seat-type parachute later favoured by pilots and some rear gunners.
5. Bennett, op. cit., p. 21
6. Ibid., p. 25
7. Ibid., p. 35
8. Centre for Air Power Studies recorded interview, 1980
9. I am indebted to the help provided by Philip Cleland, Ralph's son, and for information on his father's career and friendship with Bennett.
10. Bennett, op. cit., p. 45
11. Ibid., p. 141
12. Wing Commander Bill Anderson OBE DFC AFC, *Pathfinders*, Jarrolds (1946), p. 49
13. Hamish Mahaddie, *Hamish: The Story of a Pathfinder*, Ian Allen (1989), p. 57
14. Chaz Bowyer, *Pathfinders at War*, Ian Allen (1977), p. 77
15. Bennett, op. cit., pp. 58–9
16. Ibid., p. 63. Unfortunately, the scheme was subsequently dropped, as it proved impractical.
17. Ibid., p. 90. A total of 117 passengers and crew lost their lives in the disaster. The U-boat captain claimed legitimacy for the attack on the grounds that the ship was in an unusual position, plotting a zig-zag course and easily mistaken, therefore, for a troop ship or enemy 'Q' ship.
18. Ibid., p. 91
19. Ibid., pp. 98–9
20. Ibid., p. 125
21. Group Captain Dand

22. *The Whitley File*, Air Britain (1986)

23. Bennett, op. cit., p. 137

24. Wing Commander David Oswald Young AFC was awarded the DFC with 76 Squadron in January 1942 and retired as Group Captain D O Young DSO DFC AFC.

25. Staton had commanded 10 Squadron early in the war and taken part in one of the first attacks on the *Tirpitz*. He later endured three years as a prisoner of the Japanese. See *Churchill's Navigator* by Sean Feast, Grub Street.

26. To feather an engine was to turn its blades to be edgewise, to stop them windmilling and prevent drag.

27. Spalding was killed just over a week later.

28. Bennett, op. cit., p. 131

29. Letter from Bennett to Ken Smith in AIR20/4782

30. His second pilot, Harry Walmsley, received the DFM.

31. Bufton had proposed Embry, with Bennett as his senior air staff officer (SASO) but, for whatever reason, Embry had not been released and Harris got what he wanted. Interestingly, Embry makes no mention of any such consideration in his biography, *Mission Completed*.

32. Harris, op. cit., p. 129

33. Ibid., p. 130

34. Later Brigadier General Jack Watts DSO DFC and Bar CD, interview and correspondence with author, 2011

35. Andrew Maitland, *Through the Bombsight*, William Kimber (1986), p. 116

36. Anderson, op. cit., p. 51

37. Interview with author and quoted in Sean Feast, *Master Bombers*, Grub Street (2008)

38. Laddie Lucas, *Wings of War*, Hutchinson (1983), p. 224

39. Interview with the author, 2011

40. Centre for Air Power Studies recorded interview, 1980

41. Mahaddie, op. cit., p. 55

42. Harris, op. cit., p. 130

43. Hajo Herrmann, *Eagle's Wings*, Airlife (1991), p. 202

Chapter 4

1. Wing Commander Alan Oakeshott DFC
2. Group Captain John MacDonald DFC and Bar AFC
3. Macdonald is largely credited as having dropped the first bombs on German soil during World War Two.
4. Bennett, op. cit., p. 168
5. Jonathan Falconer, *The Bomber Command Handbook*, Sutton (1998), p. 189
6. 15 Squadron had originally been chosen but, in the event, it was 7 Squadron that was given over to PFF
7. Bennett, op. cit., p. 169
8. AIR14/2701, 11 August 1942 – 109 was associated with the force but established independent of it.
9. Robert Murray Buchan – Angus to his friends – had been awarded the DFC while flying with 51 Squadron in 1941.
10. They were also equipped with the first Mosquitoes in very small numbers.
11. Middlebrook, op. cit., p. 299
12. Bill Grierson, *We Band of Brothers*, J&KH (1997), p. 172
13. Letter from Harris to Carr in AIR14/2714, 20 June 1942
14. Grierson, op. cit., p. 299
15. AIR14/2701 Formation of Pathfinder Force, 21 August 1942
16. AIR14/2714 Headquarters 4 Group to all station commanders, 28 June 1942
17. Happily, he retired as Group Captain W H Swetman DSO DFC. He died in 2014 in his 95th year.
18. AIR14/2714
19. Gordon Musgrove, *Pathfinder Force*, Macdonald and Jane's (1976), p. 8. 35 Squadron had moved from RAF Linton-on-Ouse, 83 Squadron from RAF Scampton and 109 Squadron from RAF Stradishall. 7 Squadron, which was already at Oakington, and 156 Squadron, which was already at Wyton, were attached.
20. Anderson, op. cit., p. 52

21. Bennett, op. cit., p. 174

22. That honour went to Flight Lieutenant Douglas Greenup.

23. Sergeant J W Smith in a 35 Squadron Halifax had the dubious honour of becoming PFF's first operational casualty.

24. Bennett, op. cit., p. 174

25. AIR25/152 ORB For PFF Headquarters

26. Middlebrook, op. cit., p. 306

27. Bennett, op. cit., p. 178

28. Wing Commander Jimmy Marks DSO DFC

29. Vincent Ashworth, *'Artie' - Bomber Command Legend*, Fighting High (2014), p. 107

30. *London Gazette* (LG), 5 Jan 1943

31. Musgrove, op. cit., p. 21

32. Ashworth, op. cit., p. 111

33. John Maynard, *Bennett and the Pathfinders*, Arms & Armour (1996), p. 98

34. SAOSAG, Vol. 1, p. 434

35. Ibid., p. 435

36. Arthur Harris, *Despatch on War Operations: 1942–45*

Chapter 5

1. SAOAG, Vol. 1, op. cit., p. 433

2. Maynard, op. cit., p. 104

3. Bowyer, op. cit., p. 30

4. Ibid., p. 31

5. Mahaddie, op. cit., p. 91

6. AIR14/2701 Letter from Bennett to Harris, 25 September 1943. It is interesting to note that in the same letter, Bennett still describes the 'failed' attack on Hannover as a paragon of success compared to the farcical raids carried out before PFF.

7. Bowyer, op. cit., p. 30

8. Lucas, op. cit., p. 228

9. Mahaddie, op. cit., p. 94

10. Interview with author, 2011

11. A 4 Group squadron based in Snaith

12. Interview with author, 2011. Fred joined 35 Squadron at Graveley but was shot down on the night of 21 June 1943, the victim of a German night fighter.

13. Correspondence with author, 2008

14. Wing Commander Bob Alexander DFC

15. Interview with author, 2008

16. Correspondence via his daughter, Marilyn Shank, 2021

17. Interview with author, 2005

18. Interview with author, 2005

19. Interview with author, 2011. Bill Peedell was killed in a helicopter crash in 1966.

20. SAOAG, Vol. 1, p. 433 fn.

21. AIR14/2701

22. Interview with Reverend Les Hood, 2007

23. Interview with author, 2008

24. Interview with author, 2011

25. Via Paul Goodwin. Paul has written his father's story – *The Last Navigator* – and has kindly allowed me to quote from his book.

26. Interview and correspondence with author, 2009

27. Walter Thompson DFC and Bar, *Lancaster to Berlin*, Goodall (1985), pp. 100–101

28. Interview with author, 2011

29. Syd Johnson, *It's Never Dark above the Clouds* (1995), p. 16

30. Ron Smith DFM, *Rear Gunner Pathfinders*, Goodall (1987), p. 49

31. Max Hastings, *Bomber Command*, Pan (1982), p. 336

32. The Halton Archive, memoires of D B Jarvis, 35th entry.

33. Jack Currie, *Mosquito Victory*, Goodall (1983), p. 144

34. Interview with author, 2007

35. The Halton Archive, memoires of Trevor Jones

36. Interview with author, 2007, and as recounted in *Master Bombers*

37. Centre for Air Power Studies recorded interview, 1980

38. Quoted in Deane, op. cit.

39. Lucas, op. cit., p. 229

40. Correspondence between 5 Group headquarters and station commanders can be found in AIR14/2205

41. Richard Morris, *Guy Gibson*, Viking (1994), p. 141

42. Mahaddie, op. cit., p. 60

43. Mahaddie recounts a sad ending to this tale. He blames his soured relationship with Gibson as the reason that Gibson declined an invitation to take dual instruction on a Mosquito at Warboys prior to returning to operations as a low-level marker and master bomber. Had Cochrane known Gibson had not been properly trained to fly the Mosquito, he undoubtedly would have forbidden him to fly. No one actually knows for certain how Gibson's aircraft was lost or whether his inexperience on the type was a contributing factor.

44. Lucas, op. cit., p. 228

45. Hastings, op. cit.

46. AIR17/2714 Minute on selection of crews for PFF duties

47. Interview with author, 2011

Chapter 6

1. Walker, op. cit., p. 85

2. See Richards and Saunders, *Royal Air Force 1939–1945*, Vol. II, p. 155

3. Air Historical Branch paper in Pathfinder Archive, unfortunately undated

4. Richards and Saunders, op. cit., p. 155

5. 'Hal' Bufton quoted in Chaz Bowyer, *Mosquito at War*, Ian Allen (1979)

6. Bennett, op. cit., p. 181

7. Ibid., p. 183

8. *Mosquito at War*, op. cit., p. 68. McMullen was awarded the Air Force Cross in the New Year Honours of 1943.

9. Ibid., p. 181

10. The ORBs vary in how Oboe is described – sometimes loosely as a 'navigational aid' and sometimes more precisely as a 'precision device' (PD).

11. *Mosquito at War,* op. cit., p. 69

12. Bennett, op. cit., p. 173

13. Bennett, op. cit., p. 183

14. Middlebrook, op. cit., p. 336

15. Bennett, op. cit., p. 172

16. Air Historical Branch paper, op. cit.

17. AIR14/2986 includes a reference to the probable use of TI markers by the enemy on Berlin on the night of 29–30 March 1943.

18. SAOAG, op. cit. Vol. 2, p. 102

19. It has similarly been suggested that Cherwell had initially reacted to the project by saying 'it stinks', prompting the scientists to give it the chemical formula for hydrogen sulphide, a gas that smells of rotten eggs.

20. Joubert de la Ferté

21. Dudley Saward

22. Later, more advanced models used 3cm wavelengths.

23. Not to be confused with the German Listening Service, also known as the Y Service.

24. Norman Ashton DFC, *Only Birds and Fools,* Airlife (2000), p. 88

25. The choice of aircraft was arbitrary. Bennett wanted all of the sets to be installed on a single heavy to streamline and simplify installation and maintenance, but that would come later. The scientists had been flying H2S sets in Stirlings and Halifaxes, and that's where they stayed.

26. Alfred Price, *Instruments of Darkness,* William Kimber (1967), p. 121

27. As recited in Terraine, op. cit., p. 437–8

28. Bennett, op. cit., p. 184

29. Herrmann, op. cit., p. 201

30. Quoted in Price, *Instruments of Darkness,* p. 131

31. AIR25/152 p. 16 refers, though this appears slightly at odds with a memorandum document (No. 34) in AIR concerning the foundation of No. 8 Group Pathfinder Force that states the group came into effect on 25 January.

32. Bennett, op. cit., p. 188

33. Bennett, op. cit., p. 185

34. Ashworth, op. cit., p. 111

35. Harris, op. cit., p. 144

36. A full and detailed account of the raid is given in Richards and Saunders, Vol. II.

37. Richards and Saunders, Vol. II, op. cit., p. 286

38. Ibid., p. 286

39. The list of destruction following this and a subsequent raid on 25–26 July was so overwhelming that Mr Krupp himself was taken ill, reportedly suffering a stroke from which he never recovered.

40. *Mosquito at War*, op. cit., p. 72

41. Bennett, op. cit., p. 199

42. Harris, op. cit., p. 173

43. Middlebrook, op. cit., p. 413

44. Harris, op. cit., p. 174

45. Bennett, op. cit., p. 200

Chapter 7

1. Maynard, op. cit., p. 111–12

2. Alan Bramson, *Master Airman*, Airlife (1985), p. 84

3. Sean Feast, *The Lost Graves of Peenemünde*, Fighting High (2020)

4. www.icaew.com/library/historical-resources/guide-to-historical-resources/wartime-service/ww2/roll-of-honour-members

5. Hilton was flying Lancaster R5868, then Q-Queenie, which was later designated S-Sugar with 467 Squadron and resides at the RAF Museum, Hendon. Betty Hilton, Raymond's wife, was a first-class tennis player who reached the quarter finals of Wimbledon (twice) and the French Open.

6. 23rd entry

7. Apprentices were affectionately known as 'Trenchard's brats' after the school's founder, Lord Trenchard.

8. Bramson, op. cit., p. 84

9. Interview and correspondence with author, 2007

10. Sooby became a well-known Pathfinder with 109 Squadron
11. *RAF Historical Society Journal,* 35, p. 18
12. Bennett, op. cit., p. 189
13. Ibid., p. 189
14. As quoted in *Pathfinders at War,* op. cit., p. 155
15. Michael Cumming, *Pathfinder Cranswick,* Fighting High (2012), p. 156
16. Citation for Thomas' OBE, 14 June 1845
17. Bennett, op. cit., p. 189
18. Bennett, op. cit., p. 187
19. AIR20/4738 Letter dated 22 May from B.Ops.2 (a) Squadron Leader D A Davies
20. Interview with author
21. Quoted in Ted Stocker, *A Pathfinder's War,* Grub Street (2009); Sean Feast from interview with author
22. The aircraft was Halifax HX232
23. The PFNTU closed its doors on 18 June 1945, with a farewell party hosted by the then station commander, Hamish Mahaddie.
24. Ashton, op. cit., p. 87
25. Interview with author, 2011. Tony went on to complete 68 trips and was awarded the DFC and Bar.
26. Interview with author
27. Bennett, op. cit., p. 190
28. Interview between author and Len Judd, McMillan's flight engineer, 2013

Chapter 8

1. See Robin Higham, *Diary of a Disaster: British Aid to Greece, 1940–1941,* University Press of Kentucky (2009)
2. Willetts was appointed Greek Officer Royal Order of George I with swords
3. See the SAOAG, Vol. IV, p. 153 onwards
4. For details on Fauquier's carreer, see Spencer Dunmore's *Above and Beyond*
5. Wing Commander Bob Barrell DSO DFC and Bar

6. Flight Lieutenant Harry Webster DFC

7. Flight Lieutenant Brian Slade DFC

8. Harris, p. 186. A timed run enabled a Pathfinder aircraft to locate and mark a target based on a timed run from a specific landmark – perhaps an island (in the case of the attack on Peenemünde), headland or other obvious geographic feature.

9. Maynard, op. cit., p. 142

10. AIR14/2701 Letter from Bennett to Harris, 25 September 1943

11. Ibid., 1 October 1943. Harris writes: 'With regard to your being allowed to fly on operations, I must repeat (as I have told you several times) that I cannot allow it.'

12. Squadron Leader Kenneth Foster DFC and Bar

13. Squadron Leader Robert McKinna DFC and Bar

14. Cook's name is perhaps best known for featuring in Don Charlwood's haunting book *No Moon Tonight*, in which the author sensed that the young man's luck would finally give out. And so it proved. Cook's regular navigator, Harry Wright, was not flying with him that night, having been in hospital with sinus trouble. Wright would himself go on to be awarded both the DFC and Bar to add to an earlier DFM, and complete 78 operations. He later wrote a fictionalised account of his experiences, *Pathfinder Squadron*, in which one of the principal characters was called 'Syd' and it was to Cook's memory that the title was dedicated.

15. Harris, op. cit., p. 185

16. Middlebrook, pp. 446–7

17. Martin Middlebrook, *The Berlin Raids*, Viking (1988), pp. 309–10

18. *The Bomber Command War Diaries*, op. cit., p. 453

19. Ibid., p. 455

20. SAOG, op. cit., Vol. II, p. 193

21. Memo from Bennett to Bomber Command, 3 November 1944 and quoted in SAOG.

22. Middlebrook, *The Berlin Raids*, p. 331

23. Deane, op. cit., p. 59

24. John Searby, *The Everlasting Arms,* William Kimber (1988), p. 167
25. SAOG, Vol. II, p. 196
26. Flight Sergeant E O Charlton of 97 Squadron quoted in *The Berlin Raids,* p. 330
27. Interview with author and subsequently quoted in Elmer's privately published memoire, *Against the Odds.*
28. Middlebrook, op. cit., p. 311
29. Searby, op. cit., p. 174

Chapter 9

1. Terraine, op. cit. p. 625
2. AIR20/4738 Letter authored to Wing Commander M H Lawson, Bomber Operations (2), 18 May 1944
3. Wing Commander Fraser Barron DSO and Bar DFC DFM
4. Squadron Leader John Dennis DSO DFC
5. AIR27/768 97 Squadron ORB
6. Correspondence between Bob Lasham and author, 2011
7. The ORB suggests they were shot down by Junkers 88s. Post-war research, however, shows claims being made by Fw 190 aircraft from III/SKG 10.
8. Correspondence and interview with author, 2011
9. Ron Smith, op. cit., p. 90
10. Interview with author, 2011
11. Bennett, op. cit., p. 232
12. SAOAG, op. cit., Vol. III, p. 142
13. AIR27/827 Quoted in the 105 Squadron ORB
14. The Pathfinder Archive – correspondence, 1990
15. Harris, op. cit., p. 210
16. Smith, op. cit., p. 91
17. AIR25/153 ORB Headquarters Pathfinder Force
18. Saunders, *Royal Air Force 1939–1945,* Vol. III, p. 157
19. SAOAG, op. cit., Vol. III, p. 143
20. Interview with author, 2011

21. Peter Johnson, *The Withered Garland*, NEP (1995), p. 217

22. Squadron Leader John Weightman DFC

23. Squadron Leader James Foulsham DFC AFC

24. Correspondence with Peter Chapman, Jeff's son, and access to Jeff's privately published memoire

25. SAOAG, op. cit., Vol. III, p. 39

26. Squadron Leader George Ingram DFC

27. Davies survived to become a POW, having been blown out of the cockpit of his burning Lancaster

28. Squadron Leader Bill Blessing DSO DFC

29. Wing Commander Stephen Watts DSO DFC

30. Chaz Bowyer, *For Valour: the Air VCs*, William Kimber (1978), p. 389. The higher authority was Air Commodore Kirkpatrick of 3 Group.

31. The full text of the letter is published in *Hamish: The Story of a Pathfinder*, op. cit., p. 95

32. *For Valour*, op. cit., p. 392 – memories of Geoff Goddard, a navigator who survived the raid

33. Interview with author, 2011

34. Chris Coverdale, *Pathfinders 635 Squadron*, privately published (DATE), pp. 198–9

35. Bill Newton Dunn, *Big Wing*, Airlife (1992), p. 139

36. *Royal Air Force 1939 – 1945*, Vol. III, p. 129

37. Interview with author, 2013

38. Musgrove, op. cit., p. 132

39. Flight Lieutenant Ken Wolstenholme DFC

40. Aside from his bravery shown in World War Two, Ken Wolstenholme's name will be forever linked with the 1966 World Cup final, and his famous commentary.

41. Newton Dunn, op. cit., p. 148 fn.

42. Von Kluge quoted in *The Royal Air Force 1939 – 1945*, Vol. III

43. Bennett, op. cit., p. 241

44. Maitland, op. cit., p. 125

45. Correspondence with author, 2011

Chapter 10

1. Philip Patrick interview with author, 2007
2. Ashton, op. cit., p. 99
3. Interview with author, 2013
4. Interview with author, 2007
5. Interview with author, 2005
6. Interview with author, 2007
7. Ashton, op. cit., p. 93
8. Interview with author, 2007
9. Interview with author, 2011
10. Interview with author, 2011
11. Interview with author, 2007
12. Interview with author, 2011
13. Johnson, op. cit., p. 17
14. Interview with author, 2007
15. Interview with author, 2011
16. Interview with author, 2007
17. Interview with author, 2007
18. Percy Cannings DFM interview with author, 2007
19. RAF Pathfinder Archive
20. Eric Wilkin interview with author, 2011
21. Interview with author, 2011
22. Interview with author 2011; recounted in Sean Feast, *The Pathfinder Companion*, Grub Street (2012)
23. Interview with author, 2007
24. Interview with author, 2007
25. Interview with author, 2007
26. Interview with author, 2005
27. Interview with author. 2007
28. Sadly, Harold Siddons took his own life in 1963 at the age of 41.
29. Interview with author, 2008
30. Interview with author, 2011
31. Interview with author, 2005

32. Interview with author; recounted in *A Pathfinder's War,* op. cit.

33. Interview with author, 2011

34. Interview with author, 2013

35. Letter in 582 Squadron archive

36. Interview with author, 2011

37. Interview with author, 2011

38. Ashworth, op. cit., p. 135

39. Ibid., p. 156

40. Squadron Leader Brian Frow DSO DFC

41. Wing Commander Alan Craig DSO AFC

42. Interview with author; Fred Phillip's personal memoire

43. Interview with author, 2011

44. Letter in 582 Squadron archive, 1 November 1986

45. Michael Renault DFC, *Terror by Night,* William Kimber (1982), pp. 87–8

46. Toliver and Constable, *Horrido,* Arthur Barker (1968), p. 172

Chapter 11

1. Harris, op. cit., p. 267

2. Author interview with former Sergeant Peter Crow, 2016

3. Smith, op. cit., p. 95

4. AIR2/8039

5. *A Pathfinder's War* – the story of Flight Lieutenant Ted Stocker DSO DFC by Sean Feast.

6. Terraine, op. cit., p. 521

7. Interview with author, 2008

8. Wing Commander Philip Patrick DFC

9. Interview with author, 2008

10. Mark Wells, *Courage and Air Warfare,* Routledge (1995), p. 205

11. Ibid.; using figures from Webster and Frankland.

12. Terraine, op. cit., p. 528

13. Ron Smith DFM, *Rear Gunner Pathfinders,* Goodall (1987)

14. Interview with author, 2008

15. Interview with author, 2016

16. Lord Balfour of Inchrye wrote about his experiences in *Wings over Westminster*, Hutchinson (1973).
17. Hastings, op.cit., p. 252 onwards
18. Feast, *Master Bomber*, op. cit.
19. Laddie Lucas, *Wings of War*, Hutchinson (1983), p. 286
20. *Pathfinder*, op. cit., p. 211
21. The Halton Archive – Memoires of Flight Sergeant Trevor Jones
22. Squadron Leader Jock Cassels DFC and Bar
23. Interview with author
24. Interview with author
25. Recounted in *The Pathfinder Companion*, op.cit
26. Interview with author
27. Dr Winfield wrote about his experiences in *The Sky Belongs to Them*, William Kimber (1976).
28. John Wainwright, *Tail End Charlie*, Macmillan (1978), p. 178
29. Interview with author
30. Interview with author, 2011. Norman went on to be awarded the DFC and Bar with 35 Squadron.
31. *Desert Song*, unpublished memoire
32. Squadron Leader Owen Milne DFC
33. Interview with Tom Mansel-Pleydell, 2012; letters contained in the Mansel-Pleydell family archive.
34. Interview with author. 2011
35. As recounted to the author by Boris Bressloff
36. A full account is given in *A Pathfinder's War*. Ted Stocker, the flight engineer leader was among the scratch crew Cribb gathered for the event, along with Cribb's successor, Stafford Coulson.
37. As recounted to the author by David Wallace, whose father had served at Little Staughton.

Chapter 12

1. Adapted from the memoires of 'Butch' Foard, Fitter II at 692 Squadron
2. Aircraft hand – an airman as yet without a trade.

3. Tea and cakes

4. 'Mag drop' is the term given to the drop in engine revolutions when on single ignition, in other words, running on the port magneto with the starboard switched off and vice versa. Normally there was a visible drop, but a problem arose when the drop was 180–200 from the 3,000 peak revs. The problem was very typically a sparking plug.

5. Musgrove, op. cit., pp. 274–5

6. From Jennie Mack Gray's own personal collection – the diary of Walter Bushby

7. Adapted from the memoires of Fred Crawley DFC who flew 73 operations, 44 with 139 (Jamaica) Squadron. Sixteen of those 44 were to Berlin. He flew his last operation on 2 May 1945.

8. There were but they were not stuck to rigidly. A tour of operations on Mosquitoes was 50, but within those 50 operations they might go to Berlin on 15 or more occasions.

9. From the anonymous 'A fragment from the diary of a bomber pilot – May 1944' in The Pathfinder Archive.

10. In PFF, 105 and 109 Squadrons were the principal marker squadrons using Oboe; 139 (Jamaica) Squadron became the marker squadron for the LNSF, using H2S. By the end of the war, Bennett was able to send more than 100 Mosquitoes to Berlin as a Main Force in its own right.

Chapter 13

1. *The Encyclopedia Britannica* 1938 edition recorded that in 1927, almost 54,000 ships had passed through the canal and that the route was being increasingly used by merchant vessels.

2. *Shipping Wonders of the World*, 7 July 1936

3. A magnificent photograph exists of the *Bismarck* passing through the canal on 16 September 1940.

4. AIR27/2217 692 Squadron Appendices – S D Watts' diary entry, 1 April

5. Flight Lieutenant Val Moore DSO DFM

6. Watts' diary entry, op. cit. 23 February

7. Bennett, op. cit., p. 203

8. Watts' diary, op. cit. Watts actually writes: 'One navigator goes LMF but I manage to [indecipherable] him out of it.'

9. Ibid.

10. Memories of Flying Officer Terry Goodwin DFC DFM, The Pathfinder Archive

11. Memories of Squadron Leader Cyril Hassall DSO DFC and Bar, The Pathfinder Archive

12. Memories of Flying Officer Ian MacDonald, The Pathfinder Archive

13. Memories of Flight Lieutenant Richard Clarkson DFC and Bar, The Pathfinder Archive.

14. AIR27/2216 692 Squadron ORB

15. Watts' Diary, op. cit.

16. Squadron Leader Cyril Hassall DSO DFC and Bar, The Pathfinder Archive

17. Bennett, op. cit., p. 225

18. *The Times*, 6 July 1944

19. Memories of Flying Officer John Page DFC, The Pathfinder Archive

20. Wing Commander Jerry Gosnell DSO DFC

21. As recounted in *The Pathfinder Companion* op. cit.

22. Flight Lieutenant Tommy Broom DFC

23. At the time a squadron leader DFC and Bar

24. Tom Parry Evans, *Squadron Leader Tommy Broom DFC***, Pen & Sword (2011), p. 146

25. Flight Lieutenant Leo Wellstead DFC DFM

26. AIR27/933 128 Squadron Appendices – report on flying accident or forced landing not attributable to enemy action

27. Flight Lieutenant George Mullan DFC

28. Memories of Flying Officer Bill Ball, The Pathfinder Archive

29. Memories of Flying Officer Frederick Hill DFC, The Pathfinder Archive

30. Broom, op. cit.

31. Ball, op. cit.

32. Hill, op. cit.

33. AIR27/2044 571 ORB

34. *London Gazette*, 27 February 1945

35. Tony Spooner, *Clean Sweep: The story of Air Marshal Sir Ivor Broom. KCB, CBE, DSO, DFC & Two Bars, AFC*, Crecy (1994)

36. Flying Officer Derek Smith DFC and Bar

37. Memories of Flying Officer Derek Smith DFC and Bar, The Pathfinder Archive

Chapter 14

1. Alex Thorne, *Lancaster Squadron at War*, Ian Allan (1995)

2. Antony Beevor, *Ardennes 1944*, Viking (2015), p. 288

3. *Royal Air Force 1939–1945*, Vol. III, op. cit., p. 268

4. The Pathfinder Archive, correspondence with Tony Farrell DFC AFC

5. Coverdale, op. cit.

6. Mange later went on to command 582 Squadron

7. Beevor, op. cit., p. 298

8. Bennett, op. cit., p. 254

9. Beevor, op. cit., p. 298

10. *Royal Air Force 1939–1945*, Vol. III, op. cit., p. 190

11. Ibid., p. 191

12. Interview with author and Bill Heane DFC, 2007, as recounted in *Master Bombers*

13. *The Pathfinder Companion*, op. cit., p. 154

14. Interview with author, 2007

15. Bennett., p. 250

16. Ibid., pp. 251–2

17. W R Chorley, *Bomber Command Losses 1944*, Midland Counties (1997)

18. Interview with author, 2007

19. *Master Bombers*, pp. 105–6; interview with former WAAF Vera Jacobs, Hayden's wife

20. Hastings, op. cit., p. 403

21. *Bomber Command War Diaries*, op. cit., p. 568

22. Green ink was used for daylight sorties and red ink for night-time operations

23. Pathfinder, op. cit., p. 256
24. Wing Commander Douglas Cracknell DSO DFC and Bar
25. Maitland, op. cit., p. 134
26. Musgrove, op. cit., p. 169
27. A full account of that final operation is given by Al Bourne, one of Ted Swales' air gunners, in *Master Bombers*, pp. 173–7
28. Interview with author; recounted in *Master Bombers*
29. Wing Commander Donald Falconer DFC AFC
30. Interview with author, 2011
31. Wing Commander Kenny Lawson DSO and Bar DFC,
32. Squadron Leader William Wishart DSO DFC and Bar
33. The gunner was Flying Officer Raymond Salvoni DFC
34. Quoted from the recommendation for the first Bar to the DFC
35. Cooper, *'We Act with One Accord' – 35 Pathfinder Squadron*, J & KH Publishing (1998), p. 209
36. AIR PFF Headquarters ORB, March 1945
37. *The Daily Sketch*, 10 April 1944
38. Interview with author; recounted in 'Bob's Crew', privately published.
39. Pathfinders, p. 258
40. Interview with author, 2011

Chapter 15

1. The Pathfinder Archive, letter to Blunt, May 1991
2. Pathfinder p
3. AIR50/32 Combat report
4. Banks was lost with his crew on their 37th operation.
5. AIR50/178 Combat report
6. Peggy Ryle, *Missing in Action: May–September 1944*, W. H. Allen (1979)
7. Chaz Bowyer, *Bomber Barons*, p. 204
8. Interview with author, 2006
9. Interview with author, 2006
10. The Pathfinder Archive, letter to Blunt, January 1989.
11. Currie, op. cit., p. 139

12. Currie, op. cit., p. 145
13. Interview with author, 2010
14. The Pathfinder Archive, letter to Blunt, April 1992.
15. In AIR2/9044 via Dave Wallace and Hugh Halliday
16. Flight Sergeant Bill Read DFM RCAF
17. The Pathfinder Archive, letter to Blunt
18. 582 Squadron Archive, letter from P A Goodridge.
19. Interview with author, 2007
20. Deane, op. cit., p. 63
21. The Pathfinder Archive, letter to Blunt
22. Simpson completed 102 operations and was awarded the DFC and DFM
23. The fate of the murdered men was uncovered by author Marc Hall. Marc Hall and the author were both invited to attend the unveiling of the memorial to the dead men with relatives of those who were murdered.
24. Via Jock Cassels and in The Pathfinder Archive
25. AIR14/1246
26. The Pathfinder Archive, letter to Blunt, February 1991
27. 582 Squadron Archive
28. The Pathfinder Archive, memoires of Chas Lockyer.

Chapter 16

1. Hastings, op. cit., p. 417
2. Richard Mead, *Dambuster in Chief*, Pen and Sword (2020), p. 40
3. Jack Slessor writing to Cochrane on the latter's retirement, states the complete opposite – that Cochrane hated self-publicity.
4. Bennett, op. cit. pp. 224–5
5. Maynard, op. cit. p. 117
6. Ibid., p. 118
7. Ibid., p. 118
8. Ibid., p. 131
9. Ibid., p. 132
10. Searby, op. cit., p. 170

11. Bennett, op. cit., p. 214
12. Searby, op. cit., p. 171
13. TNA – AIR20/4738 Letter from Bufton, dated 17 April 1944
14. Ibid., p. 171
15. Deane, op. cit., p. 73
16. Correspondence between the author and Norman Westby DFC and Bar, 2010
17. Jennie Gray, *Pathfinder Aircrew*, Perardua Books (2022)
18. Johnson, op. cit., p. 213
19. Deane, op. cit., p. 72
20. As recounted by Chris Coverdale in his privately published photographic record of Bennett's life.
21. Interview with author, 2011
22. Interview with author, 2011
23. SAOAG, Vol. III, p. 154
24. Probert, *Bomber Harris: His Life and Times*, Greenhill (2001), p. 228
25. Quoted in Richard Morris, *Cheshire*, Viking (2000), p. 155
26. Ibid., p. 155
27. Ibid., p. 156
28. *Bomber Command War Diaries*, op. cit., p. 501
29. Bennett, op. cit., p. 230
30. Harris, op. cit., p. 135
31. Slessor, op. cit., p. 373
32. A newspaper article in the *Sunday Graphic* of 21 December 1944 does at least credit Daniels as 'Master Bomber No. 1' and says he was 'the first man to direct, as Master Bomber, an RAF raid on Germany.'
33. Daniels' logbook records the operation with the words 'Pathfinder Operations. R/T broadcast to Main Force.'
34. Musgrove, op. cit., p. 219
35. Interview with author, 2011
36. Bennett, op. cit. A full list of casualties is published in *Hamish* op.cit., p. 123 onwards
37. Brian Rapier, *Halifax at War*, Ian Allan (1987), pp. 46–7